LANDLORD/TENANT RIGHTS IN ONTARIO

Ron McInnes, LL.B., LL.M.

Self-Counsel Press
(a division of)
International Self-Counsel Press Ltd.
Canada U.S.A.

Printed in Canada.

Self-Counsel Press acknowledges the financial support of the Government of Canada through the Book Publishing Industry Development Program for our publishing activities.

First edition: December 1972
Tenth edition: September 1994; Reprinted: February 1996; May 1997
Eleventh edition: December 1998

Canadian Cataloguing in Publication Data

McInnes, R. W. (Ronald William), 1944-
    Landlord/tenant rights in Ontario

    (Self-counsel legal series)
    ISBN 1-55180-201-5

    1. Landlord and tenant — Ontario — Popular works. I. Title.
II. Series
KE0259.2.M33 1998   346.71304'34   C98-910754-X
KF590.Z9M33 1998

Self-Counsel Press
(a division of)
International Self-Counsel Press Ltd.

1481 Charlotte Road
North Vancouver, BC V7J 1H1
Canada

1704 N. State Street
Bellingham, WA 98225
U.S.A.

LANDLORD/TENANT RIGHTS IN ONTARIO

CONTENTS

NOTICE TO READERS

INTRODUCTION AND HISTORY

Suspicion and, sometimes, animosity have been characteristics of the relationship between landlords and tenants in recent years. The landlord* is often viewed as a wealthy and unfeeling landowner whose only interest is to get the rent and give little in return. The tenant, in the eyes of the landlord, is often seen as a second-class citizen who at any time might destroy the landlord's property and run off without paying the rent.

This attitude is not as prevalent between persons in other business relationships. Its existence in the landlord-tenant situation may be due to the ongoing or permanent nature of the relationship and the fact that it involves one of the necessities of life — shelter. Another factor may be that both landlords and tenants are unaware of, or have misconceptions about, their legal rights and obligations. Landlords may have better access to legal advice but this does not necessarily mean that they always limit their actions to what the law permits.

This book is designed to acquaint both the landlord and the tenant with a working knowledge of the law regarding the landlord-tenant relationship. It is hoped that this knowledge will enable both parties to know their rights and help them determine when it is preferable to come to an amicable agreement rather than carry on a legal battle. Court disputes are usually lengthy, complicated, and expensive, and can intensify bad feelings on both sides. Where a relationship is to continue, litigation is rarely helpful.

---

*Throughout this book, the term "landlord" when it applies to individuals should be read to include "landlady" as well.

Many, but by no means all, landlords are corporations. For this reason, the pronoun "it" is usually used throughout this book when referring to a landlord. However, some landlords are individuals renting out a single unit — often a room or apartment in their homes. Some small landlords incorporate for business or tax reasons but, in all other respects, carry on as before.

Before 1970, landlord and tenant law in Ontario was antiquated. The rules were based on concepts of land law (rather than the more modern contract law) and were particularly inappropriate to residential tenancies. Many sections of the legislation were phrased in such a way that even lawyers found them difficult to understand. Tenant rights, even if the tenant understood the law, were virtually non-existent.

On January 1, 1970, the first modernization of the Landlord and Tenant Act in over 50 years came into effect in Ontario, and brought about some small measure of legal equality between Ontario tenants and their landlords. The amendments were enacted following an extensive 10-year study of the problems in tenancy law by the Ontario Law Reform Commission. Not all of the recommendations of the Law Reform Commission were adopted by the government but, at public hearings before the enactment of the legislation, tenant activists did force some changes that improved the legal position of the tenant. These new provisions made up Part IV of the act. On July 1, 1972, further amendments to Part IV of the act were brought into force by the Ontario government. These were introduced with no prior notice and given very little publicity. The basic thrust of these changes was to improve the position of the landlord.

The Residential Premises Rent Review Act, 1975, brought rent review to Ontario. At the same time, further amendments to the Landlord and Tenant Act gave tenants security of tenure, brought mobile home parks within the protection of the legislation, expanded tenants' legal remedies in many important areas, and made provision for notices of rental increases.

In 1979, the Ontario legislature passed the Residential Tenancies Act, an entirely new act governing all phases of the relationship between landlords and tenants of residential premises. However, most of the provisions in this act were declared by the Supreme Court of Canada to be beyond the province's power. Therefore, the government was able to bring into effect only those provisions dealing with rent review and the setting up of a new tribunal known as the Residential Tenancy Commission. This became effective on August 17, 1979, and marked the beginning of an entirely new system of rent review in Ontario.

In June 1987, another amendment to the Landlord and Tenant Act was passed by the Ontario legislature extending the benefit of Part IV of the act to boarders, roomers, and lodgers.

Effective January 1, 1987, new provisions for rent control were introduced in the Residential Rent Regulation Act, 1986. With the exception of certain transitional provisions, the Residential Tenancies Act was repealed. In 1992, the Rent Control Act replaced the Residential Rent Regulation Act.

The Residents' Rights Act received Royal Assent on May 31, 1994. It amended certain provisions of the Landlord and Tenant Act, the Rent Control Act, and the Rental Housing Protection Act, as well as some other legislation. Its primary effect was on housing where "care services" are provided and on apartments, such as basement suites, within houses.

The Tenant Protection Act was passed and received Royal Assent on November 28, 1997. However, it did not come into force until June 17, 1998. As well as making significant changes to the previous law, this act consolidates all of the legislation related to residential tenancies, and repeals the

Rent Control Act, Part IV of the Landlord and Tenant Act, the Rental Housing Protection Act, the Municipal Amendment Act, the Residents' Rights Act, and the Land Lease Statute Law Amendment Act where they dealt with residential tenancies. The balance of what was the Landlord and Tenant Act has been renamed the Commercial Tenancies Act.

The Tenant Protection Act is, therefore, now the complete code of law for residential tenancies and its provisions prevail over any conflicting sections in other legislation. A complete copy of this act is reproduced in Appendix 3, which you should refer to for the exact wording of a particular section.

Considering the number of legislative changes over the years, it is not surprising that both landlords and tenants are often confused about their legal rights. Always remember that the explanations given in this book are intended for people without legal training and so must be somewhat simplified. It is therefore recommended that, in serious matters, a lawyer be consulted before any action is taken. However, as this book is intended to be primarily a "self help" aid, explanations of proceedings are provided to encourage you to represent yourself whenever possible.

1

WHAT TYPES OF RESIDENCES DOES THE ACT COVER?

a. RESIDENTIAL UNITS

Except where a specific exemption applies, the Tenant Protection Act applies to all residential units, including social housing. The act applies to a single family house, to an apartment in a highrise building, and to everything in-between — including many types of housing that you might not ordinarily think of as rental residential premises.

The term "residential unit" is defined in the act as "any living accommodation used or intended for use as residential premises." This includes "a site for a mobile home or site on which there is a land lease home used or intended for use as rented residential premises" and "a room in a boarding house, rooming house, or lodging house and a unit in a care home."

"Residential complex" is another term often found in the act. It may be —

(a) a building or related group of buildings in which one or more rental units are located,

(b) a mobile home park or land lease community,

(c) a site that is a rental unit, or

(d) a care home,

and includes all common areas, services, and facilities available for the use of residents. Everything from a single family house to a group of highrise buildings is included under this definition.

The Tenant Protection Act applies to all rental units despite any other act and despite any agreement or waiver to the contrary. If a tenant has signed a lease containing any provision contrary to the act, it cannot be enforced by the landlord. The act also overrides the provisions of any other legislation except the Ontario Human Rights Code.

The term "residential purposes" used in previous legislation was held by the courts to refer to the use of the premises and not the relationship between the owner and the person renting. A building may not qualify as a "residential complex," but a residential tenancy subject to the act can exist between an owner and a person leasing the entire building and renting units to others. This same reasoning applies to the relationship between an owner and a charitable corporation that rents a house for use as a group home, unless the group or its particular activity is exempted by another section of the act.

1. Premises that are exempt from the act

The term "residential unit" does not include premises occupied for business or agricultural purposes with living accommodation attached under a single lease, unless the tenant occupying the living accommodation is not the same person using the premises for business purposes. In other words, business and agricultural leases are not covered by the act, even in the situation where the tenant is renting both a store and an attached apartment (or a farm with a farm house), if there is only one lease covering the entire premises. If there are separate leases for the business and residential portions or if the tenant occupying the residence is not the same person carrying on the business, the living accommodation portion falls within the definition of residential unit.

Other exempt accommodations are vacation homes or rooms, premises situated on a farm or in a non-residential building where occupation is related to employment, short-term emergency shelters, hospitals, and retirement and nursing homes. Also exempt, are premises where the occupants are required to share a bathroom or kitchen facility with the landlord or a member of the landlord's family where the landlord or the family member lives in the same building. This last exemption limits the application of the act and means that many boarding and rooming houses do not really qualify for the protection provided by the act.

The act does not apply to living accommodation provided by a non-profit housing co-operative for its members. This exemption is discussed in section **c.** below.

2. Superintendent's premises

The act makes specific provision for "superintendent's premises." A building superintendent, janitor, or security guard who receives the use of an apartment as part of the employment arrangement, is covered by the act. However, the tenancy may be terminated, effective immediately, when the employment has been terminated. The former superintendent must then move out within seven days.

b. MOBILE HOMES AND LAND LEASE HOMES

The definition of "residential unit" includes "a site for a mobile home or site on which there is a land lease home used or intended for use as rented residential premises." A rented site for a mobile home is a rental unit for the purposes of the act even if the mobile home on the site is owned by the tenant.

A "mobile home" is defined as a dwelling that is designed to be made mobile and constructed as a permanent residence for one or more persons. Travel trailers and tent trailers were specifically excluded in previous legislation but are included in this act. A "mobile home park" refers to the land on which one or more occupied mobile homes are located. This includes the rental units and the land, structures, services, and facilities that are owned by the landlord but are intended for the common use and enjoyment of the tenants. Note that only one mobile home is necessary to qualify as a mobile home park. Trailer parks for tourists and vacationers are excluded by another section of the act.

A "land lease home" is a dwelling, other than a mobile home, that is a permanent structure where the owner of the dwelling leases the land used or intended for use as the site for the building. Likewise, a "land lease community" is defined as the land on which one or more occupied land lease homes are situated, and includes the rental units and the land, structures, services, and facilities that are owned by the landlord but are intended for the common use and enjoyment of the tenants. Note again, that only one land lease home is necessary to qualify as a land lease community.

Part V of the Tenant Protection Act deals specifically with mobile home parks and land lease communities, and the provisions of that part apply in any case where there is conflict with a provision in any other part of the act. This means that, subject to Part V, the protective provisions of the Tenant Protection Act outlined in this book are fully applicable to persons living in a mobile home whether they rent the mobile home or rent only the land on which the mobile home is situated. Similarly, all persons living in a home they own, but renting the land on which it is situated, are also protected.

Part V is discussed in more detail in chapter 11.

c. NON-PROFIT HOUSING CO-OPERATIVES

The relationship between a non-profit housing co-operative and a person occupying a unit as a member is not regarded as a landlord and tenant relationship and no part of the Tenant Protection Act applies to it.

A non-profit housing co-operative is a co-operative that meets all of the following conditions:

(a) The primary object of the co-operative is to provide housing to its members.

(b) The co-operative's activities are to be carried on without the purpose of profit for its members.

(c) On the dissolution of the co-operative, the property will be transferred to non-profit housing co-operatives or charitable organizations.

This definition is found in the Co-operative Corporations Act and is adopted into the Tenant Protection Act.

A housing co-operative may have units that are occupied by persons who are not members of the co-operative. The Co-operative Corporations Act contains provisions for the designation of housing units as non-member units. In these situations, the Tenant Protection Act does apply to the relationship, and the co-operative has many of the obligations of an ordinary landlord and must use the procedures set out in the act. However, there are numerous exceptions related to subletting, assignment, and rent regulation for co-operatives.

If a co-operative does not come completely within the definition, the Tenant Protection Act still applies to all aspects of the relationship between the occupant and the co-operative. However, this would now be a very rare situation.

d. CARE HOMES

A "care home" is a residential rental building or unit that is occupied or intended to be occupied by persons for the purpose of receiving care services. The receipt of these services need not necessarily be the primary purpose of the occupancy. "Care services" include such things as health care services, rehabilitative or therapeutic services, or services that provide assistance with the activities of daily living. A list of some of the specific services included is set out in regulations under the act.

Some special provisions relating to care homes are set out in Part IV of the Tenant Protection Act and, where these provisions conflict with a provision in any other part of the act, the rules in Part IV apply.

Care homes do not include living accommodation occupied for penal or correctional purposes, or accommodation that is subject to various acts dealing with hospitals, homes for the aged, and nursing homes. The term also does not include short-term living accommodation provided as emergency shelter, or living accommodation in a care home occupied on a short-term respite care basis. The term also excludes living accommodation occupied for the purpose of receiving rehabilitative or therapeutic services where the person occupying the accommodation and the person providing it have agreed that the period of occupancy will be for a specified duration, or will terminate when the objectives of the services have either been met or it is decided that they will not be met. For this exemption to apply, the intention must be that the accommodation is provided for no more than one year. No guidance is provided in the act as to how to determine when the objectives of the services have been met or if they will not be met.

e. SOCIAL HOUSING

Social housing includes —

(a) housing owned, operated, or administered by the federal or provincial government or an agency of either of them;

(b) a rental unit located in a non-profit housing project developed under certain government programs listed in the regulations;

(c) a rental unit provided by a non-profit housing co-operative to tenants in non-member units;

(d) certain rental units provided by an educational institution that are not otherwise exempt under the act; and

(e) a rental unit owned, operated, or administered by a religious institution for a charitable use.

Because these units are intended for use by a limited number of persons and rent is usually geared to income, these types of accommodation are eligible for only some of the protections provided by the act.

Social housing units where the rent is geared to income are exempt from the rule limiting rent increases to once every 12 months. Likewise, such units are exempt from the requirement for notice of rent increase. Generally, the rules in the act regarding the setting of rent and rent increases do not apply to this type of rental unit. The tenants of such units are not permitted to assign or sublet.

2

WHAT IS A TENANCY AGREEMENT?

The term "lease" is not used in the Tenant Protection Act. However, throughout this book you will find it used interchangeably with "tenancy agreement."

Section 1(1) of the act provides that —

> "tenancy agreement" means a written, oral, or implied agreement between a tenant and a landlord for occupancy of a rental unit and includes a licence to occupy a rental unit.

A written tenancy agreement is often referred to as a "lease." However, a tenancy agreement doesn't need to be in writing for it to be binding. The agreement may be written, oral, or merely implied from the circumstances.

The reference to a "licence" in the definition of a tenancy agreement was added to counter attempts by some landlords who argued that they were not in a tenancy situation and that therefore, the tenant did not have the protection of the act. "Licence" is a legal term for an arrangement where the "licensee" does not have the exclusive right to possession of the premises. These arguments were quite technical but this definition has made them irrelevant.

a. TENANCY AGREEMENTS

A tenancy agreement or lease is a contract between a landlord and a tenant that sets out, among other things, the premises or unit to be rented, the duration of the tenancy, the amount of the rent, and the terms of payment. It may include other

8

binding conditions to which both parties agree, such as pre-payment of the last month's rent, payment of utilities, and a few other matters specific to the particular house or apartment that are not prohibited by the legislation. House leases, for example, often contain a number of provisions relating to lawn and garden maintenance and insurance or other similar requirements.

Most of what is found in a written lease is of minimal importance to a tenant. Virtually all provisions governing the landlord-tenant relationship are dictated by the Tenant Protection Act and cannot be varied by the parties. Anything inconsistent with the act is void. Rent is controlled by Part VI of the act and may not be increased more than once a year. Even if a termination date is specified, all tenancies automatically continue on the same terms on a month-to-month basis until proper written notice is given by either the landlord or the tenant.

1. Landlord's obligation to provide items not in the tenancy agreement

There is usually no obligation for a landlord to provide, or continue to provide, items that are not specified in the tenancy agreement (such as, a swimming pool or a party room). However, ceasing to provide such items may be relevant to the rent that can be charged (see chapter 8). Agreements can be very hard to prove if not in writing, but there may be cases where a tenant can prove that the landlord's oral promise to provide such amenities was the reason the tenant signed the lease. He or she could then obtain an order for immediate termination of the lease or damages.

2. What may be in a tenancy agreement

The parties may agree between themselves to anything they want in a tenancy agreement, provided that it does not conflict with the Tenant Protection Act. In a few cases, the act specifically permits the parties to reach their own agreement and the provisions of the act apply only where they have not done so.

All terms of the tenancy agreement must be specifically agreed to by both parties for them to be binding. Many disputes could be avoided if, at the time of entering into the tenancy agreement, greater effort was taken to define the respective rights and obligations so that both parties knew exactly what they were. This, of course, is one benefit of a written lease or tenancy agreement. Remember, though, that provisions found in the act are always binding, regardless of what is or is not in the lease.

The major disadvantage of a written lease for a tenant is that it is usually a standard form document (either from a stationery store or the landlord's own form). It may include clauses providing additional benefits for the landlord that are not permitted by the law. Landlords are usually reluctant to alter standard forms and, unfortunately, tenants seldom read such documents carefully before signing. If the tenant (and, possibly, the landlord) is not familiar with the legislation discussed in this book, he or she may feel legally bound whereas this is often not the case.

In the past, many leases contained a clause that waived the tenant's right to any protective legislation. In residential tenancies, such clauses are no longer legal and their inclusion is meaningless. The rules contained in the act apply regardless of the wording of a written lease.

A clause found in many leases and not specifically precluded by the Tenant Protection Act is one by which the tenant gives up the right to sue the landlord for any damage or injury to the tenant, the tenant's family, or their property while on the landlord's premises. Such clauses are probably not legally binding in most circumstances but a tenant should try to have them removed from the lease before signing it. Adequate insurance, especially liability insurance, is recommended. If a problem does occur, consult a lawyer for professional advice.

3. Duration of a tenancy agreement

In written leases, the period for which the tenancy is to run is usually specified by an exact date in the body of the lease (e.g., September 1, 1998, to August 31, 1999). This is referred to as the "term" of the tenancy. Written tenancy agreements are usually for a fixed term of a year or more. Where no term is specified, and in most cases where there is no written lease, the period during which the tenancy agreement runs conforms to the period for which rent is paid (i.e., daily, weekly, monthly, or yearly).

A lease is not terminated automatically on the final date of the term. When the tenancy agreement expires, the law requires an automatic extension on a monthly basis, on the same terms, unless proper written notice is given to terminate or increase rent. The act requires landlords or tenants who want to end any type of tenancy to notify the other in writing. To terminate a monthly or term tenancy, a tenant must give at least 60 days' notice ending on the final date of the term or a period of the tenancy. To terminate a daily or weekly tenancy, at least 28 days' notice is required. The final date of a periodic tenancy is the day before the next rental payment would be due. The time periods and reasons for a notice of termination by a landlord are discussed in chapter 6.

Unless there is a specific provision permitting it, neither the landlord nor the tenant can terminate a fixed term agreement early. It is binding on both parties until the end of the term. This provides more security to the landlord since the landlord is limited to specific causes for termination while the tenant could otherwise terminate on 60 days' notice without giving a reason.

4. Changing the terms of a tenancy agreement

The terms of the tenancy agreement are agreed to by both parties for the entire duration of the tenancy. No terms of a written lease may be changed except by mutual agreement.

In the past, some landlords used a tax or other "escalation clause" as a way of altering the lease during its term. This clause provided that if taxes or certain other costs rose during the time the lease was in effect, the tenant would pay for the increase with extra rent. However, with the introduction of rent control and specific limits on rent increases, this procedure is no longer available. Most landlords now offer a maximum one year lease to take full advantage of any permitted rent increases. However, a longer term lease providing that rent will increase each year by the amount permitted by the act is binding provided that the landlord gives the required notices of rent increase (see chapter 8).

5. Rent payments

Unless agreed otherwise, rent is payable at the end of each month. Most tenancy agreements, however, require payment in advance at the start of the month. Rent is due on the agreed date and may be sued for by the landlord at any time after that day. There is no 15-day "grace" period as some tenants think. It is the tenant's obligation to get the rent to the landlord on or before the due date. Claiming that "the cheque is in the mail" is not sufficient.

A landlord is not required to accept an amount that is less than the entire rent due. It may refuse partial payment and proceed as if none of the rent had been paid. Payment should be in cash unless the parties agree to some other method. Usually cheques are acceptable. In order to have some proof of payment, a tenant should always demand a receipt or retain cancelled cheques. The act requires the landlord to provide receipts on request at no charge.

6. Renting to minors

It is commonly thought that if a tenant is under the legal age of 18, he or she is not bound by the terms of the lease signed. However, in most cases this is not true. A minor is bound by the terms of a contract that provides for a "necessary" item, such as food, clothing, or living accommodation. In addition, the Ontario Human Rights Code provides that a 16- or 17-year-old person who has withdrawn from parental control cannot be discriminated against with respect to accommodation, and any contract for such accommodation can be enforced against him or her.

7. Signing and delivering a tenancy agreement

In most cases, a tenant entering into a lease, deals with the building superintendent or rental agent rather than with the actual landlord or owner (which may, in fact, be a large corporation). The tenant usually signs the lease before it is signed by the landlord or its representative.

Where there is a written lease, landlords are required to deliver a copy to the tenant within 21 days of it being signed or renewed. This copy must be an exact duplicate of the one retained by the landlord. Where a landlord does not comply with this provision, the obligations of the tenant (including the obligation to pay rent) cease temporarily after the 21 days. A landlord need only deliver a copy of the lease at this point in order to reinstate the agreement and claim any rent withheld. However, it would appear from court decisions that a landlord cannot enforce any other obligations of the tenant that occurred or became due after the 21 days but before delivery of the copy of the lease.

The act also requires that every written tenancy agreement set out the legal name and address of the landlord to be used for giving notices under the act. If the tenancy agreement is not in writing, the landlord must give the tenant written notice of the legal name and address of the landlord within 21 days after the tenancy begins. The obligations of the tenant cease temporarily until the landlord has complied with these requirements as well.

It goes without saying that you should never sign a lease unless you have read it and feel sure that you fully understand

13

the obligations it includes. Although most leases are offered in a standard printed form, you may ask to have a clause struck out of the agreement if you do not agree with the obligation it imposes.

Provisions that are now illegal under the Tenant Protection Act should not appear in the lease, and there should be no opposition to having these deleted. Whether a landlord will agree to delete other clauses will depend on how much it wants a tenant at that particular time.

A tenant should also be very careful about signing "offers to lease" since these often require you to sign a lease that you have not yet seen. These documents may be as binding as an actual lease and you do not usually have any right to change your mind after signing.

Of course, in many cases, your only choice will be to sign the lease as is or forget the apartment. This is an unfortunate situation and the only way to counter it is through economic and social pressure. Tenant groups throughout the country are very active in redressing such inequities. The tenant's only tool is negotiation and since landlords are organized into pressure groups, tenants would be wise to follow their example. Tenant associations can be formed within a single building, neighbourhood, or city, or on a province-wide basis. The act provides certain protections for tenants who are active in such organizations.

b. JOINT TENANCY ARRANGEMENTS

Particular types of problems may arise when more than one person is occupying rented premises. If two or more people are tenants under one tenancy agreement (whether oral or written), they are each responsible for the whole rent regardless of the arrangement amongst themselves as to how much is to be paid by each. If one of the tenants leaves, his or her share of the rent must be absorbed by the remaining tenants.

14

If this person leaves without the consent of the other tenants, they may, of course, sue in Small Claims Court for that person's share of the rent on the basis of their agreement with him or her. This, however, has no effect on the rent owed to the landlord which must be paid by the remaining tenant(s) if they wish to remain in the unit.

Ontario courts have not yet had to determine the question of whether one of two or more joint tenants can unilaterally terminate a lease by giving a notice of termination to the landlord. An English court has ruled that such a notice would be effective in England and would terminate the tenancy for the other tenants as well. They would have no right to remain unless a new tenancy was entered into with the landlord. However, an Ontario court might not reach the same conclusion.

In situations where several persons are living in one apartment but only one person has actually signed a lease with the landlord, these other persons have no rights under the Tenant Protection Act unless there is either specific or implied recognition of their tenancy by the landlord. If the recognized tenant abandons the premises or gives notice of intention to vacate, the other persons have no right to remain on the premises. On the other hand, they are under no obligation to the landlord to pay any arrears of rent that may be due. Such persons are not joint tenants. In most cases, they are treated as trespassers and may be evicted without notice and without requiring the landlord to comply with the procedures in the act.

There are also situations where people come into a rented apartment, begin living with a friend and sharing the rent, but do not come to any agreement with the landlord or sign a lease. Such persons are not joint tenants. Landlords have been known to make a claim for additional rent when additional persons begin occupying the premises. The landlord has no legal right to make such a claim; lawful rent is based on the unit, not on the number of occupants. Once premises have been rented, the tenant may use them for any lawful purpose not prohibited by the tenancy agreement. "Lawful," however, also means not in violation of any by-laws prohibiting overcrowding that may be in effect in the municipality in which the apartment is situated.

Some tenancy agreements contain a clause listing the persons who will occupy the premises, and providing that the occupancy is limited to these persons. In such cases, a tenant who allows other persons to live in the apartment is in breach of the tenancy agreement and perhaps subject to eviction. The landlord may also seek a order compelling these other persons to move out.

The situations discussed here should not be confused with subletting or assigning, which are discussed in chapter 4.

3
HOW HAS THE LAW
BEEN MODERNIZED?

a. DOCTRINE OF FRUSTRATION

In law, a contract is considered to be "frustrated" if the particular thing with which the contract is concerned ceases to exist or ceases to be useful for the purpose intended, through no fault of either of the parties. The Frustrated Contracts Act sets out how a court is to adjust the rights of the parties in the event of such an unanticipated occurrence. This act applies to tenancy agreements.

Before the Frustrated Contracts Act became applicable to the landlord and tenant situation, the law was that, in the absence of anything contrary in the tenancy agreement, a tenant had to continue to pay rent even though the rented property could no longer be used for the intended purpose or had even been destroyed completely. The best a tenant could hope for was a clause in the lease permitting an abatement of rent during such times, but few leases allowed a tenant to terminate the lease completely.

Under present law, it is possible for the court to declare the lease at an end when the premises are no longer usable as living accommodation. One judge has held that a lease was frustrated because of the breakdown of air conditioning equipment. This was a particularly severe problem because the premises were located over a laundromat and, without the air conditioning, were not habitable during the summer. The tenant was relieved from paying rent for the number of months during which the heat was unbearable, although in these circumstances, the lease was not terminated.

b. MATERIAL COVENANTS

A "covenant" may be defined as a promise in an agreement. "Material covenants" are essential promises and include such things as the landlord's obligation to provide adequate heat and services, proper repairs, and "quiet enjoyment." Quiet enjoyment is a term implied in every tenancy agreement (even when not written) that means that the landlord will allow the tenant undisturbed occupation of the premises during the term of the lease.

Recent court cases broadened the concept of quiet enjoyment to include protection against substantial interference with the tenant's enjoyment of the rented premises. One judge stated, "The remedy is available where the judge thinks the tenant is deprived of a significant benefit of the tenancy for a significant period of time." Excessive noise caused or permitted by the landlord may be sufficient to constitute a breach of this covenant. Likewise, construction dust and barriers could be sufficient even if the repairs are being made in order to comply with the Tenant Protection Act. However, these breaches will usually result only in an abatement of rent and will rarely be so severe as to justify termination of the tenancy.

Under section 11 of the Tenant Protection Act, a tenant is justified in withholding rent where the landlord is in breach of a material covenant. The landlord cannot sue for this rent until it lives up to its side of the bargain. This is what is meant by covenants being "interdependent." Whether a tenant can completely terminate the lease by virtue of this section is doubtful since, until the end of the term or the end of the period of notice in a periodic tenancy, the landlord can rectify the breach and again assert the right to collect rent from that point. This section offers only temporary relief from payment of rent while a landlord is in breach of its obligations. Part IX of the act sets out the only procedure for applying for an order declaring a tenancy agreement to be terminated.

Remember that a provision in the act is not the same as a covenant in the lease. For this purpose, it does make a difference whether the lease repeats the requirement set out in the legislation. However, it is possible that the statutory provision will be construed as an "implied" covenant in the lease or tenancy agreement

It is also worth noting that the new legislation contains a specific provision that the landlord not interfere with the reasonable enjoyment of the rental unit or the residential complex in which it is located by the tenant or members of his or her household. If the Ontario Rental Housing Tribunal or the courts decide that this replaces the implied covenant in the tenancy agreement, it may be less useful as a basis to justify withholding rent. This problem should not exist where the lease contains a specific covenant for quiet enjoyment.

In any case, it should be noted that minor deficiencies or inconveniences will not be enough to justify withholding rent. The problem must be so serious that it almost becomes impossible to continue living there. Reasonable notice and time to rectify the problem should always be given to the landlord before rent is withheld.

c. PARTS OF THE LEASE BINDING ON FUTURE PARTIES

Section 12 of the Tenant Protection Act was enacted to abolish the ancient rule of landlord and tenant law that only those provisions in a lease that referred to something in existence became binding on parties other than those who signed the original agreement. Such covenants were said to "run with the land" and were binding on other persons who took over the agreement, such as a subtenant or a purchaser from the landlord. Covenants relating to things not in existence might

19

include things such as agreements to rebuild in case of fire or to make certain alterations to the premises.

Under the present law, all provisions in a tenancy agreement are binding on persons who subsequently take over the agreement whether from the landlord or from the tenant, and are not regarded as merely personal arrangements between the original parties.

d. MINIMIZING LOSSES

When either a landlord or a tenant becomes liable to pay any amount as a result of a breach of a tenancy agreement, the person entitled to claim the amount has a duty to take reasonable steps to minimize his or her losses. This legal principle is referred to as "mitigation of damages."

An example is where a tenant moves out without giving sufficient notice before the end of a fixed term tenancy. While the landlord has a claim against the tenant for the rent for this additional time, the landlord must also attempt to re-rent the unit as quickly as is reasonably possible, and is only entitled to claim actual loss of rent against the tenant. If the landlord fails to make such efforts, it may lose its entitlement to claim all or part of the damages.

Similarly, the amount of damages that a tenant can claim for damage to property caused by the landlord's failure to make repairs is restricted if the tenant does not do everything reasonably possible to minimize such damage. This might include making the repairs or having them made promptly and then claiming against the landlord for this cost.

e. THE ONTARIO RENTAL HOUSING TRIBUNAL

The present legislation has created an entirely new independent body called the Ontario Rental Housing Tribunal. The tribunal has been given exclusive jurisdiction to determine all applications brought under the Tenant Protection

Act, as well as any other matters that the act gives it jurisdiction of. This includes evictions, maintenance and repair issues, rent matters, and approving rent increases above the guideline.

For a full discussion of the tribunal; its duties, rights, and powers; and all other matters pertaining to its involvement in landlord-tenant disputes, please refer to chapter 14.

4

WHAT RIGHTS DOES A TENANT HAVE?

a. SECURITY OF TENURE

The effect of the provisions in Part III of the Tenant Protection Act (previously in an amendment to the Landlord and Tenant Act) restricting the landlord's ability to terminate a tenancy and evict the tenant, is referred to as "security of tenure." This means that a tenant cannot be evicted merely on the whim of a landlord. The landlord must give proper notice and, if necessary, be able to establish before the Ontario Rental Housing Tribunal that the tenant is guilty of some specific type of misconduct or that the landlord requires the unit for one of the specific reasons set out in Part III. Any eviction that does not go through this process is illegal.

The introduction of security of tenure for residential tenants in Ontario was a major breakthrough at the time. With the introduction of "vacancy decontrol" of rent control in the Tenant Protection Act, it has assumed even greater importance. Vacancy decontrol and other aspects of rent control are discussed fully in chapter 8.

The basic security of tenure rules are as follows:

(a) A tenancy may be terminated only under the provision in the Tenant Protection Act.

(b) A notice of termination is required unless the landlord and tenant have mutually agreed to terminate the tenancy.

(c) If a tenancy for a fixed term ends and has not been renewed or terminated, the landlord and tenant are deemed to have renewed it as a monthly tenancy agreement. A periodic tenancy is deemed to be renewed for another week, month, year, or other period depending on the terms of the agreement.

(d) A landlord cannot recover possession of a rented unit unless the tenant has vacated or abandoned the unit, or the landlord has obtained an order of the tribunal evicting the tenant.

Both an agreement to terminate and a tenant's notice to terminate are void if they are given at the time the tenancy agreement is entered into, or as a condition of entering into the tenancy agreement. A unit is not regarded as "abandoned" if the rent is not in arrears.

b. PRIVACY

The right to possession of premises has always carried with it the right of privacy and the right to use the premises for any lawful purpose. Any restrictions were required to be spelled out in the tenancy agreement. Tenants have now been guaranteed by legislation the right to privacy in their own homes, and this cannot be affected by any term in the lease.

The landlord may enter the rented premises without written notice only under one of the following four circumstances:

(a) In a case of emergency

(b) If the tenant consents at the time of entry

(c) To clean the premises if the tenancy agreement requires the landlord to clean the unit at regular intervals (such entry must be between 8:00 a.m. and 8:00 p.m. unless specified times are set out in the tenancy agreement)

(d) To show the unit to prospective tenants if all of the following conditions are met:

(i) A notice of termination has been given by either the landlord or tenant, or they have agreed to a termination

(ii) The landlord enters the unit between 8:00 a.m. and 8:00 p.m.

(iii) Before entering, the landlord informs or makes a reasonable effort to inform the tenant of the showing

There are also certain circumstances where a landlord may enter a rental unit after having given the tenant at least 24 hours' written notice. These circumstances are —

(a) to carry out a repair or do work in the unit,

(b) to allow a potential mortgagee or insurer to view the unit,

(c) to allow a potential purchaser to view the unit, or

(d) for any other reasonable reason for entry specified in the tenancy agreement.

The written notice must state the reason for entry, the day of entry, and a time between 8:00 a.m. and 8:00 p.m.

It is worth repeating that entry for any reason other than that specifically set out in the act must be found in the tenancy agreement. Otherwise, the landlord is breaching the covenant for quiet enjoyment. Where there is no tenancy agreement specifically providing for any additional rights of entry, the landlord may not enter without consent except for the specific purposes set out above.

Under the Tenant Protection Act, an illegal entry by a landlord is an offence. Any person who knowingly attempts to commit an illegal entry, and every director or officer of a corporation who knowingly concurs, is guilty of an offence. The maximum fine for an individual is $10,000 and for a corporation, $50,000.

1. Political canvassers and tradespeople

Section 22 of the Tenant Protection Act makes it an offence for a landlord to stop political candidates or their agents from coming through a building for the purpose of canvassing or distributing election material. Breach of this provision is an offence under the act and the maximum fine for an individual is $10,000 and for a corporation, $50,000.

There are no specific prohibitions in the act against restricting cleaners or milk and bread deliveries by giving a monopoly to certain tradespeople, even where a fee is charged by the landlord for such a monopoly. However, a landlord cannot stop a tradesperson actually called to the building by a tenant unless such a provision is in the lease.

2. Alteration of locks

Tenants have a privacy interest in limiting access to their unit. Likewise, the landlord has a legitimate interest in being able to get into the unit in the case of an emergency. However, changing locks has been used in the past by some landlords as an illegal method of eviction, and it was primarily for this reason that access limitations were put into the legislation.

The act provides that a landlord shall not alter the locking system on a door giving entry to the unit or complex without giving the tenant replacement keys. This includes doors giving access to the entire apartment building. Breach of this provision is an offence under the act and the maximum fine for an individual is $10,000 and for a corporation, $50,000.

A tenant may not alter locks without the consent of the landlord. This includes chain locks and similar anti-burglary devices.

c. REPAIRS

1. Landlord's responsibilities

According to section 24 of the Tenant Protection Act, a landlord must not only provide, but also maintain, the rented unit and the rental building in which it is located in a good state of repair and fit for habitation during the tenancy. In addition, the landlord must comply with all health, safety, housing, and maintenance standards. These standards are usually found in municipal property standards by-laws, but the act sets out standards for areas where there are none. The by-laws vary from one municipality to another and copies may usually be obtained at local municipal offices. The fact that the tenant knew that the premises were in a bad state of repair at the time of moving in is irrelevant to the obligations of the landlord.

2. The tenant's responsibilities

The tenant is only responsible for the ordinary cleanliness of the premises (except where the tenancy agreement requires the landlord to clean them) and the repair of any damage caused willfully or negligently by the tenant, his or her family, or guests. These responsibilites are considered good house-keeping. They include things such as emptying outside water pipes in winter, cleaning windows, replacing light bulbs, and other little jobs that a reasonable tenant would do. They do not include damage caused by forces or persons over which the tenant has no control.

A tenant is not required to leave the premises in a perfect state of repair when he or she leaves, as long as any damage that there is, is minor and can be considered part of the ordinary use of the premises (e.g., nail holes for the hanging of pictures).

3. Enforcing responsibilities for repair

A tenant may apply to the Ontario Rental Housing Tribunal to enforce the landlord's responsibilities for repair (see chapter 14). An application may be made even after the tenant has vacated the unit. If the tribunal determines that the landlord has breached the repair obligations, the tribunal may do one or more of the following:

(a) Terminate the tenancy

(b) Order an abatement of the rent

(c) Authorize a repair that has been made or is to be made and order its costs to be paid by the landlord to the tenant

(d) Order the landlord to do specified repairs or other work within a specified time

(e) Make any other order that it considers appropriate

In determining the remedy to be given, the tribunal will consider whether the tenant or former tenant advised the landlord of the need for the repairs before applying to the tribunal. Under the previous legislation, courts dealing with similar types of applications took a dim view of tenants who failed to notify the landlord in writing and give a reasonable time in which the repairs could be performed. Termination of a tenancy was ordered only when the repairs were substantial or rendered the premises unfit for habitation.

In all but the most urgent cases, the landlord should be notified in writing about the need for repairs and given a reasonable time in which to perform them. If this produces no results, a tenant should then apply to the tribunal for an order that the landlord repair the damage.

Tenants often ask whether they can make necessary repairs and deduct the cost from the rent. Where the repairs are urgent, it is probably wise to have the repairs made first and apply to the tribunal later for the necessary order for payment. The tribunal can order repayment through deductions from rent, which avoids the possibility of eviction for non-payment of rent. The pitfall occurs if the landlord objects and the tribunal later rules that the repairs were not urgently required or were more expensive than was necessary under the circumstances.

4. Abatement of rent

The act specifically allows the tribunal to award an abatement of rent — the first time the term "abatement" has appeared in the legislation. Under previous legislation, rent abatements or reductions during the period of non-repair were given in a number of cases under a general clause enabling a judge to make such further order as he or she considered appropriate. In one case, tenants were granted a reduction in rent for the period when the air conditioning, swimming pool, and sauna were out of order. A major difficulty in these cases, however, is providing evidence on what the proper reduction in rent should be. The abatement will vary depending on the degree of interference with the use of the premises. Courts often do not value the inconvenience as highly as the tenant and many awards in the past were relatively modest. How the tribunal will deal with such applications remains to be seen.

An abatement of rent may also be obtained in cases where the repairs being made by the landlord substantially interfere with the tenant's reasonable enjoyment of the premises. This could include such things as noise, dust, construction barriers, and shutting off electricity or water. However, the interference must be substantial enough to warrant a reduction of rent.

5. Withholding rent

Even though repairs are a requirement under the act, there is still doubt as to whether a tenant is justified in withholding all of the rent because of the failure of the landlord to make repairs, especially where there is no specific provision regarding repairs in the lease itself. In such cases, the repair provision may not be considered a "material covenant" as discussed in chapter 3. At present, it is not advisable for the tenant to withhold all rent without following legal advice.

6. Decorating

Decorating is not normally regarded as a repair, and a landlord is not required to decorate unless it is specified in the lease. It is possible, however, that a severe need of decorating may be said to fall under the repair section. Such things as minor paint jobs, however, may now be the obligation of the tenant.

7. Liability for loss, damage, or injury

An Ontario court has determined that since the landlord is responsible for repairs, it is also liable for any loss or damage caused to the tenant as a result of the failure to make such repairs. This may involve the tenant suing either in Small Claims Court (where the loss is under $6,000) or in Ontario Court (General Division) (if the loss is more than the Small Claims Court allows), and would cover situations such as being injured by falling down broken stairs or having furniture ruined because of a leaking roof.

Most written leases contain a clause saying that the landlord is not responsible for any injury, loss, or damage to the tenant or his or her family or guests as a result of any occurrences on the rented property. The Ontario Court of Appeal has held that this clause is not enforceable in residential tenancies. The landlord is legally obligated to keep the premises in good repair and is, therefore, liable for any injury, loss, or damage that results from the failure to keep the premises repaired. The "exculpatory" clause is an attempt by the landlord to contract out of an obligation under the act and this is not permitted.

Another effect of the change in responsibility for repairs has been to impose legal liability on a landlord for damage to the property of neighbouring landowners that results from the failure of the landlord to make proper repairs to rented premises. Previously, the tenant, as occupier of the premises, would have been solely liable for the damage.

Obviously, these obligations will make landlords more careful about the condition of their rented property, and they may wish to include a provision for periodic inspection in their leases. Properly used, this could benefit all parties (see Appendix 2).

d. VITAL SERVICES AND MAINTENANCE STANDARDS

Part VII of the Tenant Protection Act recognizes that there will be a great temptation for landlords to have their present tenants vacate a rental unit so that they can enter into a new tenancy agreement with a new tenant at a new and higher rent. One method of attempting to encourage tenants to vacate is to withhold vital services or to allow the maintenance of the building to fall below reasonable standards. A "vital service" is defined as fuel, hydro, gas, or hot or cold water.

This part of the act generally gives the responsibility for preventing such action to municipalities. Part VII contains provisions formerly found in the Municipal Amendment Act (Vital Services), 1994.

Under the act, the local municipal council is empowered to pass by-laws for such things as the following:

(a) Requiring every landlord to provide adequate and suitable vital services to every unit

(b) Prohibiting a supplier from ceasing to provide the vital service until a notice has been given by an official

(c) Requiring a supplier to promptly restore the vital service when directed to do so by an official

(d) Authorizing an official to enter into agreements with suppliers of vital services to ensure that adequate and suitable services are provided for rental units

The municipality may also pass by-laws stating that the person who contravenes or fails to comply with the by-law is guilty of an offence for each day on which the offence continues. They may also provide that every director or officer of a corporation who knowingly concurs in such an offence is also guilty of an offence. A vital services by-law may classify buildings or parts of buildings, and designate the classes to which it applies; designate areas in the municipality in which the by-law applies; and establish standards for the provision of adequate and suitable vital services. By-laws may also be passed to prohibit a landlord from ceasing to provide a vital service except when necessary to alter or repair the rental unit, and then only for the minimum period necessary. They may also provide that a landlord is deemed to have caused the termination of a vital service where the landlord fails to pay the supplier and the service is cut off.

If a supplier intends to discontinue a vital service because the landlord has breached its contract with the supplier whether through failure to pay or otherwise, the supplier must first give notice to the clerk of the municipality at least 30 days before ceasing to provide the service.

A vital services by-law does not apply to a landlord where the tenant has expressly agreed to obtain and maintain the vital services for the rental unit. In other words, if the vital services are not included in the rent, the tenant is responsible for paying the bills and maintaining the service. This arrangement is common with house leases and may be found in other tenancies as well where the utilities are separately metered.

If a landlord does not provide a vital service in accordance with the by-law, the municipality may enter into an agreement with the supplier to have the service continued. The municipality may register a lien against the property for the costs it incurs in doing so, together with an administrative fee. The municipality may also direct the tenant to pay all or part of the rent to the municipality to cover the cost of the service and such payment does not constitute a default in payment of rent under the tenancy agreement. If the rent exceeds the amount the municipality has spent, the balance will be remitted to the landlord.

The act provides that certain municipal officials may enter and inspect a building or part of a building in order to determine compliance with a vital services by-law, or direct a tenant to pay rent to the municipality. However, officials may not enter a rental unit unless they have obtained the consent of the occupant after informing the occupant of his or her right to refuse permission, or unless they have obtained a warrant under the act authorizing the entry.

In most cases, the municipality in which the residential complex is located will have a property standards by-law, and the municipality is fully responsible for enforcing its provisions through municipal work orders. Any complaint should be directed to the property standards department of the municipality.

In areas where there are no property standards by-laws, a regulation under the act prescribes maintenance standards that are applicable to a residential complex and the rental units in it. Where these prescribed maintenance standards apply, a current tenant may apply in writing to the Minister of Municipal Affairs and Housing who will then have an inspection made and, if satisfied that the prescribed maintenance standards are not being met, may issue a work order requiring the landlord to comply.

e. ASSIGNMENT AND SUBLETTING

The Tenant Protection Act deals specifically with assignment and subletting and sets out the obligations, options, and consequences of each procedure.

A tenant will want to assign a rental unit when he or she wishes to vacate the rental unit permanently. Subletting is used by those who are leaving temporarily — such as taking an extended vacation or students going home for the summer. Subletting only gives the subtenant the right to occupy the rental unit for a certain period of time ending on a specified date before the end of the original tenant's term, and giving the original tenant the right to resume occupancy on that date. A subtenant has no right to continue to occupy the rental unit after the end of the subtenancy.

A tenant may bring an application before the tribunal for an order evicting a subtenant in the same manner as a landlord may. This could be because the tenant requires the premises for his or her own use, because of non-payment of rent, or on the basis of any other applicable ground under the act. A tenant may also apply to the tribunal for an order for compensation from an overholding subtenant after the end of the subtenancy. This would be based on the rent that was charged, calculated daily, until the subtenant moves out or is evicted.

1. Benefits and liabilities

The legislation clearly sets out that all tenants have the right to assign or sublet a rented apartment or house. However, assignment or subletting does not necessarily terminate the lease or tenancy agreement.

Once a tenant has assigned a rental unit to another person (an "assignee"), the tenancy agreement continues to apply. The assignee is liable to the landlord for any breach of the tenant's obligations. The assignee may also enforce any of the landlord's obligations under the tenancy agreement or the act where such breach or obligation relates to the period after the assignment. The former tenant remains liable to the landlord only for any breaches of the tenant's obligations that occurred before the assignment and may enforce any of the landlord's obligations for the same period. Likewise, the former tenant may carry on a proceeding commenced under the act before the assignment provided that, if the benefits or obligations of the new tenant may be affected, the new tenant may either join in or continue the proceeding on his or her own.

After a subletting, the original tenant remains entitled to the benefits of the tenancy agreement or the act. He or she is also liable to the landlord for the breaches of the tenant's obligations under the tenancy agreement or the act (including breaches by the subtenant). The subtenant is entitled to the benefits of the subletting agreement or the act, and is liable to the tenant for the breaches of the subtenant's obligations under the subletting agreement or the act during the sub-tenancy.

2. Consent

The consent of the landlord must be requested for either an assignment or subletting. If the landlord gives consent, it is entitled to charge the tenant for reasonable out-of-pocket expenses incurred in giving such consent. This could include such things as the cost of obtaining income information, credit checks, or references. It is not intended to cover a flat "stand-ard" fee which may or may not bear any relation to actual expenses. The act does not define "reasonable expenses" so an itemized list of the charges should be requested before payment is made. However, this does not apply to the situation where the tenant asks the landlord to find a new tenant or where the tenant simply wants the lease cancelled.

There is no obligation on the landlord to provide a new tenant for the premises. The tenant must find the subtenant or assignee and make the arrangement personally with that person.

A tenant may seek the consent of a landlord for the assignment of a rental unit without specifying a potential assignee (the person to whom the unit is to be assigned). This may occur where the tenant has not yet located an assignee but wishes to know that the landlord is prepared to consent, at least in general terms. If the landlord gives such consent, it may still refuse consent at a later date to an assignment to a specific person whom it does not find acceptable.

Where the landlord either refuses consent or fails to re-spond to a request for consent within 7 days in the case either of an assignment or an assignment to a specific assignee, the tenant is entitled to give the landlord notice of termination within 30 days after the date he or she made the request. The date for termination to be specified is 30 days or such lesser period as may be otherwise required under the act. Presumably, a shorter period would apply only to a daily or weekly tenancy.

Where a tenant feels that the landlord's refusal to consent to a subletting or assignment to a specific subtenant or assignee is arbitrary or unreasonable, the tenant (whether or not he or she is still in possession) may apply to the tribunal for an order making this determination. If the tribunal determines that the landlord has unlawfully withheld consent, the tribunal may do one or more of the following:

(a) Order that the assignment or sublet is authorized

(b) Where appropriate, authorize another assignment or sublet proposed by the tenant

(c) Order that the tenancy be terminated

(d) Order an abatement of the tenant's or former tenant's rent

The tribunal may also establish terms and conditions for the assignment or sublet. An order from the tribunal authorizing an assignment or sublet has the same legal effect as if the landlord had consented to it.

The act provides no guidance as to what constitutes arbitrariness or unreasonableness in withholding consent. Cases under previous legislation held that a landlord did have some control over who could occupy the building under an assignment arrangement. A landlord could refuse consent to a subtenant or assignee proposed by an existing tenant if the landlord maintained a "waiting list" and had a policy of offering vacancies to persons on that list. In such a situation, the tenancy was terminated and the existing tenant was freed of all further obligations.

3. Rent control

An assignee is not treated as a new tenant for the purpose of rent control under the act. He or she simply takes over the rights and obligations (including payment of rent) of the tenant under the tenancy agreement. An assignee pays the same rent as the original tenant until such time as an increase is permitted under Part VI of the act. No doubt landlords would prefer to try to rent to a new tenant at a higher rental if the market permits, and will try to find a way to refuse consent. The tenant's options, as explained above, are to seek a tribunal order that the landlord is being arbitrary or unreasonable, or simply give a notice of termination. The latter should satisfy the tenant's needs in most cases — unless the purpose is to transfer the tenancy to a friend or relative at a favourable rent.

In a somewhat ironic twist, there are now situations where it is in the landlord's interest to have a tenant assign rather than terminate. Where a tenant has been in occupation of the rental unit since before the commencement of the new act and is paying less than maximum rent, and where the market will not permit the landlord to increase rent to a new tenant, the landlord is potentially better off with an assignment so that the maximum rent ceiling is retained for a possible future increase.

The rent control rules are applicable to subleases and a tenant may not charge a subtenant a greater rent than he or she was paying to the landlord. This includes subletting to more than one person where all rent payments together exceed what is charged by the landlord. Any fee, commission, or key deposit charged to a subtenant or to an assignee for permitting occupancy is also unlawful.

There are some specific rent rules for situations where a person occupies a rental unit as the result of an assignment obtained without the consent of the landlord, or where a subtenant continues to occupy a rental unit until after the end of the subtenancy and the tenant has abandoned the rental unit. In these cases, the landlord may negotiate a new tenancy agreement at a new rent with the assignee or subtenant. If such agreements are entered into within 60 days after the landlord discovers the unauthorized occupancy, the lawful rent becomes the rent first charged to this person.

However, if no tenancy agreement is entered into and neither the landlord nor the tenant applies to the tribunal for an order evicting the person within 60 days after the landlord discovers the unauthorized occupancy in the case of an assignment and after the end of the subtenancy in the case of a sublease, the person's occupation of the rental unit is deemed to have the same effect as an assignment with the consent of the landlord from the date the unauthorized occupancy began. The person cannot thereafter be evicted on this basis nor can the rent be increased except in accordance with Part VI of the act.

4. Who may assign or sublet

The sections in the act related to assignment and subletting apply to all tenants, regardless of whether the tenancy is periodic, fixed, contractual, or statutory. However, they do not apply to a tenant of a superintendent's premises.

Under prior legislation, a monthly tenant probably had no right to sublet or assign. A judge had stated that the rationale of the automatic statutory continuation of tenancies on a monthly basis ("statutory tenancy") was not to create perpetual arrangements that could be controlled by tenants. As early as 1982, an Ontario appeal court held that a "statutory tenant" had no such right. The case involved a situation where the term of a lease was ending and the tenants wanted to move out but wished to sublet their apartment to relatives. Although the case was decided on the basis that the subletting provision in the act was intended to protect only existing tenants and only as long as they remained in the premises, some argue that this decision applied only to the statutory extension arising after the expiration of a lease and did not apply where the tenancy has been on a monthly basis from the beginning. The specific provision in the new act has now made this argument irrelevant.

Tenants who are residents in social housing do not have a right to sublet or assign (see chapter 1). Since occupants of these units usually have their rents established in accordance with their incomes and since there is always a long waiting list for such units, it is not appropriate to permit subletting or assignment. In any case, such units are usually rented on a monthly basis and, with proper notice, the tenancy agreement may be readily and quickly cancelled by the tenant.

Other tenants without the right to sublet or assign are tenants of non-member units in non-profit housing co-operatives, student or staff occupants of some units provided by an educational institution, and occupants of units in a non-profit residential complex owned or operated by a religious institution for a charitable use.

5. Cancelling leases

Many landlords have, in the past, preferred to cancel the original lease and enter into a new one with the new tenant. There were several reasons for this. On a subtenancy, the original tenant might disappear and the landlord would want to have an agreement with the new tenant so that the landlord would be able to sue the new tenant for rent, if necessary. The landlord may also wish to lease the premises for a longer term. Under the new legislation, there is also the compelling reason for being able to set a new (and higher) rent. If a new lease is entered into, the obligations of the original tenant under the old lease cease unless there is some agreement to the contrary.

6. Rights of subtenants

There is a hazard that a subtenant who is subletting from the original tenant should be aware of. A case in the Ontario Supreme Court involved a situation where the subtenant's name did not appear on the lease and there was apparently no specific consent by the landlord to the subtenancy. When the original tenant agreed with the landlord to vacate the premises, the court held that, "due to legislative oversight," the subtenant did not even have the right to be notified of or dispute the landlord's claim for possession in eviction proceedings under Part IV of the Landlord and Tenant Act.

This decision could cause great difficulty to persons subletting directly from a prior tenant where the landlord's consent has not been obtained. If the original tenant were to breach the tenancy agreement or even agree with the landlord to surrender the lease, the subtenant would have no right to dispute any action for possession of the premises and could seek only monetary damages from the original tenant.

This unfortunate legal situation could also be used as a device where developers, who are temporarily renting houses while awaiting municipal clearance to proceed with their development, could quickly obtain possession of these houses when required. All they would have to do would be to rent the houses first to a person (or corporation) under their control who would be prepared to surrender the original lease at the developer's convenience. Once that is done, the subtenant loses all rights of possession.

As was the case with previous legislation, there is no specific provision in the act that a subtenant must be advised and given the opportunity to be heard at a hearing into an application brought by the landlord to the tribunal. However, there was a decision by the Ontario Court of Appeal under the previous legislation that a subtenant, where the subtenancy had been consented to by the landlord, was entitled to notice of an application by the landlord and to be heard at the hearing. The new act states that "other persons directly affected" are parties to an application to the tribunal in addition to the landlord and the tenant.

Under the law, a subtenant has no greater right than a tenant and, if the tenant's tenancy is terminated, the subtenant has no right to remain in possession of the unit. The subtenant's only course of action would be to enter into a new lease with the landlord provided, of course, that the landlord is prepared to do so. Under such circumstances, the former subtenant would become a new tenant at whatever new rent he or she is able to negotiate with the landlord. See chapter 8 for a discussion on rules regarding rent.

Subtenants should always make sure that the consent of the landlord is obtained. Every tenant should be certain that the "landlord" is actually the owner of the premises and not just a tenant.

f. SEIZURE OF A TENANT'S BELONGINGS (DISTRESS)

"Distress" is the common-law right of a landlord to "distrain" (i.e., seize without a court order) the furniture and goods of a tenant who is 15 days behind in paying the rent. This was abolished in Ontario in 1970 for residential tenancies.

Certain provisions in the Innkeepers Act permitted rooming house or lodging house owners to seize personal belongings for arrears of rent. The legislation was amended in 1987 to prohibit such seizures.

Apart from the offence discussed below, the act does not specifically provide for the return of distrained belongings. If the tenant is still in occupation of the premises, it might be possible to bring an application to the tribunal under a related heading (e.g., illegal entry by landlord, interference with reasonable enjoyment, altering locking system, or harassment), and seek an order for return of property under the tribunal's authority to "make any other order that it considers appropriate." This would certainly be a faster process but, in most cases, the tenant would have been illegally evicted at the same time that the belongings were seized.

Where a landlord does wrongfully distrain or seize goods or belongings, the tenant's remedy is usually to sue the landlord. This action will be brought in the local Small Claims Court if the value of the goods is under $6,000 and in Ontario Court (General Division) if the value is higher. The tenant may ask for an order for return of the goods wrongfully held. If the goods are no longer in the possession of the landlord, the action would be for their value. The procedure in Small Claims Court is quite informal but if it is necessary to commence proceedings in Ontario Court (General Division), a lawyer should be consulted. See chapter 15 for more information on these courts.

The abolition of distress has no effect on the right of a landlord or any other person who has been successful in a legal action to collect the amount of the court judgment from the losing party. This may involve seizure of goods and belongings of a tenant by the sheriff in order to satisfy the judgment. This section of the Tenant Protection Act covers only the situation where a landlord seizes the goods of a tenant on its own initiative without the necessary legal action having been taken.

There are specific provisions in the act dealing with what a landlord may do with belongings apparently abandoned by a vacating tenant or when a tenant dies (see chapters 5 and 6).

A landlord who seizes a tenant's property illegally for non-payment of rent or other obligation under the tenancy agreement, is guilty of an offence under the act and may be fined up to $10,000 ($50,000 for a corporation).

g. ACCELERATED RENT

Before the enactment of Part IV of the Landlord and Tenant Act, many leases contained a clause that if the tenant defaulted in the payment of rent or breached any other term in the lease, a substantial portion of the rent for the remainder of the term (usually 3 months' rent) became due immediately.

That legislation placed severe limitations on when such a penalty clause could be enforced.

Section 14 of the Tenant Protection Act now makes such a provision in a tenancy agreement void and it should no longer appear in a lease. If it does appear, it is not enforceable.

h. POSTDATED CHEQUES

A landlord may not ask for postdated cheques for the rent. A tenant may, for the sake of convenience, voluntarily give the landlord postdated cheques for the duration of the tenancy but does so at his or her peril. Cheques and other like instruments, such as promissory notes, occupy a special position in the law and the holder of such a document may, in some cases, sue the person who signed for the amount on the face of the document without ever being required to prove that the object (in this case, occupation of rented premises) for which the cheque was intended as payment was ever, in fact, given. While this is not always the result, the simplest way of avoiding problems is not to give the landlord postdated cheques. It may also save the cost of a stop payment order to the bank should there be a problem during the tenancy.

i. DISCLOSURE OF INFORMATION BY A LANDLORD

Previous legislation required that the legal name and address of the landlord be conspicuously posted and that this name and address could be properly used by a tenant beginning any legal action against the landlord. This latter provision was thought necessary to counter the practice of some landlords of creating a number of sham corporations and either disguising the true ownership of the building or at least complicating the situation to the extent where many legal actions begun by tenants were lost due to technicalities. This has been replaced by the requirement, discussed in chapter 2, that this information be in the lease or be provided to the tenant within 21 days.

42

The landlord was also required to post conspicuously, and maintain posted, a copy of Part IV of the Landlord and Tenant Act or a summary of it. A prescribed summary was set out as a regulation published under that act. There is no similar provision in the Tenant Protection Act.

j. PETS

Provisions in tenancy agreements prohibiting the presence of animals in or around a residential rental building are now void.

The activities or propensities of certain pets may still provide a basis for termination of the tenancy and eviction in certain circumstances (see chapter 6).

k. PROTECTION FROM HARASSMENT

A tenant has a right to live in peace in the rental unit throughout the entire period of occupancy. Even if he or she is ordered evicted, this right continues up until the day on which the actual eviction order becomes enforceable.

During this period, a landlord must not at any time substantially interfere with the reasonable enjoyment of the rental unit or the building in which it is located for all usual purposes by a tenant or members of his or her household. This includes continuing to supply all vital services, care services, or food that the landlord is obliged to supply, or not deliberately interfering with the reasonable supply of these services by others. It is an offence under the act to withhold the reasonable supply of a vital service, care service, or food, or interfere with its supply.

The act also contains a very broad provision that a landlord shall not harass, obstruct, coerce, threaten, or interfere with a tenant. It is an offence to harass, hinder, obstruct, or interfere with the tenant in the exercise of —

(a) securing a right or seeking relief under this act or in the court,

43

(b) participating in a proceeding under this act, or

(c) participating in a tenants' association or attempting to organize a tenants' association.

In addition, it is an offence to harass a tenant in such a manner that the tenant is induced to vacate the rental unit. In such cases, the tenant may also be awarded compensation for any higher rent he or she has to pay at a new unit for up to one year as well as all reasonable moving, storage, and other expenses.

It is an offence for any landlord or superintendent, agent, or employee of the landlord to knowingly harass a tenant or interfere with a tenant's reasonable enjoyment of a rental unit or the rental complex in which it is located.

As with other offences, the maximum penalty on conviction is a fine of up to $10,000 for an individual and $50,000 for a corporation.

l. ENFORCEMENT OF RIGHTS

A tenant or former tenant may apply to the Ontario Rental Housing Tribunal (see chapter 14) in any of the following cases:

(a) A landlord has unlawfully withheld consent to an assignment or sublet.

(b) A landlord has breached its obligations regarding repairs.

(c) A landlord, superintendent, or agent of the landlord illegally entered the rental unit.

(d) A landlord, superintendent, or agent of the landlord has illegally changed locks without giving the tenant replacement keys.

(e) A landlord, superintendent, or agent of the landlord has withheld the reasonable supply of any vital service, care service, or food that it is the landlord's obligation to supply.

(f) A landlord, superintendent, or agent of the landlord has substantially interfered with the reasonable enjoyment of the rental unit for all usual purposes by the tenant or a member of his or her household.

(g) A landlord, superintendent, or agent of the landlord has harassed, obstructed, coerced, threatened, or interfered with the tenant.

(h) A landlord has given a notice in bad faith that it requires the tenant's unit for its own use or that of a member of its immediate family.

(i) A landlord has given a notice in bad faith that the rental unit has been sold and the purchaser requires the premises for his or her own use of that of his or her immediate family.

(j) A landlord has given a notice in bad faith that it intends to demolish, convert, repair, or renovate the rental unit and requires vacant possession.

Any such application must be made within one year after the alleged conduct occurred.

If the tribunal determines that a landlord, a superintendent, or an agent of a landlord has done one or more of the activities set out in paragraphs (c) to (j) above, the tribunal may —

(a) order that landlord, superintendent, or agent not to engage in any further activities of that nature;

(b) order an abatement of rent;

(c) order that the landlord pay to the tribunal an administrative fine not exceeding the greater of $10,000 or the monetary jurisdiction of the local Small Claims Court;

(d) order that the tenancy be terminated; and

(e) make such other order that it considers appropriate.

Where a tenant has been induced to vacate the rental unit by any of the conduct referred to above, the tribunal may, in addition, order the landlord to pay compensation to the tenant for —

(a) all or any portion of any increased rent that the tenant has incurred or will incur for a one-year period, and

(b) reasonable out-of-pocket, moving, storage, and other similar expenses that the tenant has incurred or will incur.

5
WHAT RIGHTS DOES A LANDLORD HAVE?

a. DEPOSITS

1. Security or damage deposits

Before the changes that came into effect on January 1, 1970, with Part IV of the Landlord and Tenant Act, the most controversial and widely reported tenancy problem concerned the landlord's right to insist on a security deposit that could be held until the termination of the tenancy and then used to pay for any damage the landlord felt the tenant had caused to the rented premises.

These security deposits were governed solely by the terms of the lease that had been entered into. The terms usually stated that all, or a portion of, the security deposit could be withheld by the landlord if the tenant breached any "covenant" (i.e., promise) in the lease. This virtually always included any type of damage, however caused, with the exception of ordinary wear and tear and, in many cases, included failure to pay rent or failure to give proper notice of termination as well. Many landlords took advantage of the money in their hands and improperly levied charges for cleaning, decorating, and normal wear and tear.

Before the original enactment of Part IV of the Landlord and Tenant Act, a tenant who felt that improper deductions were made from the security deposit could only recover by suing the landlord in Small Claims Court. Needless to say, few did this and as a result many were cheated.

Section 117 (2) of the Tenant Protection Act defines "security deposit" in the following terms:

> "security deposit" means money, property, or a right paid or given by, or on behalf of, a tenant of a rental unit to a landlord or to anyone on the landlord's behalf to be held by or for the account of the landlord as security for the performance of an obligation or the payment of a liability of the tenant or to be returned to the tenant upon the happening of a condition.

In practice, most deposits were given in the form of money, as a guarantee that the landlord would have some funds available to repair the unit if the tenant caused damage and vacated without rectifying the problem. The definition in the act widens the meaning to include any type of security held by the landlord for the performance of any obligation by the tenant. This wide definition is to prevent a landlord trying to get a security deposit by making it appear to be something else.

2. Rent deposits

Since 1970, it has been illegal for a landlord to demand or receive a security deposit for damage. Instead, landlords are permitted to require prepayment of an amount not exceeding the rent for one month at the time the tenancy agreement is entered into. This deposit must be credited against the last rent payment due either under the tenancy agreement or immediately preceding some other proper termination of the tenancy. Where the tenancy is weekly or daily (as may be the case in a rooming house or boarding house), the maximum deposit can only be for the amount of the rent for one week or one day, as the case may be. Under any rental arrangement, the maximum deposit permitted by law is one month's rent.

This money may not be used by the landlord for repairs or to cover arrears of rent for any other period. A landlord may also not require a tenant to pay the last month's rent at the time it would normally become due and then return the rent deposit at a later date. Under the arrangement permitted by the act, the tenant has prepaid the last month's rent and is entitled to occupation of the premises without any further payment for that month.

Other types of "deposits" for keys, carpets, keeping of pets, or other such situations are similarly unlawful.

In addition, landlords are required to pay 6% interest on any deposit held by them. This interest rate is set out in the act and does not change from year to year. The interest must be paid out to the tenant during each year throughout the duration of the tenancy and may not be held back until the tenancy is terminated. If the interest is not paid when due, the tenant may deduct it from the next rent payment.

If the rent is legally increased during the tenancy, the landlord may require the tenant to increase the deposit to the amount of the new rent. Breach of any of these provisions for deposits may subject the landlord to a fine of $10,000 ($50,000 for a corporation).

For some time after the original enactment of these changes, there was disagreement as to whether a prepayment of rent could be demanded in monthly or weekly "periodic" tenancies since such tenancies are only for one month or less. On one side, it was argued that these tenancies terminate at the end of each week or month and are then renewed for a further like period. This means that there is no other later period for which prepayment of rent can be applied. On the other hand, it was argued that since a period of notice exceeding the rental period must be given prior to termination (28 days for weekly tenancies; 60 days for longer tenancies), the prepayment of rent can be demanded and is applicable to that rental period "immediately preceding the termination of the tenancy."

The prevailing view now is that rental deposits can be required for short periodic tenancies. This is confirmed by the new act which makes specific reference to deposits for tenancies of one month or less.

It is important to note that, except in a few unusual circumstances, the rent deposit must be agreed to either before or in the tenancy agreement. The act does not give the landlord the right to demand it at any later time.

New landlords remain responsible for crediting the deposit in payment of the last month's rent, even if these amounts were not transferred to them when they bought the property from the landlord to whom the deposits were paid. Once a tenant makes a prepayment deposit for the last month's rent, that month's rent is paid (subject only to any "top up" if the rent has been increased and the original deposit has not).

3. Deposits with offers to lease

Some landlords require a deposit when a prospective tenant signs an offer to lease. In most cases, this deposit is intended only as insurance that the person will enter into a tenancy agreement and the amount of the deposit will then be credited against the rent. Often this deposit is equal to the first and last months' rent and will be applied accordingly.

There is, however, no legal requirement that the arrangement be handled in this manner and, as a prospective tenant, you should be careful to ascertain what will be done with the deposit before signing the documents. If, for whatever reason, you do not or cannot enter into the tenancy, you can almost always expect to lose this deposit. You may also be liable for damages if the landlord is unable to rent the apartment to some other tenant for the same period at the same rent.

Unless otherwise specified, you have the right to withdraw the offer at any time prior to it being accepted (i.e., signed) by the landlord or its representative. In these cases, the deposit should be returned. However, most offers to lease contain a provision that the applicant cannot withdraw for a specified number of days (the "irrevocable" period). In any case, it may prove very difficult to determine exactly when the offer was accepted by the landlord. In the rare case that the payment was solely a prepayment of rent, the tenant would have a valid claim for its return but this may be offset by the landlord's claim for damages where the offer had, in fact, been accepted. A discussion of the landlord's duty to minimize such damages is found in chapter 3.

4. Suing for damage

Although security deposits for damage are illegal, a tenant may still be sued for damage to the premises in Small Claims Court. If the tenant is still living in the apartment, the landlord can apply to the tribunal for an order for compensation for "undue" damage caused willfully or negligently by the tenant or someone the tenant permits in the building.

It is always wise for the tenant and the landlord to jointly fill in and sign a "rental unit condition report" before moving in. Each party should then keep a copy of the report for reference at the end of the tenancy. All defects should be noted. An example of such a form may be found in Appendix 2.

b. DISPOSING OF ABANDONED PROPERTY

Before the Tenant Protection Act, there were no clear guidelines on the rights and obligations of landlords concerning property left behind by a tenant after termination of a tenancy or abandonment of a residential unit.

Under the act, a landlord may sell, retain for the landlord's own use, or otherwise dispose of property left in a rental unit or the building. However, where an order is made to evict a tenant, the landlord may not dispose of the tenant's property until at least 48 hours after the enforcement of the eviction order. During this time, the landlord must make the property available to be retrieved by the tenant either from the rental unit or some place nearby.

If a landlord follows these requirements, it is not liable for whatever type of disposal of the property is used. The act leaves it open for landlords and tenants to agree to terms other than those set out in the act for disposal of the tenant's property. Presumably, this could include storage for a longer time and the charging of storage fees.

Different provisions apply where the tenant dies leaving property in the rental unit. These are discussed in chapter 6.

c. OVERHOLDING BY THE TENANT

Section 45 of the Tenant Protection Act states that the landlord is entitled to compensation when the tenant does not vacate the premises after proper notice to terminate has been served on or given to the tenant. This compensation for use and occupation is normally equal to the rent (on a daily basis) formerly charged for the premises. The landlord may apply to the tribunal for an order for payment. In calculating the amount owing, the tribunal will deduct the amount of any rent deposit or interest owing on a deposit.

Before the amendments to the Landlord and Tenant Act, if the tenant did not vacate after the landlord gave notice, he or she would be liable to pay at the rate of double the yearly value of the land and, in cases where the tenant gave the notice and then did not vacate, he or she would have to pay double the rent.

d. REINSTATEMENT OF A TENANCY

Even after notice has been given, it may be waived and the tenancy reinstated if the parties agree, or if the landlord fails to apply for an eviction order within 30 days after the date specified in the notice.

Landlords used to fear that if they accepted arrears of rent or compensation for the period during which a tenant or other occupant remained in possession of the unit after a notice of termination was given, this was an indication of an agreement to reinstate the tenancy. They were also afraid to give a notice of a rent increase for the same reason. Section 45 makes it clear that more than just acceptance of money or giving a rent increase notice during this period is required to waive a notice of termination, reinstate a tenancy, or create a new tenancy. There must be a specific agreement.

A landlord who has a claim for rent or compensation during the period after which notice of termination has been given, may either sue for this amount in court or include the claim in an application to the tribunal for an eviction order.

e. COMPENSATION

1. Compensation from an unauthorized occupant

A landlord is entitled to compensation for an unauthorized occupant's use and occupation of the unit. Presumably, this covers subtenants who remain in the unit after the end of their subtenancy or after the tenancy of their sublandlord (the original tenant) has been terminated. It would also cover trespassers.

This enables the landlord to be compensated without establishing a tenancy with the unauthorized occupant.

2. Misrepresentation of income

Non-profit co-operatives and landlords of social housing rented on a geared-to-income basis may apply to the tribunal for an order for payment of the amount of money the tenant should have paid based on actual income. Such applications may only be brought while the tenant is in possession. Otherwise, a court action is required.

f. SELECTING PROSPECTIVE TENANTS

Because of the landlord's limited ability to evict tenants, it is very important for landlords to take particular care in selecting tenants at the outset.

In selecting prospective tenants, landlords may use income information, credit checks, credit references, rental history, guarantees, or other similar business practices. The use of "income information" will, of course, enable the landlord to determine whether or not a prospective tenant is receiving social assistance. Discrimination in accommodation because of receipt of public assistance was, before the Tenant Protection Act, prohibited under the Ontario Human Rights Code. Inclusion of this provision in the Tenant Protection Act required an amendment to the code so that landlords may use such information provided they do so in the manner prescribed in new regulations to be made under the Ontario Human Rights Code.

g. HARASSMENT

Just as a landlord is prohibited from harassing a tenant, a tenant is prohibited from harassing, obstructing, coercing, threatening, or interfering with a landlord. Not all landlords are large corporations. Many landlords are women, seniors, or members of a visible minority. They are as vulnerable to harassment as are many tenants.

A tenant who harasses or interferes with a landlord while securing a right or seeking relief under this act, or in the court, or in participating in a proceeding under the act is guilty of an offence and subject to a maximum fine of $10,000.

6

TERMINATION OF A TENANCY

A tenancy does not terminate automatically just because the end of the specified term has been reached. A tenancy may only be terminated in accordance with the Tenant Protection Act, which requires a written notice of termination unless there is a written agreement between a landlord and tenant to terminate the tenancy. Both an agreement to terminate and a tenant's notice to terminate are void if given at the time the tenancy agreement is entered into or as a condition of entering into it.

A tenant may give a notice of termination without specifying a reason. However, a landlord can only give a notice of termination that sets out a reason recognized as valid under the act.

a. TYPES OF TENANCIES

The validity of a notice of termination depends, in part, on the nature of the tenancy.

Basically, there are two types of residential tenancies. There are "fixed term" tenancies, which have a specified termination date (usually, but not always, set out in a written lease), and there are "periodic" tenancies, which have no specified termination date but are entered into for a daily, weekly, monthly, yearly, or other period. In either situation, the required type and length of notice must be given by either a landlord or a tenant before the tenancy is terminated.

A tenancy agreement for a fixed term is considered to be automatically renewed on a monthly basis if it comes to an end before it is terminated or a new agreement is made. A periodic tenancy is deemed to be renewed for another day, week, month, year, or other period depending on the original arrangement. In both situations, the tenancy is renewed on the same terms and conditions but is subject to the rent increases permitted under the act.

b. BREAKING A LEASE

Only rarely is there any provision in a fixed term lease that allows a tenant to terminate the lease before the end of the term. If the tenancy agreement is periodic, a tenant can give notice in the proper form and move out at the end of the notice period. Where the lease is for a specified term, however, the tenant is legally stuck with it for that period. As stated in chapter 3, even the landlord's failure to perform a material covenant of the lease may not give a tenant the right to terminate the agreement entirely.

Holding a noisy party in the hope that the landlord will break the lease is not the answer either. Courts have held that where a tenant, by means of excessive noise or other objectionable conduct, forces the landlord to terminate the lease, the tenant will be deemed to have "abandoned" the lease, and will still be liable for any loss suffered by the landlord from lost rental or costs of reletting.

If a tenant does break the lease, the landlord has a duty to minimize its loss. In general contract law, whenever a contract is broken, the party who will suffer loss because of the breach is under an obligation to minimize this loss as much as he or she reasonably can under the circumstances. This is referred to as "mitigation of damages" (see chapter 3). In other words, where a tenant unlawfully breaks a lease and moves out, the landlord is under an obligation to re-rent the apartment or house as soon as possible and reduce the loss.

A landlord who can relet the premises only at a lower rent or for a shorter period than under the original lease, may be reluctant to do so if it thinks that it could still collect rent from the original tenant. However, failure to relet the premises would probably mean that the tenant would only be liable for the difference between what the tenant owed and what the landlord could reasonably have recovered from another tenant. A landlord may also have other apartments or houses vacant that it might try to rent first and thus build up its claim against the defaulting tenant for unpaid rent. In any case, it is often very difficult to prove what a landlord did or did not do to minimize damages.

A Supreme Court of Canada case has confirmed that a landlord is permitted to claim damages against a defaulting tenant for losses and expenses reasonably incurred even after the premises have been re-rented to a new tenant.

To summarize, a landlord is required to re-rent premises that have been unlawfully vacated by a tenant as soon as possible and on the best terms possible. A defaulting tenant will be liable only for the period during which the premises are actually vacant and for any actual expenses necessarily incurred by the landlord in finding a new tenant. In some cases, this may include the cost of minor repairs, redecorating and, perhaps, a reduction in rent. Despite the provision for minimization of losses, it can still be costly to terminate a lease illegally.

c. AGREEMENT TO TERMINATE

A landlord and tenant may at any time mutually agree to terminate a tenancy. A written agreement signed by both parties and specifying a termination date will be enforced by the tribunal if an application is made within 30 days of the termination date by filing the agreement with the court.

Under the act, an agreement to terminate is void if given at the time the tenancy agreement is entered into or as a condition of entering into it. However, there is an exception in the regulations for certain arrangements between students and educational institutions that provide accommodation.

d. NOTICES OF TERMINATION

1. General provisions

Any notice, by either a landlord or a tenant, to terminate a tenancy must be in a form approved by the tribunal and must —

(a) identify the rental unit,

(b) state the date on which the tenancy is to terminate, and

(c) be signed by the person giving notice or the person's agent.

If the notice is given by a landlord, it must also set out the reasons for and details of the termination and inform the tenant that —

(a) if the tenant does not vacate the rental unit, the landlord may apply to the tribunal for a eviction order, and

(b) the tenant is entitled to dispute any such application.

Generally, notice to end a tenancy agreement, by either a landlord or a tenant, has to be given not less than 28 days before the last day of a daily or weekly tenancy, and 60 days before the last day of a monthly, yearly, or fixed term tenancy. For the purpose of calculating the 60 days, February is treated as if it had 30 days (i.e., a notice given by January 1 is effective for the last day of February and a notice given by February 1 is effective for the last day of March).

In some cases, the period of notice required is shorter. There are also a few situations where a longer period of notice is required. See the discussion under section **e**.

The termination date specified in the notice must be the last day of a fixed term tenancy or the last day of a period of a periodic tenancy. The latter is often, but not always, the last day of a month (especially for monthly tenancies). It is always the day before the date on which rent is due for the next period.

Whatever period of notice is required, it must consist of "clear" days. This means that neither the day the notice is given or the day it is to be effective is counted in deciding whether there has been sufficient notice.

Failure to give sufficient notice or to have it be effective on the correct date may render the notice void and the entire process may have to be started again. However, some court decisions have accepted less than perfect compliance, especially where the landlord was aware of the tenant's intention in time. Landlords are treated much more strictly than tenants regarding notices.

An application for eviction must be brought before the tribunal within 30 days after the termination date specified in the notice or the notice becomes void. There is one exception to this requirement. The time limit does not apply to a notice based on the tenant's failure to pay rent. This gives the landlord and tenant some flexibility in working out a payment schedule for arrears without the landlord having to give a new notice if the tenant defaults. An eviction application is, of course, not required if the tenant vacates the rental unit on or before the date in the notice of termination.

There are also certain circumstances where the notice becomes void if the tenant rectifies his or her default within a specific period. In these cases, there is nothing that the landlord can do to keep the notice in effect and proceed to an eviction. If arrears of rent are involved, the tenant can make the payment to the landlord or to the tribunal. For more detail, see section **e.2**.

After the date in the notice terminating the tenancy, the landlord is no longer entitled to rent. However, a landlord is entitled to compensation for use and occupation of the rental unit after that date. This amount will be calculated daily based on the previous rent.

During the period after the notice has been given, the notice is not considered to have been waived just because the landlord accepts arrears of rent or compensation or gives the tenant a notice of rent increase. A specific agreement between the landlord and tenant is needed to reinstate the tenancy or create a new one.

2. Methods of giving notices

A number of methods for giving a written notice are set out in the act. These methods are —

(a) handing it to the landlord or tenant,

(b) handing it to an employee of the landlord who has authority in the residential complex,

(c) handing it to an apparently adult person in the rental unit (for delivery to a tenant, subtenant, or occupant),

(d) leaving it in the mailbox where mail is ordinarily delivered,

(e) leaving it at the place where mail is ordinarily delivered to the person where there is no mailbox,

(f) sending it by mail to the last known address where the person resides or carries on business, or

(g) any other means allowed in the rules.

A notice given by mail is deemed to have been given on the fifth day after mailing.

Delivery by courier is not included in the list. This method might qualify as handing it to the person or an apparently adult person in the unit but there is no easy way of proving actual delivery by this method should proof later be required for an application to the tribunal. It is no longer acceptable to give a notice to a tenant by "posting" or taping it to the door of the rental unit.

A notice that is not given in one of the methods set out in this list is still considered to have been validly given if it is proven that its contents actually came to the attention of the person for whom it was intended within the required time.

e. WHEN THE LANDLORD WANTS TO TERMINATE AT THE END OF A PERIOD OR TERM

A lease or tenancy does not come to an end on the date given in a written lease or on the final day of a periodic tenancy. The lease or tenancy is automatically renewed. The landlord must give notice to terminate any tenancy and it can only do so for reasons specifically set out in the Tenant Protection Act.

The following are recognized by the act as valid reasons for a landlord to terminate a lease at the end of a period or term of a tenancy:

(a) The landlord requires possession for occupation by him or herself or certain family members (the landlord's spouse or a child or parent of one of them).

(b) The rental unit has been sold and the purchaser requires the unit for occupation by him or herself or certain family members (the purchaser's spouse or a child or parent of one of them).

(c) The landlord requires possession for demolition, conversion to a non-residential use, or extensive repairs or renovations (120 days' notice required).

(d) The tenant persistently failed to pay rent on the due date.

(e) The tenant no longer meets the qualifications for a geared-to-income rental unit.

(f) The rental unit was provided as part of an employment arrangement and the employment has ended.

(g) The tenancy arose through the purchase of a proposed condominium unit and the purchase has been terminated.

There are some specific requirements for the first three reasons. There are no special provisions for the other reasons. The appropriate form and length of notice must be given and an application made to the tribunal if the tenant fails to vacate the unit.

1. Possession for personal occupation

A landlord requiring possession of the rental unit for personal occupation must satisfy the tribunal that the notice is given in good faith and that the occupation will be by the landlord, the landlord's spouse, or a child or parent of one of them. The burden of proof is clearly on the landlord and the test of good faith is interpreted as being a genuine intention to occupy the premises, not a test of whether the landlord's proposal is reasonable.

Cases under the previous legislation held that it is only necessary for landlords wishing to occupy a rental unit in their buildings to show that this desire is in good faith and not primarily for the purpose of evicting a particular tenant. The landlord may choose any unit in the building and the reasonableness of that choice is not relevant, although the fact that there are other similar units in the building that are vacant will cast doubt on the landlord's good faith. It is even sufficient if the landlord requires only part of the unit. However, it must be for residential purposes. Under previous legislation, evictions were ordered in some cases where the landlord wanted the unit for an office.

A minimum of 60 days' notice is required and the termination date specified must be the last day of a period of the tenancy or the end of the term of a fixed term tenancy. A tenant who receives such a notice may, at any time before the termination date, terminate the tenancy on an earlier date by giving 10 days' written notice to the landlord.

There seems to be a reasonable argument that the landlord's right to terminate for personal occupancy should be limited to residential complexes containing not more than three rental units, as is the case with a purchasing landlord. However, the legislature has not imposed any such limitation.

(a) Corporate landlords

Since the earliest days of this legislation, there has been an issue around whether a corporate landlord could use possession for personal occupancy as a basis for an eviction. It is clear that most corporations cannot. However, some relatively recent cases have held that, in certain circumstances, a sole shareholder may be able to terminate a tenancy for personal occupation. There has even been a suggestion that an officer or shareholder of a small family corporation should be able to do so.

The reasoning of the courts has been based on the definition of "landlord" which, in both the old and new acts, includes "the person permitting occupancy of a rental unit." If the sole shareholder (or, possibly, major shareholder or officer) of a small corporation personally performs all the usual duties and responsibilities of a landlord, including the leasing function ("permitting occupancy of the rental unit"), then the individual shareholder qualifies as a landlord and can use this ground to terminate a tenancy.

One of two co-owners of a building or rented unit might also qualify, especially if the co-owners are not incorporated, and if he or she has been given authority by the other co-owner. The Tenant Protection Act does not address this issue or provide any guidance. It does exempt from the definition of "tenant" —

> "a person who has the right to occupy a unit by virtue of being —
>
>> (a) a co-owner of the residential complex, or
>>
>> (b) a shareholder of a corporation that owns the complex,"

but the significance of this is not obvious. The more pressing issue is whether such a person, particularly a shareholder, is a "landlord" and entitled to take possession of a unit for personal occupation.

(b) Co-ownership

Co-ownership of buildings is treated somewhat differently from corporate ownership, and the legislation provides a degree of protection for tenants.

In the early 1980s, a practice developed of converting rental buildings into co-ownerships, with each "owner" having a percentage interest in the building and an exclusive right to occupy one dwelling unit in the building. The Supreme Court held that such "owners" qualified as "landlords" and could evict existing tenants in their particular unit if they wished to move in.

In 1983, the Ontario legislature took action to prevent this by an amendment to the Landlord and Tenant Act. Where a person purchased an interest in a building with an agreement that entitled the purchaser to reside in an apartment in that building, the act provided that a writ of possession (eviction order) would not be granted for personal or family occupation unless either the building had no more than six dwelling units, or the purchaser, his or her spouse, or the child or parent of either had previously occupied the unit.

This restriction has been kept in the new act and the required number of units in the building has been reduced to four. Eviction orders will not be made on applications by either existing landlords or purchasing landlords where the claim is based on an agreement that entitles the landlord to reside in the unit unless —

    (a) the building has no more than four dwelling units, or

    (b) the landlord, his or her spouse, or child or parent of either has previously been a genuine occupant of the unit.

There is other legislation that says that, under these circumstances, no one can advertise an apartment for sale that will give the purchaser the impression that he or she will be able to evict an existing tenant.

2. Possession by a purchaser

Another reason for the landlord to terminate a lease which did not appear in earlier legislation, provides that a landlord may give notice of termination on behalf of a proposed purchaser. The requirements in the event of a sale of the rental property are discussed in further detail in section j.

3. Demolition, conversion, or repairs or renovations

Termination for demolition, conversion, or repairs or renovations requires a minimum 120 days' written notice ending on the final day of the term or period of the tenancy.

Where the notice is for demolition, the tribunal will not make an eviction order unless satisfied that the landlord intends in good faith to carry out the demolition and has obtained all necessary permits or other authority that may be required.

Where the notice is for conversion, the conversion must be to a purpose other than residential premises. This would include such things as a hotel, an apartment hotel, and many of the other types of "accommodation" that are exempt from the act, as well as commercial or industrial uses where zoning by-laws permit such uses. There are specific provisions dealing with conversion to condominiums and changes from rental premises to owner-occupied premises and these are discussed in section **i**.

Where a tenancy is terminated for proposed demolition or conversion to something other than residential use, and the residential complex contains at least five units, the landlord must also compensate the tenant with an amount equal to three months' rent unless the landlord can offer the tenant another rental unit that the tenant finds acceptable. In the case of a demolition, compensation or alternate accommodation is not required if the landlord was ordered to demolish the unit or building by some governmental authority.

Where the notice is for repairs or renovations, these must be so extensive that they require a building permit and vacant possession of the rental unit. The notice given by the landlord must inform the tenant that he or she has a "right of first refusal" (i.e., first chance) to occupy the premises again after the repairs or renovations are completed and, if the tenant wishes to do this, he or she must give the landlord written notice of that intention before vacating the unit. To retain this right, the tenant must also inform the landlord in writing of any subsequent change of address. When the tenant moves back, the landlord may not increase the rent to more than what it could have lawfully charged if there had been no interruption in the tenancy but may apply to the tribunal for a rent increase over the guideline if capital expenditures are involved (see the discussion in chapter 9).

Where termination is for repairs or renovations, compensation or the provision of another rental unit acceptable to the tenant may also be required under certain circumstances. The building or complex must contain at least five residential units and the repair or renovation must not have been ordered under the authority of any other legislation. As in the case of proposed demolition or conversion, three months' rent compensation or alternative accommodation is required where the tenant does not intend to return to the rental unit after the repairs or renovations are complete. Where the tenant has given notice to the landlord that he or she wishes to have a right of first refusal to occupy the unit again after the repairs or renovations, the compensation is limited to the lesser of three months and the time the unit is under repair or renovation.

The definition of "residential complex" in the act includes a group of related buildings as well as a single building. Through a legal procedure known as "severance," a residential complex that initially had five or more residential units might be legally altered to two or more complexes, each having fewer than five residential units. This procedure cannot be used by the landlord as a way to avoid compensation to a tenant. When a notice of termination is given for demolition, conversion, or repair or renovation within two years after the severance, the landlord must still compensate the tenant or offer another acceptable rental unit.

f. WHEN THE LANDLORD WANTS TO TERMINATE BEFORE THE END OF A PERIOD OR TERM

In situations where a tenant is not meeting his or her obligations under the tenancy agreement, the landlord may be entitled to terminate the tenancy before the end of the term or a period of the tenancy. The landlord can only do this for the reasons listed below, and a notice to terminate the tenancy in the approved form must be given to the tenant.

The following are valid reasons for a landlord to terminate a lease or tenancy before the end of a period or term of a tenancy:

(a) The tenant has failed to pay rent.

(b) The tenant has caused undue damage to the rental unit or the residential complex.

(c) The conduct of the tenant substantially interferes with the reasonable enjoyment of the complex by the landlord or another tenant, or it substantially interferes with another lawful right, privilege, or interest of the landlord or another tenant.

(d) The number of persons occupying the rental unit results in a contravention of health, safety, or housing standards required by law.

(e) The tenant is carrying on an illegal business or has commited an illegal act on the premises.

(f) The tenant has misrepresented his or her income in a residential complex where rent is geared to income.

(g) An act of the tenant seriously impairs or has impaired the safety of any person. This would include something done by an animal kept by the tenant as a pet.

Each of these reasons has its own specific provisions in the act. In some cases, the tenant can take corrective action that will nullify the notice.

1. Failing to pay tent

Rent is payable on the date it is due. If the rent is not paid on that date, the landlord may give notice of termination to be effective not earlier than the 7th day after the notice is given in the case of a daily or weekly tenancy, and the 14th day after the notice is given in all other cases. The notice must set out the amount of rent due and specify that the tenant may avoid termination by paying that rent before the notice of termination date. If the tenant pays the rent within that time or at any time before the landlord applies to the tribunal to terminate the tenancy, the notice of termination becomes void. In fact, it will become void if the tenant pays the rent plus the landlord's expenses and any costs ordered by the tribunal any time before an eviction order becomes enforceable.

2. Causing undue damage

Where the tenant or a person permitted in the building by the tenant willfully or negligently causes undue damage to the building, the landlord may deliver a notice of termination which provides for a termination date not earlier than the 20th day after the notice if given, sets out the grounds for termination, and requires the tenant to pay the landlord the reasonable costs of repair or to make the repairs within 7 days. If the tenant makes the repairs, pays the costs, or makes other arrangements satisfactory to the landlord, the notice under the section becomes void within that 7-day period.

3. Interfering with reasonable enjoyment

Where the tenant or some person permitted in the residence by the tenant conducts himself or herself in such a way that interferes with the reasonable enjoyment of the landlord or other tenants, the landlord may deliver a notice of termination that provides a termination date not earlier than the 20th day after the notice is given, sets out the grounds for termination, and requires the tenant to stop the conduct or activity or correct the omission within 7 days. If the tenant does so within the 7-day period, the notice of termination becomes void.

4. Contravening health, safety, or housing standards

Where the number of persons occupying the rental unit contravenes health, safety, or housing standards by-laws, the landlord may also give notice of termination to be effective not later than the 20th day after the notice is given, set out the details of the grounds for termination, and require the tenant, within 7 days, to reduce the number of persons occupying the unit to comply with the by-laws. If the tenant does so within 7 days, the notice of termination is void.

In those situations where a notice has become void, the tenant is not given the opportunity to rectify the situation in the event of a repeat offence. If a notice of termination under one of these sections (damage, interference with reasonable enjoyment, or overcrowding) or its equivalent under Part IV of the Landlord and Tenant Act has become void as a result of the tenant's compliance with the terms of the notice, but the tenant contravenes any of those sections again within six months or contravenes the section with an illegal act, notice may be given to be effective not earlier than the 14th day after the notice is given. Under this section, it need not be a repeat contravention of the same section before the opportunity to rectify is lost.

The following three grounds are regarded as more serious, and the tenant is not given any opportunity to put the tenancy back into good standing.

5. Committing an illegal act

Where a tenant commits an illegal act or carries on an illegal business in the rental unit or building, a landlord may give notice of termination that provides a termination date not earlier than the 20th day after the notice and sets out the grounds for termination. An illegal act can be established without the tenant having been convicted of a criminal offence.

6. Misrepresenting income

The same procedure and time period as for the commitment of an illegal act applies where notice is given because the tenant has misrepresented his or her income for one of the types of rent geared-to-income accommodation referred to in chapter 1.

7. Committing an act that impairs the safety of a person

Where the allegation is that the tenant or a person permitted in the building by the tenant commits an act that seriously impairs the safety of any person (and this act occurs in the residential complex), notice of termination may be given that provides a termination date not earlier than the tenth day after the notice is given. This notice must set out the details of the reasons for termination.

Remember that the tenant always has the right to have the issue decided by the tribunal and the tenant cannot be forced to vacate without an eviction order by the tribunal. The landlord must start an application for eviction before the tribunal within 30 days of the termination date on the notice in order to be in a position to obtain an eviction order. Failure to bring this application in time renders the notice void. Where there is a 7-day period for rectification, the application cannot be started until this period expires.

g. APPLICATION BY THE LANDLORD TO THE TRIBUNAL

A landlord may apply to the tribunal for an order terminating a tenancy and evicting the tenant without notice to the tenant in the following three situations:

(a) The landlord and tenant have entered into an agreement to terminate the tenancy or the tenant has given the landlord notice of termination, but the tenant has failed to vacate the premises.

(b) The landlord has previously made an application for termination that resulted in a order or settlement allowing the landlord to apply again if the tenant did not meet certain specified conditions and the tenant has not met those conditions.

(c) The landlord believes that the tenant has abandoned the rental unit. (A unit is not regarded as "abandoned" if the rent is not in arrears.)

In an agreement to terminate or a tenant's notice of termination, the landlord must file an affidavit verifying the agreement or notice and make the application within 30 days after the specified termination date. If the tribunal makes an eviction order, the tenant may make a motion to the tribunal, within 10 days and on notice to the landlord, to have the order set aside. No further action may be taken to evict the tenant until the motion is considered by the tribunal. If the tribunal

71

sets the order aside, it will then hear the application on its merits. If it does not set the order aside, the eviction will then proceed.

Essentially the same procedures and requirements apply in the case of an application for an eviction order based on a previous order arising from a mediated settlement. An application under this section must be made not more than 30 days after the failure of the tenant to meet a condition in the order or settlement.

In addition to the above situations, a landlord may apply to the tribunal without notice for an order terminating the tenancy of a superintendent who does not vacate within 7 days after his or her employment is terminated. A landlord may also apply for an order evicting a person whose occupancy has not been authorized through either the assignment or subletting provisions. An application under this latter provision must be made no later than 60 days after the landlord discovers the unauthorized occupancy. The act does not indicate whether notice of the application must be given to the ex-superintendent or the unauthorized occupant.

h. WHEN THE TENANT WANTS TO TERMINATE

Where a tenant gives notice to terminate a monthly tenancy or to terminate at the end of a lease term, the landlord may enforce the termination by bringing an application to the tribunal within 30 days of the termination date. If a tenant gives such a notice and then decides to stay, the notice will lapse unless the landlord brings the application in time.

A tenant's notice to terminate is void if given at the time the tenancy agreement is entered into or as a condition of entering into it.

i. CONDOMINIUM CONVERSIONS

Special rules apply where a rental complex is converted to a condominium — a use which is non-rental but still residential.

Other uses in the same category, such as conversion to a co-operative, are not specifically dealt with in the act.

With the repeal of the Rental Housing Protection Act (see chapter 9), it is likely that more rental apartment buildings will be converted to condominiums. Under the previous legislation, municipal approval was required and such approval could only be given if the owner of the property could provide other comparable rental housing in the same area or there was a sufficient supply of rental housing otherwise available in the area. In Toronto, where the vacancy rate for apartments has been extremely low in recent years, virtually any proposal would adversely affect the supply of rental housing.

The Tenant Protection Act provides lifetime security for many tenants when a rental building is converted to a condominium. A landlord may not give a notice of termination for personal occupation or for the personal occupation of a purchaser to a tenant who is in the unit on either the date the building is registered as a condominium or the date that an agreement of purchase and sale is entered into for a "proposed unit." A "proposed unit" in this context is a unit in a building intended as a condominium. Such units are usually sold conditionally and occupied by the purchaser before the condominium is officially registered.

However, the tenant only gets this security of tenure when the building fits in a certain time slot. If at least one unit in the building was rented before July 10, 1986, the protection applies immediately. If the first unit was rented after that date, the protective provisions do not apply until either two years after the day on which the first rental unit was first rented, or two years after June 17, 1998, whichever is later. For these tenants, the protection will not start until June 17, 2000, or later.

The tenant of a unit in a building converted to a condominium also has a right of first refusal to purchase his or her unit provided that person was a tenant on the date of registration of the building as a condominium. The landlord must advise the tenant that an acceptable offer to purchase has been received and that the tenant has 72 hours to agree to purchase the unit at the same price and on the same terms and conditions. However, this does not apply where the unit has been previously purchased since the registration. If the tenant has previously declined the opportunity to purchase the unit but remains in possession as a tenant of the purchaser, he or she does not get a second chance if that purchaser decides to sell the unit. As discussed in section **e.2.**, such tenants cannot be evicted because the landlord (including the new landlord) or a purchaser wishes to occupy the unit.

In addition, the right of first refusal does not apply when the offer received is to purchase more than one unit. It would be unfair to the landlord or vendor if the sale of a block of units could be thwarted by a tenant buying a single unit — not to mention the difficulty in determining what price and other terms apply to the sale of that unit. The tenant may continue in occupation as a tenant of the purchaser and, although this is not entirely clear, may still have a right of first refusal if the purchaser later decides to sell the individual unit.

These provisions and protections are only available to tenants who are in occupancy at the time of conversion. A tenant who rents a condominium unit at a later time from either the developer or a purchaser, has only the rights of any other residential tenant. At present, however, this includes the probably unintended benefit that condominium developers (or "declarants") and individual condominium unit owners are precluded from evicting a tenant from a unit on behalf of a proposed purchaser when the unit is sold. That section, as presently written, applies only where the building contains no more than three residential units. Very few condominium buildings will be this small.

j. SALE OF A RENTAL UNIT

The sale of the rental unit is not usually of concern to a tenant. A change of landlord has no effect on the tenant's rights under the Tenant Protection Act. The new landlord simply steps into the shoes of the old landlord. The tenancy agreement does not change and the rent does not change.

However, if the rental unit is a single family house or a condominium unit and the new owner is an individual, he or she may wish to occupy the unit or have it occupied by certain immediate family members. In such cases, it is possible to have the tenant evicted at the end of the term or period of the tenancy. While the previous legislation did not deal specifically with this situation, procedures were developed and accepted by the courts in order to accomplish this result. Now, the Tenant Protection Act recognizes this as a legitimate reason for terminating a tenancy at the end of the term or a period of a tenancy, and specific procedures are set out in the act. However, you should also refer to the discussion concerning condominium conversions in section **i.** above.

The owner or landlord may give notice to the tenant on behalf of a purchaser after an agreement of purchase and sale has been entered into. The purchaser must, in good faith, require possession for the purpose of residential occupation by the purchaser, the purchaser's spouse, or a child or parent of one of them. At least 60 days' notice must be given and the date for termination must be the day a period of the tenancy ends or the end of the term of a fixed term tenancy.

A tenant who receives such a notice may, at any time, terminate the tenancy on a specified earlier date by giving at least ten days' notice to the landlord.

For a discussion of the landlord's right to allow a potential purchaser to view the unit, see chapter 4, section **b.** This procedure only applies to a residential complex containing no more than three residential units. In other words, no building larger than a triplex qualifies for this special treatment for purchasers. In addition, a room in a rooming house, boarding house, or care home comes within the definition of a residential unit, which further limits the size of building which can qualify. The limitation is for "residential units" not "rental units" so all living quarters are counted, not just those that are rented or intended for rental.

An unintended result of the wording in the act is that condominium developers and probably individual condominium unit owners as well may not use this section to evict a tenant from a unit on behalf of a proposed purchaser when the unit is sold. The section, as presently written, applies only where the building contains no more than three residential units. Very few, if any, condominium buildings will be this small. Although the purchaser could go through with the deal and later evict the tenant in order to assume personal occupation of the unit (see section **e.2.**), many purchasers will not want to take on this burden. There will probably be an amendment or "clarifying" regulation soon.

In the past, timing was often a concern in sale situations if it was uncertain whether the tenant would move out following the notice or insist on an eviction order being obtained. Purchasers usually insist on the premises being vacant at closing so they can move in. However, before the closing date, the purchaser may not be legally entitled to bring an eviction application. Legally, the purchaser qualifies under the wide definition of "landlord" in the act but, even so, the purchaser may not wish to take on the burden of having a tenant evicted. This presented the seller with a major problem if an application for eviction could not be commenced and concluded prior to the closing date. Sometimes the only practical method was to pay off the tenant (a month's free rent, moving costs, etc.) in exchange for a written agreement to vacate on or before the closing date. Now that the act makes it clear that an eviction application can be commenced prior to the termination date on the notice, there should be fewer problems for landlords.

There is one sale situation where a tenant retains security of tenure. If a severance or subdivision arrangement results in a rental unit becoming a property which can be sold separately from other property of which it was previously a part, a landlord may not give notice of termination to the tenant on the basis that he or she wishes to occupy the unit, or has sold it to a purchaser who wishes to occupy it, in cases where the tenant was in occupation at the time of consent to the severance or approval of the subdivision.

k. KEEPING PETS

The act contains some additional requirements where the basis for termination relates to the fact that the tenant is keeping a pet. A landlord cannot refuse to permit a tenant to keep a pet or pets in the rental unit or around the building. Further, the act contains no provision that would permit the landlord to even limit the number of pets that a tenant can keep (unless it violates a health by-law).

The presence of an animal, however, may form the basis of an application based on an allegation that the tenant has done something that substantially interferes with the reasonable enjoyment of the complex by the landlord or another tenant, or that seriously impairs or has impaired the safety of any person in the residential complex. In such cases, the tribunal cannot issue an eviction order without being satisfied that —

(a) the past behaviour of an animal of that species has substantially interfered with the reasonable enjoyment of the premises by the landlord or the other tenants,

(b) the presence of an animal of that species has caused the landlord or another tenant to suffer a serious allergic reaction, or

(c) the presence of an animal of that species or breed is inherently dangerous to the safety of the landlord or the other tenants.

Even if satisfied that criteria (a) or (b) has been met, the tribunal shall not order an eviction or make any other order concerning the animal if it is satisfied —

(a) for (a) above, that the particular animal kept by the tenant did not cause or contribute to the substantial interference, or

(b) for (b) above, that the particular animal kept by the tenant did not cause or contribute to the allergic reaction.

In reaching its decision, the tribunal may not consider a "no pets" provision in the lease or in any other agreement between the landlord and tenant.

These provisions may not apply where the tenant is renting a unit in a condominium. In such situations, a "no pets" provision in the condominium by-laws may be enforceable against the tenant.

l. DEATH OF TENANT

Previous legislation contained no provisions to deal with a situation where a tenant died. The Tenant Protection Act now provides that if a tenant dies and there are no other tenants in the unit, the tenancy is deemed to be terminated 30 days after the death of the tenant.

Until the tenancy is terminated, the landlord is under an obligation to preserve any property of the deceased tenant in the unit or building, other than property that is unsafe or unhygienic, and to afford the executor of the tenant's estate or a member of the tenant's family reasonable access to remove the tenant's property.

After the 30-day period has expired, the landlord may sell, retain for its own use, or otherwise dispose of the property.

However, during the six months after the tenant's death the executor or a member of tenant's family may claim any property that the landlord has sold and the landlord must pay the proceeds of the sale to the estate after deducting any arrears of rent and reasonable out-of-pocket expenses related to storage or sale of the property. During the same period, the landlord must return any property retained for the landlord's own use on a demand from the executor or a member of the family of the deceased.

The act leaves it open for the landlord and the executor to enter into an agreement on terms other than those set out in the legislation concerning the termination of the tenancy and disposal of the tenant's property.

m. SUPERINTENDENT'S PREMISES

There is a special provision for a rental unit occupied by a superintendent. "Superintendent's premises" is defined in the act as a rental unit used by a person employed as a janitor, manager, security guard, or superintendent, and located in the residential complex where the person is so employed. Because of the employment relationship and the fact that these persons are not tenants in the usual sense, they are not given the same protection or security of tenure by the act, although the landlord and superintendent are free to enter into their own tenancy agreement.

In the absence of some other agreement, a superintendent's tenancy terminates on the day the employment is terminated. It is not necessary for the landlord to give the superintendent any notice of termination of the tenancy. After the employment is terminated, the superintendent must vacate the premises within one week. During this week, the landlord may not charge or receive rent or compensation from the superintendent.

If the superintendent fails to move out within the week, the landlord must apply to the tribunal for an order evicting the superintendent.

n. MORTGAGES

In most cases, a landlord will have financed the acquisition of the building or condominium unit by taking out a mortgage, or will have subsequently mortgaged the premises to obtain money for other purposes. Until recently, a default by the landlord in payment of the mortgage potentially had very serious effects for a tenant. The mortgagee (lender and holder of the mortgage) was not bound by the leases or tenancy agreements that the owner entered into after the mortgage, and was not required to follow the procedures of the Landlord and Tenant Act in order to evict tenants. Except in the case of an apartment building, the mortgagee often wanted the property vacated immediately so it could be sold.

In 1991, the Mortgages Act was amended to provide some of the protections then found in Part IV of the Landlord and Tenant Act for tenants of residential premises in situations where the mortgage goes into default. Generally, these amendments applied to all tenancies whether entered into before or after 1991, and to all mortgages whether registered before or after the tenancy agreement was entered into, or before or after 1991. The amendments apply despite any agreement to the contrary that any of the parties might enter into.

A mortgagee who takes possession of any rental residential premises is now deemed to be a landlord, and is subject to the tenancy agreement and the provisions of the Tenant Protection Act. This means that a mortgagee may now only get vacant possession of residential premises following the applicable provisions of the Tenant Protection Act, including the provisions concerning notice, reasons for termination, and time periods.

If a tenant has prepaid the last month's rent, he or she is not required to pay again for that month even though the payment was made to the previous landlord rather than the mortgagee. The mortgagee is also required to pay the 6% interest on the prepayment from the date the mortgagee takes possession.

There are special provisions for the sale of rented single family homes, including condominium units, provided that a tenancy was not in existence when the original mortgage was officially registered. In such cases, the mortgagee may, on 60 days' written notice in proper form to the tenant, obtain possession on behalf of a purchaser who, on closing, will be occupying the premises or permitting certain members of his or her family (as specified in the Tenant Protection Act) to occupy the premises. The purchaser in such cases must provide a written undertaking that the home is required for such occupation. If the purchaser does not subsequently occupy the premises, the tenant retains the right to re-occupy them or, if they are occupied by another tenant, the original tenant has a right of action for damages against the purchaser.

A single family home does not include a duplex or a triplex. However, it does include a "primary dwelling" in which up to two "subsidiary" apartments or rooms are rented out. A mortgagee may show a single family home to prospective purchasers on reasonable notice and at reasonable times.

Where the tenancy was in existence at the time of the registration of the mortgage, the tenant's rights supersede those of the mortgagee. In other words, the mortgagee is bound by the terms of the lease and the legislative requirements in the same way as is a landlord. Tenants of single-family homes whose tenancy predated the mortgage cannot be evicted under these special provisions. However, in most cases, before the mortgagee will loan any money to the landlord, it insists that the landlord have all tenants sign an agreement that the mortgage will have priority over the leases. The Mortgages Act does not address the situation where the home is subject to a tenancy agreement when the mortgage is registered but the tenant has signed such an agreement subordinating his or her rights to the mortgagee. Probably, the tenant is in the same position as if the tenancy came into effect after the mortgage.

A mortgagee may not attempt to indirectly evict a tenant by interfering with the supply of services to, or the reasonable enjoyment of, the residential premises. This constitutes an offence that could result in a fine of $5,000 in the case of an individual and $25,000 in the case of a corporation.

The legislation includes the following other provisions:

(a) A mortgagee who obtains possession or title to the residential premises must serve notice on all tenants of the change.

(b) A tenant who receives notice and in good faith pays rent to the mortgagee, is released from the obligation to pay rent to anyone else.

(c) After a mortgage has gone into default, tenants are required to co-operate with the mortgagee by providing certain information.

(d) A tenant who has paid a security deposit that has not been applied to the last month's rent can make a claim for repayment from the proceeds of the sale, provided there are sufficient funds after certain other creditors are paid.

o. EVICTIONS

A landlord may not evict a tenant or in any way take possession of the rented unit (except where it has been abandoned) without an order from the Ontario Rental Housing Tribunal authorizing the eviction or possession.

A landlord may apply to the tribunal (using an application form approved by the tribunal) for —

(a) an eviction order,

(b) an order for the payment of arrears of rent,

(c) an order for compensation where a tenant has remained in possession after the end of the tenancy,

(d) an order for damages, or

(e) an order for payment of money where the tenant has misrepresented his or her income.

A single application can include a request for more than one order. A landlord may also bring an application just for the money items without seeking an eviction order as long as the tenant is still in possession of the unit. If the tenant has moved out, the landlord would have to sue in Small Claims Court (see chapter 15).

Under the earlier legislation, it was unclear whether the landlord had to wait until after the termination date on a notice before starting the application for eviction (although there was no doubt that any order for eviction could not be effective before the termination date). Many court offices would not accept the application before the termination date. Under the Tenant Protection Act, it is now clear that a landlord may start an application for an eviction order immediately after serving a notice of termination unless there is a specific provision against this somewhere else in the act or there was in Part IV of the Landlord and Tenant Act.

One such provision is that where there is a seven-day period during which the tenant may remedy the reason for the eviction notice (e.g., damage, interference with reasonable enjoyment, overcrowding), the application cannot be started until that time has expired.

In addition, a landlord may not apply to the tribunal for an eviction order based on non-payment of rent before the date for termination specified on the notice. Even where the landlord brings an application on this basis, the tenant has until the date that the eviction order becomes enforceable to rectify the situation and reinstate the tenancy. A tenant does this by paying, either to the tribunal or to the landlord, all the rent in arrears and any compensation owing for the period after the date in the notice of termination, together with any costs ordered by the tribunal and the fee paid by the landlord to make the application to the tribunal. If this is done, any order for arrears of rent, compensation, or eviction of the tenant based on arrears of rent becomes void. However, if the application and ensuing order of the tribunal were based on an additional ground for termination, that part of the order still remains in effect and the tenant would still be subject to eviction.

Evictions are carried out by sheriff's officers, usually about a week after the sheriff is instructed by the landlord to enforce the eviction order. If necessary, the tenant and his or her belongings will be physically removed and locks will be changed. Contrary to popular belief, there is no rule preventing winter evictions.

7

FURTHER TENANT PROTECTION

a. REFUSAL TO GRANT EVICTION

In any application brought by a landlord for an eviction order, the tribunal has discretion to postpone or refuse to grant an eviction order. In addition, the act contains other provisions to protect the tenant against unwarranted eviction. The tribunal may (regardless of any provision in the Tenant Protection Act or in the tenancy agreement) either —

- (a) refuse to grant the application unless satisfied in all the circumstances that it would be unfair to refuse, or

- (b) order that the enforcement of the eviction order be postponed for a period of time.

In addition, the tribunal must refuse to grant an eviction order where it is satisfied that —

- (a) the landlord is in serious breach of its responsibilities under the Tenant Protection Act or under any material part of the tenancy agreement;

- (b) the reason for the application being brought is that the tenant has complained to a government authority of the landlord's violation of a statute or a municipal by-law dealing with health, safety, housing, or maintenance standards;

- (c) the reason for the application being brought is that the tenant has attempted to secure or enforce his or her legal rights;

(d) the reason for the application being brought is that the tenant is a member of a tenants' association or is attempting to organize a tenants' association; or

(e) the reason for the application being brought is that the rental unit is occupied by children (but is not over-crowded).

The tribunal cannot issue an eviction order in a proceeding based on demolition, conversion to non-residential rental use, renovations, or repairs until the landlord has complied with its obligations to compensate or provide alternate accommodation for the tenant as required (see chapter 6).

Together with the requirement that the landlord give reasons for terminating a tenancy and satisfy the independent tribunal, these provisions increase the security of tenure of Ontario tenants. The provisions are especially important to tenants who want to insist on their rights under the rent control rules without fear of retaliation by the landlord. A tenant can never be legally evicted without a tribunal order.

b. EVICTION OF A SUBTENANT

All of the provisions in the act allowing a landlord to give notice of termination before the end of a period or term of the tenancy and then seek an eviction order, can also be used by a tenant where a subtenant is in violation of any of those provisions.

A tenant who has sublet a unit may apply to the tribunal for an order for compensation for use and occupation where the subtenant remains in possession of the rental unit after the end of the subtenancy. The subtenant must still be in possession of the rental unit at the time of the application. Similarly, a tenant may apply for an order for the payment of arrears of rent.

A tenant (or sublandlord) may also apply, in the same manner as a landlord, for compensation for damage to the unit by the subtenant.

c. TERMINATION BY A TENANT

In certain situations, the tribunal may order a tenancy terminated before the end of a period or the term of tenancy on an application by a tenant. This remedy is open to the tribunal where it makes certain determinations on the application. See the discussion on enforcement of rights in chapter 4.

d. OTHER APPLICATIONS TO THE TRIBUNAL

A landlord may apply to the tribunal for certain orders other than termination of tenancies and evictions. These claims may only be brought before the tribunal if the tenant is still in possession of the rental unit. If the tenant has vacated the rental unit, the landlord would have to pursue the claim in court — Small Claims Court where the amount is $6,000 or less and Ontario Court (General Division) for larger amounts.

The landlord may apply for —

(a) an order for the payment of arrears of rent,

(b) an order for payment of compensation for use and occupation of a rental unit,

(c) an order for compensation where the tenant or a person permitted on the premises by him or her willfully or negligently causes undue damage, or

(d) an order for the payment of money where a tenant has misrepresented his or her income so as to pay a lower rent than would otherwise have been required.

8
RENT CONTROL

Some form of rent regulation has existed in Ontario since 1975. It is useful to review the history of these regulations as many people are unclear about which rules are presently in effect.

The initial statute governing rents was the Residential Premises Rent Review Act, 1975, which applied only to buildings occupied before January 1976. This was replaced in 1979 by the Residential Tenancies Act, which attempted to introduce a comprehensive scheme governing all aspects of residential tenancies but continued to exempt from rent review units renting for $750 monthly or more. In 1986, the Residential Rent Regulation Act was passed extending rent review to all rental units in Ontario regardless of the amount of rent being paid or when the building was occupied. This legislation also created an Ontario-wide Rent Registry intended to record the maximum legal rent for every rental unit in the province and established a Standards Board to attempt to ensure proper maintenance of all rental properties in Ontario.

Moratorium legislation became law on April 22, 1991. This was an amendment to the Residential Rent Regulation Act which effectively deemed void all rent increases, including phase-in orders, in excess of the 6% statutory guideline where the first effective date of the rent increase was October 1, 1990, or later. Some limited scope for landlords to apply for increases above the statutory guideline was permitted but justification on the basis of capital expenditures and financing costs was eliminated.

On August 10, 1992, the Rent Control Act came into effect, replacing all previous rent review and rent regulation legislation except for a few transitional provisions to deal with matters still outstanding under the Residential Rent Regulation Act. This legislation provided a new and more restrictive method for calculating the annual percentage increase (the "rent control guideline") and gave additional grounds for tenants to challenge even a guideline increase. An important change from previous legislation was that newly built residential buildings or complexes were given a five-year exemption from rent control.

Effective June 17, 1998, Part VI of the Tenant Protection Act replaced the Rent Control Act. Although the general scheme is still much the same for tenants who remain in their apartments or houses ("sitting tenants"), there is no longer a limit on rents for the first rental period for tenants who move or who rent for the first time. This practice is called "vacancy decontrol." However, once the tenant moves in, rent increases are again governed by the annual guidelines and the other rules apply as well.

All new rental units (as described below in section **c.**) are permanently exempt from controls on rent amounts.

a. THE RULES RELATING TO RENT

The basic rules relating to rent today can be summarized as follows:

(a) No landlord can charge more rent than the lawful rent permitted under Part VI of the Tenant Protection Act.

(b) No landlord can increase rent by more than the guideline percentage.

(c) Rent cannot be increased more than once every 12 months.

(d) Rent cannot be increased without giving 90 days' written notice of rent increase in the prescribed form.

(e) Landlords and tenants may not enter into an agreement for a rent higher than that permitted by the act.

Rules (b) to (e) have exceptions in certain circumstances. Rule (a), however, requires some further explanation.

Unless otherwise prescribed by regulations, the rent being charged to a tenant on the day before the Tenant Protection Act came into effect is regarded as the lawful rent. In cases where that amount exceeded what was permissible under the Rent Control Act, the lawful rent is the amount that it was lawful to charge on that day.

The regulations also deal with unusual situations so that these situations cannot be used as a technique to get around the general rules. Where a landlord offers a discount in rent at the beginning of or during a tenancy, or where the landlord charges a higher rent for the first rental period of a tenancy and subsequently lowers it, the lawful rent will be calculated in accordance with these rules. Otherwise, a landlord might establish a fictional "lawful rent" that exceeds what is actually being charged so that it has the option at a later date to impose a penalty or significantly raise the rent to take advantage of an improved market, or to force out a troublesome tenant.

Part VI of the act contains provisions that put a limitation period on claims that rent was illegal or that an increase in rent was unlawful. Rent charged one or more years earlier is considered lawful unless an application challenging it is made within one year after the date that amount was first charged. An increase in rent is considered lawful unless an application challenging it is made within one year after the date of the increase. These provisions do not take effect until six months after the act is proclaimed in force, so tenants have a reasonable period (i.e., until December 17, 1998), to challenge existing illegal rents and unlawful increases in rent.

It is an offence under the act for any person to charge more rent than that permitted under the act. The maximum fine for doing so is $10,000 for an individual and $50,000 for a corporation. Directors or officers of corporations may be personally liable if they knowingly concur in the offence. Proceedings must be commenced within two years after the date on which the offence was committed.

b. WHAT IS RENT?

For the purpose of this act, rent is defined very broadly. It includes any amount paid or given to the landlord for the right to occupy a rental unit and for any services and facilities, privilege, accommodation, or anything else the landlord provides relating to occupancy of the unit (even if there is a separate charge for it). "Services and facilities" include —

(a) furniture, appliances and furnishings,

(b) parking and related facilities,

(c) laundry facilities,

(d) elevators,

(e) common recreational facilities,

(f) garbage facilities and services,

(g) cleaning and maintenance,

(h) storage facilities,

(i) intercom systems,

(j) cable television,

(k) heating facilities and services,

(l) air-conditioning facilities,

(m) utilities, and

(n) security services.

A decrease in a service or facility is treated as having the same effect as an increase in rent.

c. WHICH RENTAL UNITS ARE COVERED BY THE RENT CONTROL RULES?

The rules relating to rent found in Part VI of the Tenant Protection Act apply to all the units that the act applies to for other purposes (see chapter 1). While there are a few special rules for specific types of rental units, rent control applies to every residential rental unit from a single family house to an apartment in a highrise building and includes a room in a boarding house, rooming house, or lodging house.

Chapter 1 of this book outlines the specific exemptions to all the provisions found in the Tenant Protection Act. These include hotels, tourist homes, vacation homes, and cottages. Where living accommodation is supplied in connection with employment on a farm or in connection with employment in some non-residential business conducted in the building or complex, the act is not applicable. Other exemptions are living accommodation provided by a non-profit co-operative housing corporation to its members (although non-profit co-operations are defined slightly differently in this legislation than in the Tenant Protection Act), as well as living accommodation in prisons, hospitals, nursing homes, some retirement homes, certain types of college residences, temporary shelters, and living accommodation where the occupant is required to share a bathroom or kitchen facility with the owner.

Another provision exempts premises that are occupied for business or agricultural purposes with living accommodation attached, and rented under a single tenancy agreement to the same person or persons. However, if there are separate tenancy agreements for the business and residential portions of the premises, or if the tenant occupying the residential part is not the same person carrying on the business or operating the farm, the living accommodation portion comes under the act.

There are two principal types of exceptions to certain sections of the rules relating to rent in Part VI of the act. The most significant of these relates to new rental units while the other consists of a variety of special situations.

1. New rental units

As part of an effort to encourage new construction of rental residential complexes, new rental units are exempt from controls on rent increases but not from the requirement for notices of rent increases or the general limit to one increase every 12 months. However, it is not only new buildings that receive the benefit of this exemption. The exemption applies to all rental units falling in any one of these three categories:

(a) not occupied for any purpose before June 17, 1998,

(b) not previously rented since before July 29, 1975, or

(c) no part of the building, mobile home park, or land lease community occupied for residential purposes before November 1, 1991.

The first category covers all new units (but is not limited to newly constructed ones). The second category extends the exemption to units not rented since the first rent review legislation was introduced. The third category was exempt under previous legislation for five years after the first unit was occupied. That exemption has now been made permanent.

2. Special types of rental units

Non-profit housing units financially supported by the federal or provincial government are exempt from most rent control regulations. So are units rented to non-members in a non-profit housing co-operative, units provided by educational institutions to students or staff (if not completely exempt from the act under another section), and units of a religious institution operated for a charitable purpose. Accommodation that is subject to the Homes for Special Care Act, the Homes for Retarded Persons Act, and the Developmental Services Act is also generally exempt from most of the rules. Notices of rent increases are required but the 12-month rule does not apply.

Although housing units owned or administered by the federal or provincial government are exempt from the rules in most cases, if the tenant occupying the rental unit pays rent to a landlord other than the government or government agency, all the rules apply. This deals with the situation where a government body rents a house or building to a person who, in turn, rents individual rooms or apartments to other persons for residential purposes.

Where a tenant pays rent on a geared-to-income basis due to public funding, neither the rule limiting rent increases to once every 12 months, nor the rule requiring 90 days' notice of a rent increase is applicable.

Care homes, mobile home parks, and land lease communities have specific rules applicable only to them. These can be found in chapters 10 and 11. For these categories, rent does not include:

(a) for a mobile home or land lease home, an amount paid to reimburse the landlord for property taxes, and

(b) for a care home, the amount a landlord charges for care services or meals.

Rental units that do not fall squarely within the requirements for an exemption are subject to Part VI of the act.

d. FIRST RENTAL TO NEW TENANTS

The lawful rent for the first rental period for a new tenant under a new tenancy agreement is the rent first charged to the tenant. This means that rent control no longer applies in the situation where a tenant first enters into a tenancy agreement for a vacant apartment or house.

This process is called as vacancy decontrol. The theory is that adjustment of rents to market value (i.e., the most the landlord can get) when units become vacant will gradually allow rents to move to market level without hardship to any individual tenant. On average, about 25% of tenants move each year and, if this continues after vacancy decontrol comes into effect, most rental units should be decontrolled within five years. Of course, much will depend on the vacancy rate in any given area. In Toronto, it is less than 1% and definitely a landlord's market, but tenants in other municipalities may not feel the squeeze as much.

The lawful rent for a unit is whatever the landlord and tenant agree on at the start of the tenancy. What the previous tenant was paying becomes completely irrelevant. The calculation of lawful rent is subject only to the rules prescribed to deal with discounts and high initial rents for the first period of a tenancy. This will prevent landlords from creating an artificially high ceiling for lawful rent when the actual rent being charged to the tenant is really a lower amount. This device could be used by a landlord to later increase the rent beyond the guideline amount, perhaps even to the level where it could use this as a device to force an unwanted tenant from the building contrary to the general protection offered by security of tenure.

Once an initial rent is agreed on between the landlord and tenant, all future increases are subject to the rent control rules as long as that tenant remains in the unit. In addition, there would be no increase on an assignment or subletting to another tenant with the landlord's consent (see chapter 4).

e. FREQUENCY OF RENT INCREASES

A landlord may not increase the rent charged to a tenant until at least 12 months have elapsed since the day of the last rent increase for that tenant in that rental unit. Where there has not been a previous increase, no increase is allowed until 12 months after the rental unit was first rented to that tenant. This does not apply to those circumstances where rent can be increased because additional services are being provided.

A tenant may not increase rent on a subletting but may provide for an increase at such time as the landlord is entitled to increase the tenant's rent.

f. NOTICE OF RENT INCREASE

Rent for an existing tenant (sometimes referred to as a "sitting" tenant) cannot be increased unless a landlord has given the tenant a written notice in a form approved by the tribunal not less than 90 days before the intended increase is to take effect. This is required even if the increase is only for the guideline percentage. The act contains no exception for a guideline increase already provided for in a lease, but it may be sufficient if the lease specifies the actual dollar amount of the new rent (provided, of course, that this is within the guideline percentage).

The form need only set out the amount of the new rent. This differs significantly from notices under earlier legislation which required that the form set out the amount of the proposed increase expressed both in dollars and as a percentage of the current rent and also inform the tenant of the maximum legal rent. Where there has been an order increasing the maximum rent by more than the statutory guideline, based on an allowance for a capital expenditure or an extraordinary operating cost increase, notice is still necessary but the landlord is no longer required to include information on the cost of taxes, heat, hydro, and water for the previous two years for the building.

If a landlord raises rent without giving sufficient time or without a proper form of notice, the increase in rent is void. The landlord would then have to give a 90-day notice before collecting any increase and would have to refund the amount of any increases collected.

A tenant is deemed to have accepted the amount of the increase unless he or she gives notice of termination at least 60 days before the increase is to come into effect.

g. AMOUNT OF RENT INCREASE

Under the new legislation, there will continue to be a statutory guideline established each year. The Ministry of Municipal Affairs and Housing will publish the guideline for each year in the Ontario *Gazette* not later than August 31 of the preceding year. The guidelines set under the Rent Control Act of 2.8% for 1997 and of 3.0% for 1998, remain in effect for those years. The guideline applies to all rent increases that are to come into effect during the calendar year for which it is established. For 1999, the guideline amount will again be 3.0%.

The guideline is calculated by adding together certain amounts allocated to operating costs and capital expenditures. The part of the guideline allocated to capital expenditures is 2% and the part of the guideline allocated to operating costs is 55% of the "rent control index." A table has been prescribed setting out certain operating cost categories relevant to maintaining a rental building, such as municipal taxes, heat, hydro, and water. These categories will be weighted components taken from the Consumer Price Index but will be based on the average change in these costs during the previous three-year period in order to level out sudden increases or decreases in any of the costs.

Statutory guideline percentages since the passing of the Residential Rent Regulation Act in 1986 have been as follows:

August 1 – December 31, 1986	4.0%
January 1 – December 31, 1987	5.2%
January 1 – December 31, 1988	4.7%
January 1 – December 31, 1989	4.6%
January 1 – December 31, 1990	4.6%
January 1 – December 31, 1991	5.4%
January 1 – December 31, 1992	6.0%
January 1 – December 31, 1993	4.9%

January 1 – December 31, 1994	3.2%
January 1 – December 31, 1995	2.9%
January 1 – December 31, 1996	2.8%
January 1 – December 31, 1997	2.8%
January 1 – December 31, 1998	3.0%
January 1 – December 31, 1999	3.0%

h. MAXIMUM RENT

The concept of "maximum rent" was originally introduced in the Residential Rent Regulation Act, in 1986. With the introduction of vacancy decontrol, maximum rent is now relevant only to tenancies where the tenant has been in continuous occupancy of the rental unit since the day before the Tenant Protection Act came into force and, even there, its relevance is limited to the difference between actual rent and maximum rent at June 16, 1998. After that, it's "use it or lose it" for landlords.

The concept was originally designed to protect landlords from losing their right to collect the maximum amount of rent for a unit where, because of market conditions or by mistake, a landlord did not charge or collect an increase equal to the statutory guideline (or such higher or lower amount as he or she was awarded under rent review) in any particular year or years. The maximum rent still increased in accordance with the statutory guideline or rent review award and, in such cases, a landlord was able to take an increase greater than the statutory guideline in a future year in order to catch up to the maximum rent for the unit without having to make an application for rent review. This information was required to be specified in the notice of rent increase and a proper notice of the increase was required to be served on the tenant. There could still only be one rent increase in any 12-month period.

The maximum rent for a rental unit under the new legislation is the maximum rent under the Rent Control Act on the day before the new provision becomes law, plus all increases allowed to be added to it and all decreases required to be subtracted from it under the Rent Control Act. The new act makes no provision for the continuation of maximum rent through nominal additions of the guideline amount where these annual percentages are not charged. Accordingly, the maximum rent concept will become irrelevant except to allow landlords one last chance to make up any gap existing on June 16, 1998, between actual rent and maximum rent for sitting tenants. The act does not specify any time limit during which a landlord has to take this increase.

This is the only situation where a landlord can increase rent beyond the guideline for a sitting tenant without an application to the tribunal other than those limited circumstances where the landlord and tenant are permitted to agree to a rent increase.

i. AGREEMENT ON RENT INCREASES AND DECREASES

Generally, the provisions of the act apply regardless of any agreement to the contrary between landlords and tenants, whether written, oral, or implied. A clause in a written lease, regardless of how formal and legal it may appear, is completely unenforceable if it is contrary to a provision in the Tenant Protection Act. However, the act does permit some types of agreements related to rent.

The landlord and an individual tenant may agree on a rent increase above the guideline if —

(a) the landlord has carried out or undertakes to carry out a specified capital expenditure, or

(b) the landlord has provided or undertakes to provide a new or additional service.

The maximum increase allowed is 4% over the guideline. The agreement cannot be effective until at least six days after it has been signed and the tenant has a cooling-off period of five days during which he or she may cancel the agreement by giving written notice to the landlord. The agreement must be in the form approved by the tribunal and must set out the new rent, the tenant's right of cancellation, and the date the agreement is to take effect. No application to the tribunal is necessary.

No notice of rent increase is required in these circumstances but the single increase within a 12-month period rule still applies. Any notice of rent increase given before the agreement was entered into becomes void when the agreement takes effect where such increase was to take effect on or after the day the agreed increase is to commence. In other words, the agreed increase replaces the increase in the notice — the two are not added together.

Where the landlord reneges on its part of the agreement, a tenant (or former tenant) may apply to the tribunal for relief. The application must be made within two years after the rent increase became effective. In such an application, the tribunal may find that some or all of the rent increase above the guideline is invalid and may order a rebate of any money owing to the tenant or former tenant.

In addition to the negotiated increases, a landlord may increase rent at any time without application to the tribunal if the landlord and tenant agree that the landlord will add to the tenancy a parking space or some other service, facility, privilege, accommodation, or thing prescribed in the regulations. The safeguards set out above for agreements to increase rent do not apply in this situation. A notice of rent increase is not required and the 12-month rule does not apply either. The amount of the permitted increase for such items is not to exceed the landlord's cost of providing them.

A landlord must decrease the rent charged to a tenant if the landlord and tenant agree that the landlord will cease to provide a parking space or any of the prescribed items. The minimum amount of the decrease for such items is the land-lord's cost of providing them.

An agreement of either type is not enforceable if entered into as a result of coercion or a false or misleading repre-sentation by the landlord or its agent.

j. APPLICATION FOR RENT INCREASE ABOVE THE GUIDELINE

A landlord may apply to the tribunal for an order increasing the maximum rent by more than the guideline for any or all of the rental units in a residential building or complex. This application must be made at least 90 days before the effective date of the first intended rent increase.

Such an increase may be sought only in one or more of the following cases:

(a) An extraordinary increase in operating costs for mu-nicipal taxes and charges or utilities such as hydro, water, or heating for the whole complex

(b) A capital expenditure related to the building as a whole or a particular rental unit or units

(c) Operating costs related to security services for the complex provided by persons not employed by the landlord (i.e., commercial security companies)

An "extraordinary" increase is an increase greater than the percentage increase for the cost in the table used to calcu-late the rent control index. There is no limit on the amount rent may be increased on this basis, but utilities are considered as a group and an increase in one may be offset by a decrease in another. The landlord cannot pick and choose just the costs that go up. On the other hand, the fact that utility costs may have gone down does not have to be considered at all where a landlord makes an application based on any tax increase, capital expenditures, or security costs.

Capital expenditures are costs necessarily incurred by the landlord for major repairs or improvements which, by their nature, are required periodically but not every year. Some examples are major roof repairs, replacement of hallway carpeting, repaving of a parking lot, and replacement of kitchen cupboards in a unit. The total cost is not added onto the rent in a single year. It is "amortized" or spread out (together with an interest charge) over a number of years depending on the "useful life" of the item. The regulations set out the time periods for various items and the interest rate to be applied.

In dealing with an application on this ground, the tribunal may disallow a capital expenditure if it finds that it is unreasonable. However, the tribunal shall not find that a capital expenditure is unreasonable if it —

(a) is necessary to protect or restore the physical integrity of the complex,

(b) is necessary to maintain maintenance, health, safety, or other housing-related standards required by law,

(c) is necessary to maintain a plumbing, heating, mechanical, electrical, ventilation, or air conditioning system,

(d) provides access for persons with disabilities,

(e) promotes energy or water conservation, or

(f) maintains or improves the security of the complex.

The order for a rental increase that the tribunal can make for capital expenditures or operating costs related to security services, is limited to 4% of the previous lawful rent. If the tribunal determines that an increase of more than 4% is justified by the costs of capital expenditures, operating costs related to security services, or both, the tribunal shall also order, in accordance with rules to be prescribed, increases in rent for the following years in an amount not to exceed 4% in any single year until the total increase has been taken. Such increases are in addition to any increases based on extraordinary increases for municipal taxes or utility charges.

The full amortized cost of the capital expenditure can be passed through to the tenant as increased rent even though the annual guideline already includes a 2% allowance for capital expenditures.

An order of the tribunal relating to a landlord's application has no effect if a new tenant enters into a tenancy agreement with the landlord and that agreement takes effect within 90 days of the first effective date of a rent increase in the order. It is assumed that the landlord's cost increases will be built into the new rent to the new tenant and the new tenant should not be subject to such an order on top of the negotiated rent.

Where an order is made that continues over more than one year and the landlord has not yet taken all of the increases permissible under that previous order, the landlord may still make another application (where cost increases warrant) and increase the rent further under the subsequent order as well, but only in accordance with prescribed rules.

Where the landlord has applied for an order for a rent increase above the rent guideline and has given the required notice of the intended rent increase, the landlord may only collect either the new rent set out in the notice, or the maximum amount the landlord could charge without the application, whichever is less.

In other words, the tenant need not pay more than the existing or maximum rent plus the guideline amount until the tribunal has ruled on the landlord's application. However, if the application is granted and the decision is not given until after the date of the intended rent increase, the tenant must make up any resulting arrears. Some may prefer to make the monthly payments rather than be faced with a large lump sum if the order is made. The tenant has the alternative under the act of voluntarily paying the higher rent pending the outcome of the application and, if that exceeds the amount eventually ordered, having the landlord owe the tenant the difference. The tribunal can order repayment through deductions from rent.

If the order is not made until three months or more after the effective date of the first rent increase, and if a tenant owes a sum of money to the landlord as a result of the order, the order may provide that the tenant pay the accumulated arrears in monthly instalments rather than by an immediate lump sum. The maximum number of monthly instalments is 12. The instalment payment provision also applies to former tenants whose tenancy is terminated while the application is pending.

The tribunal is to determine the percentage rent increase justified by following prescribed rules, make an order for that amount, and set the period during which it may be taken (also prescribed in rules or regulations). Previous legislation had required that a capital expenditure increase would be removed from the rents for the residential unit or complex once the landlord had collected the amount spent from the tenants over the projected useful life of the capital item. The date on which this component was to be deducted from the maximum rent was set out in the order. It is unlikely that this will be continued under the new act. The amount will be permanently included in the rent and compounded annually by the guideline increase.

The previous legislation also specified that a capital expenditure that became necessary as a result of neglect or was unnecessary, would not be considered. That safeguard is missing from the Tenant Protection Act but may be the basis of an argument by a tenant against the landlord's application as to whether the expenditure is "reasonable."

The new rules regarding capital expenditures will generate significant additional rental revenue for landlords —

approximately double what could be recovered under the previous legislation.

It will be the landlord's decision whether to apply for such increases for the whole building or just certain units. Where capital expenditures relate to only certain units (for example, new appliances or new bathroom fixtures), the increase can only be sought for those units. However, if some units are below "market" rent when compared to others, the landlord may wish to seek increases based on other costs only for those units. In this case, there will be allocation rules to govern how the increase is to be applied. A portion of the total units in the building will not have to bear the entire cost as a rent increase — only a proportionate share of the cost.

k. APPLICATION TO REDUCE RENT

A tenant may apply for a rent reduction if there —

(a) are reduced or discontinued services or facilities to the complex as a whole or to the tenant's unit, or

(b) is a reduction in municipal taxes and charges for the complex.

The previous legislation had also permitted an application where there was inadequate maintenance of the building or complex as a whole or of the tenant's unit. A list of "services and facilities" can be found in section **b.** in this chapter.

A former tenant may apply when services or facilities were reduced or discontinued while he or she was a tenant. However, all applications on this basis must be started within one year of the reduction or discontinuance. An order on a tenant application may reduce the rent charged completely or for a specified period where there has been only a temporary reduction in a service. A rent rebate may also be ordered. The order takes effect from the day the reduction or discontinuance occurred.

The process for a rent reduction based on a reduction in municipal taxes or charges is found in detailed rules in the regulations. For complexes or buildings of a certain size, the municipality will be required to notify the landlord and the tenants that rent is reduced by a certain percentage and when the reduction takes effect.

A tenant or former tenant of a rental unit may apply to the tribunal for an order that the landlord, superintendent, or agent of the landlord repay any money collected or obtained in contravention of this act, the Rent Control Act or Part IV of the Landlord and Tenant Act. This would include illegal deposits, illegal rent amounts, and other "key money" offences. A prospective tenant may also make an application for return of an illegally collected deposit. The act also permits a subtenant to make an application if the tenant has collected an amount illegally. However, no order for such repayment may be made unless the application is filed within one year after the collection or retention of the money.

1. RENT REGISTRY

A computerized province-wide Rent Registry was created by the Residential Rent Regulation Act in 1986. It was intended to record rental anniversary dates and maximum rents for every private rental unit in Ontario. It was continued under the Rent Control Act with some changes.

Under the Tenant Protection Act, the registry no longer exists. Maximum rents are largely irrelevant now except for tenants who have not moved since the new legislation came into effect. Their rent is deemed lawful six months after the act becomes law (i.e., December 17, 1998), unless it was challenged in an application within a year after it was first charged. It is presumed that existing tenants know what they are paying, can calculate the guideline increase, and know whether there has been an increase within 12 months. New tenants have no need of the information since their rent will be whatever they negotiate with the landlord in their first tenancy agreement.

m. ILLEGAL ADDITIONAL CHARGES

Unless otherwise prescribed, no landlord of a rental unit shall, directly or indirectly —

(a) collect, attempt to collect, or require from a tenant or prospective tenant a fee, premium, commission, bonus, penalty, key deposit, or other like amount of money — whether or not the money is refundable;

(b) rent any portion of the rental unit for rent that, together with all other rents payable for other portions of the unit, is greater than the rent the landlord lawfully may charge for the entire rental unit; or

(c) require or attempt to require a tenant or prospective tenant to pay any consideration for goods or services, as a condition for granting the tenancy or continuing to permit occupancy of a rental unit, if that consideration is in addition to the rent the tenant is lawfully required to pay.

The act also provides that no superintendent, property manager, or other person who acts on behalf of a landlord shall, directly or indirectly, with or without the authority of the landlord, do any of these things.

The regulations exempt a number of types of payments which might otherwise appear to be illegal. These include the actual cost of additional or replacement keys, refundable key deposits if not more than the cost of replacement, NSF (not sufficient funds) bank charges (including up to $20 as an administrative charge), and charges up to $250 to transfer to a different unit in subsidized housing.

A tenant who sublets his or her unit is subject to the same rules. The act states that, unless otherwise prescribed, no tenant and no person acting on behalf of the tenant shall, directly or indirectly —

(a) sublet a rental until for rent that is greater than the rent lawfully charged by the landlord;

(b) sublet any portion of the rental unit for rent that, together with all other rents payable for all other portions of the rental unit, is a sum greater than the rent that is lawfully charged by the landlord;

(c) collect, or attempt to collect, or require from any person any fee, premium, commission, bonus, penalty, deposit, or other like amount of money for subletting a rental unit or any portion of it, for surrendering occupancy of a rental unit, or for otherwise parting with possession of a rental unit; or

(d) require or attempt to require a person to pay any consideration for goods or services as a condition for the subletting, assignment, or surrender of occupancy or possession in addition to the rent the person is lawfully required to pay.

The second point in both the above lists is designed to prevent the situation where a landlord (or a tenant) "subdivides" a unit and rents portions to several people separately for a total rent that exceeds the lawful rent that could be charged for the entire unit.

n. OFFENCES REGARDING RENT

A landlord may be prosecuted under Part VI of the Tenant Protection Act, in Provincial Offences Court for doing or attempting to do any of the following:

(a) Requiring or receiving an illegal security deposit

(b) Failing to pay 6% interest annually on a rent deposit

(c) Failing to apply a rent deposit to the last month of a tenancy

(d) Failing to provide a receipt for rent when requested

(e) Charging rent in an amount greater than permitted by the act

(f) Requiring a tenant to pay the rent proposed in an application before an order is made

(g) Charging or collecting a fee, bonus, penalty, key deposit, or otherwise collecting or requiring amounts in addition to the lawful rent (see section **m.**)

A tenant may also be charged under the final point for illegal charges on a subletting.

An individual who is convicted of an offence is liable to a fine of up to $10,000 and a corporation is liable to a fine of up to $50,000. A director or officer of a corporation who knowingly concurs in an offence is also personally liable.

9

PROTECTION OF RENTAL HOUSING

In 1986, the Ontario government became concerned about the number of rental units that were disappearing from the market as a result of demolition or conversion to other uses. The government's response was the Rental Housing Protection Act, which was initially temporarily enacted but was later made permanent.

Essentially, that act provided that no rental residential property, or part thereof, could be —

(a) demolished,

(b) converted to a condominium, co-operative, hotel, apartment hotel, or any use other than rental residential property, or

(c) renovated or repaired, whether or not a tenant is in occupation, to the extent that vacant possession would be required,

unless the council of the municipality in which the property was located approved. However, a municipality was allowed to approve a proposal only if one of the following conditions was met:

(a) The owner of the property provided other accommodation for the current tenants in comparable rental housing at the same rents in the same areas.

(b) The building had to be demolished or renovated because it was proven to be unsafe for human habitation.

(c) The council believed the proposal would not adversely affect the supply of rental housing in the area.

The prohibition applied even if the building was vacant at the time of the application. The act only applied where there were four or fewer rental units, if a conversion to a condominium was planned. Tenants had to be notified of any application to the municipality for approval.

The Rental Housing Protection Act has been repealed by the Tenant Protection Act. In place of the provisions for the preservation of rental housing generally, the new act provides certain benefits for tenants directly affected by termination of their tenancy for the purpose of demolition, conversion, or repairs or renovations.

Where the building is converted to a condominium, a tenant retains some limited security of tenure in the unit and also has a right of first refusal to purchase the rental unit.

In cases of demolition or conversion to some use other than a condominium, the tenant must, with certain exceptions, be given three months' rent as compensation, or be offered another acceptable rental unit. Where the tenancy is terminated for repairs or renovations, the tenant has a right of first refusal to occupy the rental unit as a tenant when the repairs or renovations are completed. Alternatively, if the tenant does not intend to return, the landlord is required to compensate him or her in an amount equal to three months' rent or offer another acceptable rental unit.

These provisions are subject to a number of exceptions and requirements. For full details, see chapter 6.

Many municipalities have by-laws restricting demolitions, conversions, and major repairs that a landlord must still comply with.

10

CARE HOMES

The Residents' Rights Act (passed on May 31, 1994) introduced the new concept of a "care home." This act gave occupants of these homes many of the same rights as those enjoyed by other residential tenants. Before this, all "accommodation occupied by a person for . . . rehabilitative or therapeutic purposes or for the purpose of receiving care" was exempted from the definition of "residential premises" and was, therefore, not governed by either the Landlord and Tenant Act or the Rent Control Act.

There are an estimated 40,000 adults living in care homes across Ontario. They tend to be mainly elderly people, former psychiatric patients, persons with developmental problems, and persons with disabilities. A commission of inquiry had found many instances where such residents were subject to abuses such as arbitrary eviction, unsafe living conditions, inadequate care, and lack of privacy.

The Residents' Rights Act has now been repealed by the Tenant Protection Act. However, a number of the protective provisions are continued under the new legislation. Part IV of the act sets out some specific provisions dealing with care homes.

The term "care home" is fully defined in chapter 1. Essentially, it is a residential rental building or unit occupied by persons for the purpose of receiving some type of care services. A list of some of the services included is set out in regulations under the act.

a. RIGHTS AND DUTIES OF LANDLORDS AND TENANTS

There must be a written tenancy agreement for every tenant in a care home. This agreement must set out what has been agreed to regarding care services and meals, and the charges for them. The agreement must contain a statement that the tenant has the right to consult a third party advocate about the agreement and to cancel the agreement within five days by written notice to the landlord.

Before entering into a tenancy agreement with a new tenant, the landlord must give the prospective tenant a Care Home Information Package (CHIP) containing information prescribed in the regulations. If a landlord fails to do this and a tenancy agreement is entered into, the landlord is prevented under the act from giving a notice of rent increase or a notice of increase in the charge for providing a care service or meals until the information package is provided.

Because of the nature of the services being provided, it is permissible to include a provision in the tenancy agreement requiring the landlord to check the condition of a tenant at regular intervals and, despite the general prohibition of this, a landlord may enter a rental unit for such purpose. However, a tenant may at any time unilaterally revoke such a provision by giving written notice to the landlord.

There is a special provision for termination of a tenancy where the occupation is solely for the purpose of receiving rehabilitative or therapeutic services. If the period of tenancy agreed to has expired and if no other tenant occupying the care home for the same purpose is permitted to live there longer than two years, the landlord may terminate the tenancy by a notice of termination. The notice period for termination depends on the type of tenancy and is the same period as for any other tenancy. A tenant, on the other hand, may terminate such a tenancy at any time on 30 days' notice.

Where a landlord gives a tenant of a care home a notice of termination for the purpose of demolition, conversion, or repairs or renovations, it is required to make reasonable efforts to find appropriate alternate accommodation for the tenant. However, the provisions for compensation for other tenancies terminated for these reasons do not apply to the tenant of a care home who chooses to take the alternate accommodation found by the landlord.

Not all provisions of the Tenant Protection Act are appropriate for this type of tenancy. For instance, a landlord may refuse to consent to an assignment or sublease to someone who does not meet the admission requirements or guidelines for the care home.

b. EVICTIONS

Part IV of the Tenant Protection Act contains a special provision for eviction from a care home, referred to as "transferring a tenant out of a care home," in cases where —

    (a) the tenant no longer requires the level of care provided by the landlord, or

    (b) the tenant requires a level of care that the landlord is not able to provide.

The tribunal may only issue an order under clause (b) if it is satisfied that appropriate alternate accommodation is available and that the level of care that the landlord is able to provide (even when combined with community-based services) cannot meet the tenant's care needs. The tribunal cannot issue a default order on such an application and, if a dispute arises, it must be sent to mediation.

c. RULES REGARDING RENT

There are a few special rules related to rent for care homes in addition to those for other residential tenancies.

If there is more than one tenancy agreement for a rental unit in a care home, the rules related to rent apply to each agreement as if it were an agreement for a separate rental unit. This recognizes and deals with situations where rooms in care homes are shared by two or more persons. Even though there is only one room, the landlord is required to deal with each occupant independently.

Rent does not include the amount a landlord charges for care services or meals. However, a landlord cannot increase a charge for providing a care service or meals to a tenant without first giving 90 days' notice. The notice must be in writing in the form approved by the tribunal and must set out the new charges. Failure to give proper notice renders the increase void and the landlord must provide a new 90 days' notice before taking any increase.

11

MOBILE HOME PARKS AND LAND LEASE COMMUNITIES

Part V of the Tenant Protection Act sets out some provisions specific to mobile home parks and land lease communities. A definition and explanation of mobile homes and land lease homes can be found in chapter 1.

Mobile homes have been covered by landlord and tenant legislation for some time but the specific reference to land lease homes appears for the first time in the Tenant Protection Act. For simplicity, this discussion will generally refer to mobile home parks, but remember that all of the provisions apply, with any necessary modifications, to tenancies in land lease communities.

The essential difference between this type of tenancy and others is that, for both mobile homes and land lease homes, the tenant owns the home and is renting only the land on which it is situated.

a. RIGHTS AND DUTIES OF LANDLORDS AND TENANTS

A tenant has the right to sell or to lease his or her home without the landlord's consent. A landlord may act as an agent of a tenant in negotiations to sell or lease the dwelling, but only under a written agency contract entered into for the purpose of beginning those negotiations. A provision in the tenancy agreement requiring a tenant to use the landlord as an agent is void.

A tenancy agreement may prohibit the tenant from selling the dwelling without first offering to sell it to the landlord. If a tenant receives an acceptable offer from another party, he or she must give the landlord at least 72 hours' notice of the offer before he or she can accept it. During this period, the landlord has the right to purchase the dwelling at the same price and subject to the same terms and conditions as are contained in the offer. Any provision in the tenancy agreement which claims to permit a landlord to purchase the dwelling at a price less than that in a prospective purchaser's offer to purchase is void. In this case the landlord may still exercise the option to purchase at the higher price.

A landlord cannot prevent a tenant from placing a "For Sale" sign in the window of the dwelling unless this is a general prohibition applicable to all tenants, and the landlord provides a bulletin board free of charge for the placing of "For Sale" advertisements that is located in a prominent place and accessible to the public at reasonable times.

Where a person has purchased or entered into an agreement to purchase a dwelling, the landlord may not refuse consent to assignment of the site.

The previous legislation specified that landlords were not permitted to charge entry and installation fees or removal and exit fees for mobile homes to and from the park other than to recover reasonable expenses actually incurred for this purpose. The landlord could also only place limited restrictions on tradespeople and could only prohibit or restrict them where they unduly disturbed the peace and quiet of the park, failed to observe reasonable rules of conduct, or violated the traffic rules of the park. The new legislation states simply that a landlord shall not restrict the right of a tenant to purchase goods or services from the person of his or her choice.

The regulations specifically allow a landlord to require a payment at the commencement of a tenancy for rental of a particular site. A landlord is permitted to set reasonable standards for mobile home equipment.

A landlord is responsible for —

(a) providing for the removal or disposal of garbage at reasonable intervals,

(b) maintaining the park roads in a good state of repair,

(c) removing snow from the roads,

(d) maintaining the water supply, sewage disposal, fuel, drainage, and electrical systems in the park in a good state of repair,

(e) maintaining the park grounds and all buildings and equipment intended for the use of the tenants in a good state of repair, and

(f) repairing damage to the tenant's property caused by the willful or negligent conduct of the landlord.

These obligations may be enforced by an application to the tribunal provided the application is made within one year after the date of the breach. The tribunal has the power to terminate the tenancy, order an abatement of rent, authorize a repair and order its costs to be paid by the landlord, order the landlord to do specified repairs within the specified time, or make any other order it considers appropriate. In determining the remedy, the tribunal shall consider whether the tenant advised the landlord of the alleged breaches before applying to the tribunal. Presumably, a tenant who does not try to resolve the problem with the landlord before applying to the tribunal will not receive the sympathy of the tribunal.

b. TERMINATION OF TENANCIES

Unless otherwise provided, the general rules applicable to termination of a tenancy apply. However, there are special provisions dealing with the disposition of a dwelling or mobile home where the tenancy has been terminated either by agreement or order of the tribunal.

The landlord shall not dispose of a dwelling or mobile home without first notifying the tenant by registered mail to the tenant's last known mailing address and by a notice in a newspaper. If the tenant has not made a claim within 60 days after the notices, the landlord may sell, retain for its own use, or dispose of the dwelling or mobile home. If the tenant makes a claim within six months after the notices, the landlord is required to pay to the tenant the amount by which the proceeds of the sale exceed the landlord's reasonable out-of-pocket expenses and any arrears of rent. If the landlord has retained the dwelling or mobile home for its own use, it is required to return it to the tenant. However, before returning it, the landlord may require the tenant to pay any arrears of rent and any reasonable expenses incurred by the landlord for the mobile or land lease home. Provided it follows these procedures, a landlord does not incur any liability for selling, retaining, or otherwise disposing of the property of a tenant.

Those sections in another part of the act dealing with disposal of the property of a tenant who dies, are not applicable where the tenant owns the mobile or land lease home.

The act provides for an extended notice of termination for conversion, demolition, or renovation. For mobile and land lease homes, the notice period must be a least one year ending on the day that the period of the tenancy ends or, where the tenancy is for a fixed term, the end of that term.

c. RULES REGARDING RENT AND OTHER CHARGES

There are some special rules regarding rent and other charges applicable only to mobile home parks and land lease communities.

For a mobile home or land lease home, an amount paid to reimburse the landlord for property taxes is not considered to be rent. It is a legal additional charge.

Despite the general provision that a new tenant may legally be charged a new rent, where a new tenant has purchased the mobile or land lease home located on the site, the landlord may not charge the new tenant a rent greater than the last lawful rent charged plus an amount prescribed in the regulations to the act (essentially, $50 or the difference between existing rent and what would have been "maximum rent," whichever is greater). For this purpose, an assignee is regarded as a new tenant.

A landlord may not charge entry or exit fees when a mobile home is moved into or out of the mobile home park. Similar fees for installation and removal of a home are also prohibited. However, the landlord may charge reasonable out-of-pocket expenses incurred during these matters. Likewise, a landlord may charge reasonable expenses for the testing of water or sewage.

For the purpose of justifying a rent increase based on a capital expenditure, if the tribunal finds that it is for infrastructure work required by a governmental authority, the tribunal may determine the number of years over which the justified increase may be taken. This is an exception to the usual 4% limit. "Infrastructure work" means work on roads, a water supply, sewage disposal, and fuel, drainage, and electrical systems, and other services prescribed in the regulations.

Interference with a tenant's right to sell or lease his or her dwelling or restricting the tenant's right to purchase goods and services from the person of his or her choice are offences under the act and may subject the landlord to a fine of up to $10,000 for individuals or $50,000 for a corporation.

12

ILLEGAL RENTAL UNITS

The Residents' Rights Act of 1994 introduced amendments to various other pieces of legislation. These changes were designed to increase the availability of rental units and to protect tenants in what had previously been "illegal" units. Although basement apartments received most of the publicity at the time, the act dealt with a variety of types of residential rental units in houses.

a. APARTMENTS IN HOUSES

It was estimated at the time the Residents' Rights Act was introduced that there were more than 100,000 illegal apartments in Ontario in houses zoned as single-family dwellings. The legislation amended the Planning Act to ensure that official plans and by-laws could not be used by municipalities to prohibit a second residential unit in a detached house, semi-detached house, or row house provided it met health and safety standards. In particular, these apartments had to meet very stringent fire safety standards. Unless the Fire Code requirements were met by July 14, 1996, these apartments became "illegal" again.

The legislation recognized that tenants previously living in these illegal units were often required to put up with poor maintenance or unsafe conditions under threat of eviction because of the illegality of the unit. Tenants were often afraid that municipal officials would order the landlord to stop renting the apartment if they lodged a complaint.

These amendments were, in turn, repealed in 1996. The legislation preserved the legality of those apartments that were "legal" as of November 16, 1995, subject to certain requirements that are too technical to discuss here. With the exception of these and previous "legal" units, municipalities are again free to pass by-laws restricting homeowners from renting out part of a single-family house and tenants living in such illegal units are again open to possible harassment and the fear of eviction.

Residential accommodations in commercial and industrial areas are discussed in section **c.** below.

b. GRANNY FLATS

Under the Residents' Rights Act, municipalities were also given flexibility to enter into long-term agreements with homeowners who wanted to install garden suites or "granny flats" on their property. These are usually small, portable, self-contained units installed in a back or side yard. Demand for such accommodation is expected to come from seniors or persons with disabilities who wish to continue living independently but require some nearby support.

The legislation also amended the Municipal Act to ensure that municipalities could not use their power to license lodging houses to regulate granny flats.

c. COMMERCIAL AND INDUSTRIAL AREAS

Because of zoning restrictions, residential accommodation is not allowed in certain areas of municipalities. These are usually areas intended for commercial and industrial uses where the municipality does not feel it is appropriate to have people living. However, sometimes landlords create apartments in unused areas of warehouses or other commercial or industrial buildings, or tenants of small studios and similar units begin to live in them, with or without the landlord's knowledge.

Municipal zoning by-laws restrict the use to which buildings in certain areas can be put. It is an offence under the zoning by-law to use the premises for any other use, including a residential use. In addition to fining the owner, the municipality can issue an order requiring the owner to cease the illegal use. This means that the owner or landlord must terminate any tenancy for residential purposes. This raises a number of additional issues and questions.

One issue is whether or not the Tenant Protection Act applies to such accommodation. The act specifically exempts premises occupied for business purposes with living accommodation attached if the occupancy for both purposes is under a single lease. Depending on the precise wording of the zoning by-law, an artist's studio may or may not be an illegal use since such studios are commonly thought of as providing living accommodation for the artist as well as a place to work. In this and similar situations, the courts have sometimes looked at the "predominant use" to determine whether it was a residential use that fell within the protection of the act. Other courts have held that it was only necessary that there be combined use without worrying about which was predominant.

One judge concluded that, since residential use alone of an artist's studio would be illegal under the zoning by-law, it must be part of a combined use which is legal under the by-law since the residence can be regarded as "accessory" to the commercial or industrial use. However, since combined uses are exempt from what is now the Tenant Protection Act, any application for eviction or other relief must be made in a court under the Commercial Tenancies Act.

Another judge also considered the issue of renting residential studios in an area zoned for industrial purposes. In that case, there was no question of a combined use in that no business or artistic endeavours were carried on. It was solely a residence. The judge concluded that this must, therefore, be a residential use to which Part IV of the Landlord and Tenant Act applied. However, the court refused to deal with the tenant's application for an abatement of rent based on the landlord's failure to repair because the lease was illegal and, therefore, unenforceable. The judge went on to say that, had the landlord been bringing an application for some relief based on the tenancy agreement or Part IV of the Landlord and Tenant Act, the court would also have refused to consider that application. An illegal contract cannot be relied on by either party and the court will not recognize any rights or obligations arising from it. In this case, it appeared that both the landlord and tenant were aware that the apartment was not legal.

A similar situation arose in a case where tenants were seeking repayment of rent they had paid for a basement apartment that had such a low ceiling it contravened a municipal by-law. The landlord had previously been ordered by the municipality to cease renting it. The tenants realized that the ceiling was low but were not aware that it was illegal. The court ordered that all rent be repaid to the tenants less the cost of hydro consumed while the tenants were there. The issue of whether the tenants were entitled to claim relief based on an illegal contract was not discussed, but their lack of knowledge of the illegality may have been a factor.

In another more recent case, the court approved an order for termination of a tenancy and eviction order for an illegal basement apartment, but denied the landlord's claim for arrears of rent. Since the apartment was illegal, the landlord could not rent it as a residential unit or charge any rent. However, since the apartment was illegal, the judge ordered the tenant to vacate immediately. There was no discussion of the illegal contract issue.

The real problem is that the municipality, under its enforcement powers for a zoning by-law, can order the landlord or owner to stop renting an illegal unit. A tenant, knowing that the municipality may order the residential tenancy to be brought to an end and the tenant to vacate on short notice, will be very reluctant to try to assert any of the rights given under the Tenant Protection Act. The landlord is also left in a quandary as to how to evict the tenant. The procedures under the Tenant Protection Act cannot be used since the reason for termination is not provided for in the act but, if it is determined to be a residential tenancy, the act applies to the tenancy.

13
WHERE DO YOU GET HELP?

a. MUNICIPAL BY-LAWS

Every municipality is authorized to enact its own by-laws for things such as adequate heat, proper repairs, safety and housing standards, sanitation, and numerous other matters that may affect rental premises. No attempt is made here to summarize these since they vary from one municipality to another. Tenants who feel their building is deficient in one of the above categories should consult their local municipal offices.

In addition to taking action under the Tenant Protection Act regarding requirements for repairs, as discussed earlier, a complaint may also be laid with the municipal authorities. When this is done, a municipal inspector will be sent out and, if the inspection reveals that the building does not comply with the relevant by-law, the municipality has authority to order the repairs to be made.

Municipalities also have power to enact by-laws regarding vital services and restricting demolitions, conversions, and major repairs or renovations. Copies of the by-laws are usually available from the municipal offices.

b. DISCRIMINATION

Discrimination regarding the provision of accommodation, including renting apartments and houses, is prohibited by the Ontario Human Rights Code. The grounds of discrimination set out in the code are —

(a) Race

(b) Place of origin

(c) Ethnic origin

(d) Creed (religion)

(e) Sexual orientation

(f) Marital status

(g) Handicap

(h) Ancestry

(i) Colour

(j) Citizenship

(k) Sex

(l) Age

(m) Family status

(n) Receipt of public assistance

The prohibition against discrimination applies to the decision of whether to accept a tenant as well as any attempt at eviction. Permissible screening devices are things such as level of income, security of income, smoking, and references from previous landlords. Landlords may not ask any questions, either in applications or interviews, that relate to any of these prohibited grounds and there must be no reference to these grounds in any advertisements or signs.

In order to conform to the Charter of Rights and Freedoms, the code prohibits discrimination based on marital status or family status for all rental accommodation. A landlord cannot refuse to rent to persons who want to live together, regardless of their marital status or sexual orientation. Similarly, buildings can no longer be designated as "adult only" despite previous restrictions. Tenants cannot be refused accommodation just because they have children.

"Housing accommodation" is defined as any dwelling place, except one that is part of a building in which the owner or his or her family resides and with whom the tenant is required to share a bathroom or kitchen facility.

The Ontario Human Rights Commission, either on its own initiative or as a result of complaints received, may initiate an inquiry into any alleged acts of discrimination. The commission may then make recommendations to the Minister of Citizenship, Culture, and Recreation who is empowered to appoint a board of inquiry to hold a hearing on the matter. This may result in a mandatory order requiring the landlord to rent the premises to the complainant and an order for compensation to the complainant.

In order to encourage people to assert their human rights, it is also an offence to discriminate against any person who has made a complaint or participated in any proceedings under the code.

Complaints or inquiries may be directed to the Ontario Human Rights Commission, 180 Dundas Street W., 7th Floor, Toronto, ON M7A 2R9. However, it is preferable to contact a local commission office which you can find in the blue pages of your telephone book.

c. LEGAL AID

Legal aid may be available to persons whose financial circumstances warrant it, but only where the matter is serious or a large amount of money is at stake. As the legal aid plan tries to cut costs, it is almost impossible to get this funding for most landlord and tenant disputes. If a certificate is given, the legal aid plan may pay all or part of the tenant's legal costs or may require repayment either at a future time or out of the judgment recovered (if any). Legal aid will not be granted for prosecuting charges or for Small Claims Court actions. Each county or region has an office where applications may be made. Check the yellow pages under "Lawyers" or the white pages under "Legal aid."

Community legal clinics are also funded by legal aid and have lawyers on staff who can give advice in minor matters without having to make a formal application for legal aid. These lawyers are usually very experienced in landlord and tenant matters, particularly eviction procedures and requirements.

A lawyer referral service is operated by the Law Society through Osgoode Hall in Toronto. If you contact this office you will be referred to a lawyer knowledgeable in the relevant area, and given a half-hour interview at no cost to determine if you have a legal case and if it is feasible to pursue the matter. The phone number is (416) 947-3330, 1-800-268-8326, or TDD (416) 361-0663.

14

THE ONTARIO RENTAL
HOUSING TRIBUNAL

The Ontario Rental Housing Tribunal is an entirely new independent body created by the Tenant Protection Act. It has been given exclusive jurisdiction to determine all applications brought under the Tenant Protection Act, and any other matters in which jurisdiction is conferred on it under the act. This includes evictions, maintenance and repair issues, rent matters, and approving rent increases above the guideline.

The role of courts in most landlord and tenant matters has almost completely been eliminated except for disposing of applications filed before the commencement of the new act. Offences are still prosecuted through Provincial Offences Court although the tribunal is empowered to assess "administrative fines" for certain types of conduct. See the discussion on enforcement of rights in chapter 4.

a. ORGANIZATION

The tribunal will have a head office in Toronto and 8 district offices — London, Hamilton, Sudbury, Ottawa, Mississauga, and 3 in Toronto. These offices will receive applications, conduct mediations, hold hearings, and provide information services and forms for landlords and tenants. As well, there will be 12 smaller customer service offices in medium-sized communities, which will receive applications and documents and provide information and document forms. The tribunal is also making arrangements with Motor Vehicle Licence Issuing Offices so that tribunal forms and brochures will be available in smaller communities. Applications and documents can be filed at these offices. For further information, you can contact the tribunal at 1-888-332-3234, or on the Internet at *www.orht.gov.on.ca.*

b. PROCEDURES

The procedures to be followed by the tribunal are not yet fully formulated. The tribunal is required to adopt the quickest method of determining questions arising in a proceeding. A Rules and Guidelines Committee will be established to adopt rules of practice and procedure before the tribunal. While this process is happening, the Minister of Municipal Affairs and Housing may establish temporary rules for the tribunal. It is intended that the hearings be very informal.

The timing of an application to the tribunal depends on the purpose of the application. When an application may be brought to terminate the tenancy and evict the tenant is discussed in chapter 6. Other types of applications may be made at any time, subject to limitation periods before which the application must be brought.

The party must complete an application form setting out the reasons for the application and what is being sought (such as reduction of rent or increase of rent over the guideline). This is then filed with the tribunal. If it is an application for termination, the notice of termination together with a certificate of service must be filed. Other documentation may be required for other types of applications. Once the required documents are filed, the applicant is given a notice of hearing specifying a date for the hearing.

A landlord applying to the tribunal for an eviction order must give the tenant a copy of the application and notice of hearing at least five days before the scheduled hearing date. A tenant wishing to dispute the application must do so by filing a dispute in writing with the tribunal within five days after being served with the notice of hearing. Other time periods may apply for other types of hearings.

If the parties consent, the tribunal may attempt to mediate a settlement between the landlord and tenant. This procedure is highly recommended to both landlords and tenants. A mediated settlement may contain provisions that contravene the act. However, the largest rent increase that can be mediated is either the maximum rent, where that is still applicable, or the sum of the guideline amount plus 4% of the previous year's lawful rent, whichever is greater.

The tribunal must determine the real substance of all transactions and activities relating to a residential complex or a rental unit, as well as the good faith of the participants. It may disregard the appearance of any transaction or the separate corporate existence of participants, and may consider a pattern of activities relating to the complex or unit. Before, during, or after a hearing, the tribunal may conduct any inquiry it considers necessary, request an inspector to conduct an inspection, question any person concerning a dispute, permit or direct a party to file additional evidence, or view the premises that are the subject of the dispute.

Where appropriate, the tribunal is authorized, subject to any regulations under the act, to require a tenant to pay a sum into the tribunal within a given time. The tribunal may establish procedures in its rules for the payment of money into and out of the tribunal. If the tenant fails to pay, the tribunal may refuse to consider the evidence and argument that the tenant would like to put forward. Under Part IV of the Landlord and Tenant Act, there was a provision that, where the landlord's claim was for arrears of rent or compensation, the tenant was required to pay the amount claimed into court before he or she could file a dispute. This section in the new legislation may be used for much the same purpose.

The tribunal is also given the broad power to dismiss an application without a hearing or to refuse to allow an application to be filed if it is of the opinion that the matter is frivolous or vexatious, has not been initiated in good faith, or discloses no reasonable claim. The tribunal may dismiss a proceeding at any time if it finds the applicant filed documents that he or she knew, or ought have known, contained false or misleading information.

The tribunal may include in an order whatever conditions it considers fair in the circumstances and may order a party to pay the costs of another party or even the costs of the tribunal itself. This is likely to be invoked only where the proceeding was commenced in bad faith and is completely without merit or, perhaps, where a party has unduly prolonged or delayed the proceeding.

The tribunal may include in an order the following general provision:

> "The landlord or the tenant shall pay to the other any sum of money that is owed as a result of this order."

This will enable the successful party to collect what he or she is owed without having to take other proceedings and saves the tribunal having to do all the calculations.

Hearings will be held at the district offices or in the major city in each county. They will be arranged on a regular schedule whenever possible. Hearings will be conducted by a single member of the tribunal and it is anticipated that, in most cases, decisions will be made immediately following the hearing and orders issued soon after. Hearings should be held much more expeditiously than was the case under the old system.

The tribunal will require fees for almost all applications other than cases involving harassment. These fees will range from $45 to $60 with the higher fee payable for applications for evictions.

c. FORMS

The various notices, certificates, applications, and other documents must be in a form approved by the tribunal. Copies of the forms as approved by the tribunal can be found on the tribunal's Web site at *www.orht.gov.on.ca*. Copies can also be obtained from tribunal offices and from Motor Vehicle Licence Issuing Offices in smaller communities.

It is not clear whether the tribunal will "approve" and allow to be used any other form of document even if it contains the necessary information. The safer procedure is to obtain the approved document from the tribunal and use it in all cases. For a list of forms available, see Appendix 1.

d. METHODS OF GIVING NOTICES AND SERVING DOCUMENTS

The methods for serving or delivering applications and other documents to the other party are the same as for giving a notice. The methods are —

(a) handing it to the landlord or tenant,

(b) handing it to an employee of the landlord exercising authority in the residential complex,

(c) handing it to an apparently adult person in the rental unit (for delivery to a tenant, subtenant, or occupant),

(d) leaving it in the mailbox where mail is ordinarily delivered,

(e) leaving it at the place where mail is ordinarily delivered to the person where there is no mailbox,

(f) sending it by mail to the last known address where the person resides or carries on business (it is deemed to have been given on the fifth day after mailing), or

(g) any other means allowed in the rules.

Delivery by courier is not included in the list. This method might qualify as handing it to the person or an apparently adult person in the unit but there is no easy way of proving actual delivery by this method.

A notice that is not given in one of the methods set out in this list is still deemed to have been validly given if it is proven that its contents actually came to the attention of the person for whom it is intended within the required time.

Various documents, such as applications and related materials, including disputes, must be filed with the tribunal. This may be done by —

(a) hand delivering it to the tribunal at the appropriate office as set out in the rules,

(b) sending it by mail to the appropriate office as set out in the rules, or

(c) any other means allowed in the rules.

A notice or document given to the tribunal by mail is deemed to have been given on either the fifth day after mailing or the date on which it was actually received by the tribunal, whichever is earlier.

The tribunal will have district offices in major centres, customer service offices in medium-sized communities, and will use Motor Vehicle Licence Issuing Offices in smaller communities.

e. DEFAULT ORDERS

Where no written dispute is filed, the tribunal may make an order for the following types of applications without holding a hearing:

(a) An application to terminate a tenancy or to evict a person (except an application based on a claim that an act or omission of the tenant has seriously impaired the safety of any person)

(b) A landlord's application for arrears of rent, compensation, damages, or the payment of the money as a result of misrepresentation of income

(c) A tenant's application for compensation from an overholding subtenant

(d) A tenant's application for repayment of money collected illegally by the landlord

(e) A tenant's application claiming that a landlord unreasonably withheld consent to an assignment or a subletting

Where such a default order is made, the person against whom it is made may, within ten days, make a motion to the tribunal to have the order set aside. The order will then not be enforced until the motion is dealt with. The tribunal may set aside the default order if it is satisfied that the respondent was not reasonably able to participate in the proceeding. If it is convinced of this, the matter then proceeds to a hearing on merits. The party that obtained the default order must be given notice that such a motion is being made.

Other types of applications do not require a written dispute and a hearing will always be held.

f. EVICTION ORDERS

An eviction order given by the tribunal does not come into effect any earlier than the date of termination set out in the landlord's notice. Where the eviction order is obtained on default, it takes effect 11 days after the order is issued, in order to give the tenant the required 10 days in which to bring a motion to have it set aside.

A landlord may not apply to the tribunal for an eviction order based on non-payment of rent before the date for termination specified on the notice. Other applications may be started as soon as the notice of termination is delivered to the tenant.

Where the landlord brings an application on the basis of non-payment of rent, the tenant has until the date the eviction order becomes enforceable to rectify the situation and reinstate the tenancy. A tenant does this by paying, either to the tribunal or to the landlord, all the rent in arrears and any compensation owing for the period after the date in the notice of termination, together with any costs ordered by the tribunal and the fee paid by the landlord to make the application to the tribunal. If this is done, any order for arrears of rent, compensation, or eviction of the tenant based on arrears of rent becomes void. However, where the application and ensuing order of the tribunal was based on an additional ground for termination, that part of the order still remains in effect and the tenant would still be subject to eviction.

Actual evictions are carried out by sheriff's officers, usually about a week after the sheriff is instructed by the landlord to enforce the eviction order. If necessary, the tenant and his or her belongings will be physically removed and locks will be changed. There is no rule prohibiting winter evictions.

g. MONETARY JURISDICTION

Where it has jurisdiction, the tribunal may order the payment of an amount of money up to $10,000 or the monetary jurisdiction of the local Small Claims Court, whichever is greater. At present, the maximum monetary jurisdiction of Small Claims Courts is only $6,000, so the $10,000 figure applies.

If you are otherwise entitled to apply under this act but are claiming more money than the tribunal has jurisdiction to order, you may instead bring your application in Ontario Court (General Division) and the court may exercise any of the powers of the tribunal. If you bring the application before the tribunal, you lose all rights to claim any amount in excess of the $10,000 limit. A subsequent court action for the remaining balance is not permitted.

If a landlord is ordered to pay a sum of money to a current tenant, the tribunal's order may provide that, if the landlord fails to pay the amount owing, the tenant may recover the money plus interest by deducting a specified sum from the rent for a certain number of rental periods. The order will set out the date by which payment must be made and interest accrues after that date at a rate applicable to general legal proceedings.

h. AGENTS

Either a landlord or a tenant may have an agent appear for them at a tribunal hearing. The agent may charge a fee but the fee cannot be based on a percentage of the amount saved or recovered in the proceeding unless it is no more than 10% of such amount for a one-year period. Such charges are referred to as contingency fees.

Landlords and tenants should be cautious in their choice of agents, especially when hiring persons making a business of acting as an agent or consultant. There have been a number of occurrences in recent years of such persons failing to follow instructions and misrepresenting the work they have done in order to claim exorbitant fees. Always get references. A reputable agent should not object to you speaking with other clients.

15

THE ROLE OF THE COURTS

While most matters are now dealt with by the Ontario Rental Housing Tribunal, some landlord-tenant disputes may still end up in court. It may be necessary to appear in Small Claims Court, Provincial Offences Court, or Ontario Court (General Division).

a. SMALL CLAIMS COURT

This is the court in which disputes involving money will be heard if not provided for in the Tenant Protection Act or if the tenant is no longer in possession of the rental unit (although the Tenant Protection Act does make some remedies available to "former tenants"). Fortunately, it is also the most informal court. If the claim is civil in nature (i.e., does not involve fines or a jail sentence), and is for $6,000 or less, you will likely proceed in Small Claims Court. If it is for over $6,000, you must proceed in Ontario Court (General Division) or drop your claim to $6,000. Cases involving arrears of rent, return of security or rent deposits, recovery of money for damages to premises, wrongful seizure of goods by a landlord, and any other monetary loss, may be heard in Small Claims Court when they do not come within the exclusive jurisdiction of the tribunal.

It is important to remember that, if you have a lawyer, you may not be able to recover all your legal fees from the other side even if you win your case. Court costs, such as the cost of issuing claims and service of documents, are always recoverable from the losing side unless ordered otherwise by the judge. Only a small amount can be recovered for lawyer's fees.

Unless you are prepared to spend a relatively large amount of money for a lawyer, you must appear on your own behalf. Fortunately, the procedure is simple. All you have to do is appear at the Small Claims Court office in the area of the premises involved or of the residence of the party being sued.

To locate the appropriate Small Claims Court, consult the blue pages of your telephone directory under the Government of Ontario, Attorney General. If in doubt about where to go, simply phone one of the offices and explain your problem. They are very helpful.

Once you are at the right office, a clerk will record all the particulars of your case and process the summons. It will cost you about $50 to $100, depending on the amount involved. If you are successful, this fee will be returned to you. Following this, you need only appear in court at the time of trial and tell the judge your story.

b. PROVINCIAL OFFENCES COURT

Landlord-tenant disputes where conduct an offence under the Tenant Protection Act are heard in Ontario Court (Provincial Division) under the Provincial Offences Act. This court is usually called Provincial Offences Court and is especially important for the tenant since most, but not all, offences relate to actions by landlords. However, don't expect the police to become involved in this process unless there is actual or threatened violence.

The Tenant Protection Act provides penalties for violation of certain sections of the act. These charges are tried before a provincial court judge by the relatively quick summary conviction procedure or by a justice of the peace. The maximum penalty is a fine of $10,000 ($50,000 for corporations). Procedure is governed by the Provincial Offences Act. There are also some provisions where the tribunal can levy an "administrative fine" of up to $10,000. See the discussion on enforcement of rights in chapter 4.

A list of offences can be found in Section 205 of the Tenant Protection Act. Subsection (1) provides that a person who "knowingly" does any of the following is guilty of an offence:

(a) Restrict reasonable access by political candidates or their representatives in contravention of Section 22

(b) Alter the locking system in contravention of Section 23

(c) Withhold the reasonable supply of a vital service, care service, or food in contravention of Section 25

(d) Harass, hinder, obstruct, or interfere with a tenant who is —

    (i) securing a right or seeking relief under the act or in court,

    (ii) participating in a proceeding under the act, or

    (iii) participating in a tenants' association or attempting to organize one

(e) Harass, coerce, threaten, or interfere with a tenant so as to induce the tenant to vacate the rental unit

(f) Harass, hinder, obstruct, or interfere with a landlord who is —

    (i) securing a right or seeking relief under the act or in court, or

    (ii) participating in a proceeding under the act

(g) Seize any property of the tenant in contravention of Section 31

(h) Obtain possession of a rental unit improperly by giving a notice to terminate in bad faith

(i) Fail to afford a tenant a right of first refusal in contravention of Section 54 or 56 (condominium conversion or repair or renovations)

(j) Recover possession of a rental unit without complying with the requirements of Section 55, 57, and 58 (demolition or conversion, repairs or renovations, and severance)

(k) Coerce a tenant of a mobile home park or land lease community to enter into an agency agreement for the sale or lease of their home

(l) Coerce a tenant to sign an agreement to increase rent above the guideline amount

In addition, it is an offence to do any of the following (presumably, whether "knowingly" or not):

(a) Furnish false or misleading information in any document filed in any proceeding or provided to an inspector or the tribunal

(b) Enter a rental unit where such entry is not permitted under the act

(c) Contravene an order of the tribunal for making repairs or ceasing other prohibited conduct under the act

(d) Unlawfully recover possession of a rental unit

(e) Give a notice to terminate a tenancy for a landlord's occupation or occupation by a purchaser in contravention of the provisions for conversion to a condominium

(f) Give a notice of rent increase or a notice of increase of a charge in a care home without first giving an information package

(g) Increase a charge for providing a care service or meals in a care home without giving 90 days' notice in the proper form

(h) Interfere with a tenant's right to sell or lease his or her mobile home

(i) Restrict the right of a tenant of a mobile home park or land lease community to purchase goods or services from the person of his or her choice

(j) Require or receive a security deposit from a tenant

(k) Fail to pay 6% interest annually on a last month's rent deposit

(l) Fail to apply the rent deposit to the rent for the last month of the tenancy

(m) Fail to provide a tenant with a receipt for rent when requested

(n) Charge rent in an amount greater than permitted under the act

(o) Require a tenant to pay rent proposed in an application for an increase above the guideline

(p) Charge or collect amounts from a tenant, a subtenant, or an assignee in contravention of Section 140

(q) Fail to comply with all of the items contained in a work order

(r) Charge an illegal contingency fee to represent a landlord or a tenant in a proceeding

(s) Obstruct or interfere with an inspector or investigator

Some of these activities also constitute offences for which the tribunal can levy an administrative fine of up to $10,000. Presumably, any information attesting to the same facts as led the tribunal to fine the person will not be allowed to proceed.

The sections of the legislation that create offences can be enforced only if someone lays a charge. This is accomplished by going to the office of the justice of the peace and swearing to the facts that constitute the offence. This is called "laying an information." To locate the nearest office, simply phone a police station.

The justice of the peace will consider the information and, in some cases, will hear and consider the evidence of the informant and any witnesses and then decide if a sufficient case has been made to proceed. If he or she refuses, the local Crown Attorney should be contacted. Once the information is accepted, the defendant will be summonsed by a provincial offences officer at no cost to the person laying the charge.

The extent to which the staff of the Ministry of Municipal Affairs and Housing will become involved in laying or prosecuting charges laid by tenants is not clear at this stage. They will certainly be involved in charges arising from their own investigations. However, it seems likely that most charges will be laid and prosecuted by individual landlords and tenants.

It is significant to note that this court is quasi-criminal in nature. This means you should have a witness to corroborate your story, as the defendant cannot be required to take the stand to testify against himself or herself. In addition, there is a higher standard of proof required than in Small Claims Court. However, there are no court costs. In some cases, you may be able to enlist the aid of the Crown Attorney who will advise you without charge and may prosecute your case in court. More often, you or your agent or lawyer will have to act as prosecutor.

When the case comes to trial, the prosecutor will have to make sure the witnesses are present and handle the presentation of evidence to the judge. As mentioned, if the situation is serious, the Crown Attorney may assist in the prosecution of the case.

One problem that should be kept in mind is that when a private citizen, as opposed to a police officer, lays a charge and the person accused is not convicted, the person laying the charge may later be sued for malicious prosecution. This is mentioned simply to warn you that you must be sure of the facts and that you are able to prove them before proceeding to lay a charge. It is a serious matter to lay a charge that is without foundation or that is laid primarily to harass the other party or to force the other party to settle a claim or some other problem that should properly be dealt with in a civil court. As set out in the list above, such harassment is, in itself, an offence under the act.

c. ONTARIO COURT (GENERAL DIVISION)

Under Part IV of the Landlord and Tenant Act, all eviction applications were brought in Ontario Court (General Division). The hearings were held using an informal procedure in what was often referred to as "Landlord and Tenant Court."

Other actions that fell within the jurisdiction of Ontario Court were enforcement of the landlord's obligation to repair, disputes involving arbitrary withholding of consent to sublet and/or charging excessive fees for subletting, and disputes over accelerated rent clauses. The responsibilities of a mobile home park landlord were also enforced in this court.

With the creation of the Ontario Rental Housing Tribunal, Ontario Court will now only finalize landlord-tenant matters started before the Tenant Protection Act became law.

A monetary claim for over $6,000 must also be brought in Ontario Court (General Division), but (except for those specifically permitted to be brought by application) this requires a full court hearing and different documentation. Use of a lawyer is highly recommended for pursuing any claim in this court. Commencement of any Ontario Court action requires the payment of charges, which are almost always recoverable later from the losing side along with a portion of the lawyer's fees.

d. COURTROOM PROCEDURE

Regardless of whether a case is criminal in nature (Provincial Court) or civil (Small Claims Court or Ontario Court [General Division]), the general procedure for presentation of the case is similar.

The person instigating the action must prove his or her case. This is done by calling witnesses. Such witnesses may not be asked "leading questions" — that is, questions that tend to suggest the answer required. Likewise, witnesses may testify only about facts of which they have personal knowledge and that are relevant to the particular issue in the trial. They may not be asked about what someone else has told them (other than the opposing party in the trial). This second-hand information is called "hearsay" evidence.

The person bringing the action may act as his or her own witness and, in civil cases, may even call his or her opponent as a witness. Any relevant documents should, of course, be brought to the trial and entered as evidence by having someone identify them. Once a witness has concluded testimony, the party on the opposite side may question or "cross-examine" that witness about what he or she has said.

Once the plaintiff (the instigator of a civil action) or the complainant (the instigator of a criminal action) has concluded the case, the defendant may ask the judge to dismiss the case on the basis that the other side has not proven the necessary facts, or may call witnesses on his or her own behalf. If witnesses are called, they are subject to the same rules of evidence and may be cross-examined.

If there is any danger that a witness may not show up for the court appearance, the party requiring the person's evidence should subpoena him or her. A subpoena is a court document requiring the witness to be present for the trial and may be obtained in the court office for the court in which the trial is being held. There is a small charge for issuing a subpoena, and sometimes travel expenses must be provided for the sheriff or process server to give to the witness.

APPENDIX 1
APPLICATIONS, FORMS, AND NOTICES

a. LANDLORD APPLICATIONS

L1 Application to terminate a tenancy for non-payment of rent

L2 Application to terminate a tenancy and evict a tenant

L3 Application to terminate a tenancy — tenant gave notice or agreed to terminate the tenancy

L4 Application to terminate a tenancy — tenant failed to meet conditions of a settlement or order

L5 Application for an above guideline increase

L6 Application for review of a provincial work order

L7 Application to transfer a care home tenant

L8 Application because the tenant changed the locks

b. TENANT APPLICATIONS

T1 Tenant application for a rebate

T2 Application about tenant rights

T3 Tenant application for a rent reduction

T4 Tenant application — landlord did not comply with an agreement to increase rent above the guideline

T5 Tenant application — landlord gave a notice of termination in bad faith

c. APPLICATIONS THAT MAY BE FILED BY A LANDLORD OR TENANT

A1   Application about whether the act applies

A2   Application about a sublet or assignment

d. NOTICES

N1   Notice of rent increase

N2   Notice of rent increase (rental unit partially exempt)

N3   Notice to increase the rent and/or charges for care services and meals

N4   Notice to terminate a tenancy early for non-payment of rent

N5   Notice to terminate a tenancy early

N6   Notice to terminate a tenancy early — illegal act or misrepresentation of income

N7   Notice to terminate a tenancy early for impaired safety

N8   Notice to terminate a tenancy at the end of term

N9   Tenant's notice to terminate the tenancy

N10 Agreement to increase the rent above guideline

N11 Agreement to terminate a tenancy

e. OTHER FORMS

Affidavit

Certificate of service

Dispute of application

Motion to set aside a default order

Statutory declaration

APPENDIX 2
SAMPLE RENTAL UNIT CONDITION FORM

RENTAL UNIT CONDITION REPORT

PRINT OR WRITE CLEARLY

Top copy to Tenant
Carbon copy to Landlord

G – Good
M – Missing
D – Damaged
B – Broken
S – Scratched or Marked

Date (1) . . . .   Date (2) . . . .

		Condition at Commencement of Tenancy	Condition at Termination of Tenancy
Exterior	Stucco and/or Siding	N/A	
	Front & Rear Entrances	G	
	Garbage Container(s)	G	
	Glass & Frames	G	
	Screens & Storm Windows	B	
	Ground & Walks	N/A	
	Keys Issued	✓	
	Keys Returned		
Kitchen	Ceiling	G	
	Walls & Trim	G	
	Floor	D	
	Countertop	D	
	Cabinets & Doors	S	
	Range – Condition & Equipment	G	
	Sink & Stoppers	G	
	Chests	N/A	
	Refrigerators – Condition & Equipment	G	
Basement	Stair & Stairwell		
	Walls & Floor	N/A	
	Furnace, Water Heater & Plumbing		
Living Room – Dining Room	Floor	G	
	Ceiling	G	
	Walls & Trim	S	
	Closets	G	
Stairwell & Hall	Treads & Landings		
	Walls & Trim	N/A	
	Ceilings		
	Closets		
Bathroom	Ceiling	G	
	Floor	D	
	Walls & Trim	S	
	Cabinets & Mirror	B	
	Tub, Sink & Toilet	G	
	Closets	G	
		G	
Bedrooms	Floor, Walls & Trim	G	
	Closets, Ceilings	G	
	Doors	All there	
		Fair	
	LIGHTING FIXTURES – throughout	All there	
	GENERAL CONDITION – Cleanliness	Fair	

ADDRESS OF RENTED PREMISES
#809-500 Sunny Blvd.
Toronto . . . .
. . . .

TENANT (Name print)
Thomas Tenant

Tenants Forwarding Address
(after termination of Tenancy)
. . . .
. . . .
. . . .

Landlord or Agent's Signature
. . . . (1)
. . . . (2)

Tenant's Signature
. . . . (1)
. . . . (2)

N.B. Further comment and detail e.g. furniture, rugs, drapes, appliances and premises as to decorating and alterations to be noted and initialled overleaf

APPENDIX 3
THE TENANT PROTECTION ACT

Her Majesty, by and with the advice and consent of the Legislative Assembly of the Province of Ontario, enacts as follows:

PART I
INTRODUCTION

Definitions   **1.** (1) In this Act,

"care home" means a residential complex that is occupied or intended to be occupied by persons for the purpose of receiving care services, whether or not receiving the services is the primary purpose of the occupancy; ("maison de soins")

"care services" means, subject to the regulations, health care services, rehabilitative or therapeutic services or services that provide assistance with the activities of daily living; ("services en matière de soins")

"guideline", when used with respect to the charging of rent, means the guideline determined under section 129; ("taux légal")

"land lease community" means the land on which one or more occupied land lease homes are situate and includes the rental units and the land, structures, services and facilities of which the landlord retains possession and that are intended for the common use and enjoyment of the tenants of the landlord; ("zone résidentielle à baux fonciers")

"land lease home" means a dwelling, other than a mobile home, that is a permanent structure where the owner of the dwelling leases the land used or intended for use as the site for the dwelling; ("maison à bail foncier")

"landlord" includes,

(a) the owner or other person permitting occupancy of a rental unit,

(b) the heirs, assigns, personal representatives and successors in title of a person referred to in clause (a), and

(c) a person, other than a tenant occupying a rental unit in a residential complex, who is entitled to possession of the residential complex and who attempts to enforce any of the rights of a landlord under a tenancy agreement or this Act, including the right to collect rent; ("locateur")

"Minister" means the Minister of Municipal Affairs and Housing; ("ministre")

"Ministry" means the Ministry of Municipal Affairs and Housing; ("ministère")

"mobile home" means a dwelling that is designed to be made mobile and that is being used as a permanent residence; ("maison mobile")

"mobile home park" means the land on which one or more occupied mobile homes are located and includes the rental units and the land, structures, services and facilities of which the landlord retains possession and that are intended for the common use and enjoyment of the tenants of the landlord; ("parc de maisons mobiles")

"municipal taxes and charges" means taxes charged to a landlord by a municipality and charges levied on a landlord by a municipality and includes taxes levied on a landlord's property in unorganized territory, but "municipal taxes and charges" does not include,

(a) charges for inspections done by a municipality on a residential complex related to an alleged breach of a health,

152

safety, housing or maintenance standard,

(b) charges for emergency repairs carried out by a municipality on a residential complex,

(c) charges for work in the nature of a capital expenditure carried out by a municipality, or

(d) any other prescribed charges; ("redevances et impôts municipaux")

"municipality" means a city, town, village, improvement district or township, a regional, district or metropolitan municipality or the County of Oxford; ("municipalité")

"non-profit housing co-operative" means a non-profit housing co-operative under the *Co-operative Corporations Act*; ("coopérative de logement sans but lucratif")

"person", or any expression referring to a person, means an individual, sole proprietorship, partnership, limited partnership, trust or body corporate, or an individual in his or her capacity as a trustee, executor, administrator or other legal representative; ("personne")

"prescribed" means prescribed by the regulations; ("prescrit")

"regulations" means the regulations made under this Act; ("règlements")

"rent" includes the amount of any consideration paid or given or required to be paid or given by or on behalf of a tenant to a landlord or the landlord's agent for the right to occupy a rental unit and for any services and facilities and any privilege, accommodation or thing that the landlord provides for the tenant in respect of the occupancy of the rental unit, whether or not a separate charge is made for services and facilities or for the privilege, accommodation or thing, but "rent" does not include,

(a) an amount paid by a tenant to a landlord to reimburse the landlord for property taxes paid by the landlord with respect to a mobile home or a land lease home owned by a tenant, or

(b) an amount that a landlord charges a tenant of a rental unit in a care home for care services or meals; ("loyer")

"rental unit" means any living accommodation used or intended for use as rented residential premises, and "rental unit" includes,

(a) a site for a mobile home or site on which there is a land lease home used or intended for use as rented residential premises, and

(b) a room in a boarding house, rooming house or lodging house and a unit in a care home; ("logement locatif")

"residential complex" means,

(a) a building or related group of buildings in which one or more rental units are located,

(b) a mobile home park or land lease community,

(c) a site that is a rental unit,

(d) a care home, and

"residential complex" includes all common areas and services and facilities available for the use of its residents; ("ensemble d'habitation")

"residential unit" means any living accommodation used or intended for use as residential premises, and "residential unit" includes,

(a) a site for a mobile home or on which there is a land lease home used or intended for use as a residential premises, and

(b) a room in a boarding house, rooming house or lodging house and a unit in a care home; ("habitation")

"Rules" means the rules of practice and procedure made by the Tribunal or the Minister under section 164 of this Act and section 25.1 of the *Statutory Powers Procedure Act*; ("règles")

"services and facilities" includes,

(a) furniture, appliances and furnishings,

(b) parking and related facilities,

(c) laundry facilities,

(d) elevator facilities,

(e) common recreational facilities,

(f) garbage facilities and related services,

(g) cleaning and maintenance services,

(h) storage facilities,

(i) intercom systems,

(j) cable television facilities,

(k) heating facilities and services,

(l) air-conditioning facilities,

(m) utilities and related services, and

(n) security services and facilities; ("services et installations")

"subtenant" means the person to whom a tenant gives the right under section 18 to occupy a rental unit; ("sous-locataire")

"superintendent's premises" means a rental unit used by a person employed as a janitor, manager, security guard or superintendent and located in the residential complex with respect to which the person is so employed; ("logement de concierge")

"tenancy agreement" means a written, oral or implied agreement between a tenant and a landlord for occupancy of a rental unit and includes a licence to occupy a rental unit; ("convention de location")

"tenant" includes a person who pays rent in return for the right to occupy a rental unit and includes the tenant's heirs, assigns and personal representatives, but "tenant" does not include a person who has the right to occupy a rental unit by virtue of being,

(a) a co-owner of the residential complex in which the rental unit is located, or

(b) a shareholder of a corporation that owns the residential complex; ("locataire")

"Tribunal" means the Ontario Rental Housing Tribunal; ("Tribunal")

"utilities" means heat, hydro and water; ("services d'utilité publique")

"vital service" means fuel, hydro, gas or hot or cold water. ("service essentiel")

the land lease home on the site is owned by the tenant of the site.

Application of Act **2.** (1) This Act applies with respect to rental units in residential complexes, despite any other Act and despite any agreement or waiver to the contrary.

Conflicts, care homes (2) In interpreting a provision of this Act with regard to a care home, if a provision in Part IV conflicts with a provision in another Part of this Act, the provision in Part IV applies.

Conflicts, mobile home parks and land lease communities (3) In interpreting a provision of this Act with regard to a mobile home park or a land lease community, if a provision in Part V conflicts with a provision in another Part of this Act, the provision in Part V applies.

Conflict with other Acts (4) If a provision of this Act conflicts with a provision of another Act, other than the *Human Rights Code*, the provision of this Act applies.

Exemptions from Act **3.** This Act does not apply with respect to,

(a) living accommodation intended to be provided to the travelling or vacationing public or occupied for a seasonal or temporary period in a hotel, motel or motor hotel, resort, lodge, tourist camp, cottage or cabin establishment, inn, campground, trailer park, tourist home, bed and breakfast vacation establishment or vacation home;

(b) living accommodation whose occupancy is conditional upon the occupant continuing to be employed on a farm, whether or not the accommodation is located on that farm;

(c) living accommodation provided by a non-profit housing co-operative to tenants in member units;

(d) living accommodation occupied by a person for penal or correctional purposes;

(e) living accommodation that is subject to the *Public Hospitals Act*, the *Private Hospitals Act*, the *Community Psychiatric Hospitals Act*, the *Mental Hospitals Act*, the *Homes for the Aged and Rest Homes Act*, the *Nursing Homes Act*, the *Ministry of Correctional Services Act*, the *Charitable Institutions*

Rental unit, clarification (2) A rented site for a mobile home or a land lease home is a rental unit for the purposes of this Act even if the mobile home or

154

Act, the *Child and Family Services Act* or Schedule I, II or III of Regulation 272 of the Revised Regulations of Ontario, 1990, made under the *Developmental Services Act*;

(f) short term living accommodation provided as emergency shelter;

(g) living accommodation provided by an educational institution to its students or staff where,

    (i) the living accommodation is provided primarily to persons under the age of majority, or all major questions related to the living accommodation are decided after consultation with a council or association representing the residents, and

    (ii) the living accommodation does not have its own self-contained bathroom and kitchen facilities or is not intended for year-round occupancy by full-time students or staff and members of their households;

(h) living accommodation located in a building or project used in whole or in part for non-residential purposes if the occupancy of the living accommodation is conditional upon the occupant continuing to be an employee of or perform services related to a business or enterprise carried out in the building or project;

(i) living accommodation whose occupant or occupants are required to share a bathroom or kitchen facility with the owner, the owner's spouse, child or parent or the spouse's child or parent, and where the owner, spouse, child or parent lives in the building in which the living accommodation is located;

(j) premises occupied for business or agricultural purposes with living accommodation attached if the occupancy for both purposes is under a single lease and the same person occupies the premises and the living accommodation;

(k) living accommodation occupied by a person for the purpose of receiving re-

habilitative or therapeutic services agreed upon by the person and the provider of the living accommodation, where,

    (i) the parties have agreed that,

        (A) the period of occupancy will be of a specified duration, or

        (B) the occupancy will terminate when the objectives of the services have been met or will not be met, and

    (ii) the living accommodation is intended to be provided for no more than a one year period;

(l) living accommodation in a care home occupied by a person for the purpose of receiving short term respite care; and

(m) any other prescribed class of accommodation.

Exemptions from rules relating to rent

4. (1) Sections 54, 55, 57, 58, 59, 92, 100 to 116, 121, 123 to 126, 129 to 143 and 189 do not apply with respect to accommodation that is subject to the *Homes for Special Care Act* or the *Homes for Retarded Persons Act*.

Same

(2) Sections 100, 114, 116, 121, 123 to 125, 129 to 139, 142, 143 and 189 do not apply with respect to a rental unit if,

(a) it has not been occupied for any purpose before the day this subsection comes into force;

(b) it is a rental unit no part of which has been previously rented since July 29, 1975; or

(c) no part of the building, mobile home park or land lease community has been occupied for residential purposes before November 1, 1991.

Developmental Services Act

(3) Sections 54, 55, 57, 58, 59, 92, 100 to 116, 121, 123 to 126, 129 to 143 and 189 do not apply with respect to accommodation that is subject to the *Developmental Services Act* and that is not otherwise exempt under clause 3 (e).

Exemptions related to social, etc., housing

5. (1) Sections 17 and 18, paragraph 1 of subsection 32 (1), sections 33, 54, 55, 57, 58 and 59, subsection 81 (2) and sections 82, 89, 90, 92, 95, 100 to 102, 108, 114, 116, 121,

123 to 125, 129 to 139, 142 and 143 do not apply with respect to a rental unit described below:

1. A rental unit located in a residential complex owned, operated or administered by or on behalf of the Ontario Housing Corporation, the Government of Canada or an agency of either of them.

2. A rental unit located in a non-profit housing project that is developed under a prescribed federal or provincial program.

3. A rental unit provided by a non-profit housing co-operative to tenants in non-member units.

4. A rental unit provided by an educational institution to a student or member of its staff and that is not exempt from this Act under clause 3 (g).

5. A rental unit located in a residential complex owned, operated or administered by a religious institution for a charitable use on a non-profit basis.

Exemption re: 12-month rule (2) Section 126 does not apply with respect to,

(a) a rental unit described in paragraph 1, 2 or 3 of subsection (1) if the tenant occupying the rental unit pays rent in an amount geared-to-income due to public funding; or

(b) a rental unit described in paragraph 4 or 5 of subsection (1).

Exemption re: notice of rent increase (3) Sections 127 and 128 do not apply with respect to increases in rent for a rental unit due to increases in the tenant's income if the rental unit is as described in paragraph 1, 2 or 3 of subsection (1) and the tenant pays rent in an amount geared-to-income due to public funding.

Exception (4) Despite subsection (1), the provisions of this Act set out in that subsection apply with respect to a rental unit described in paragraph 1 of that subsection if the tenant occupying the rental unit pays rent to a landlord other than the Ontario Housing Corporation, the Government of Canada or an agency of either of them.

Same (5) Despite subsection (1), the provisions of this Act set out in that subsection apply with respect to a rent increase for rental units described in paragraph 4 of that subsection if there is a council or association representing the residents of those rental units and there has not been consultation with the council or association respecting the increase.

Part VI not applied, rent geared to income 6. (1) If a tenant pays rent for a rental unit in an amount geared-to-income due to public funding and the rental unit is not a rental unit described in paragraph 1, 2 or 3 of subsection 5 (1), Part VI does not apply to an increase in the amount geared-to-income paid by the tenant.

Assignment, sublet not applied, rent geared to income (2) Sections 17, 18, 82, 89, 90 and 95 and subsections 81 (2) and 125 (3) do not apply to a tenant described in subsection (1).

Application to determine issues 7. (1) A landlord or a tenant may apply to the Tribunal for an order determining,

(a) whether this Act or any provision of it applies to a particular rental unit or residential complex;

(b) any other prescribed matter.

Order (2) On the application, the Tribunal shall make findings on the issue as prescribed and shall make the appropriate order.

PART II
RIGHTS AND DUTIES OF LANDLORDS AND TENANTS

TENANCY AGREEMENTS

Name and address in written agreement 8. (1) Every written tenancy agreement entered into on or after the day this section comes into force shall set out the legal name and address of the landlord to be used for the purpose of giving notices or other documents under this Act.

Copy of tenancy agreement (2) If a tenancy agreement entered into on or after the day this section comes into force is in writing, the landlord shall give a copy of the agreement, signed by the landlord and the tenant, to the tenant within 21 days after the tenant signs it and gives it to the landlord.

Notice if agreement not in writing (3) If a tenancy agreement entered into on or after the day this section comes into force is not in writing, the landlord shall, within 21 days after the tenancy begins, give to the tenant written notice of the legal name and address of the landlord to be used for giving notices and other documents under this Act.

Failure to comply

(4) Until a landlord has complied with subsections (1) and (2) or subsection (3), as the case may be,

    (a) the tenant's obligation to pay rent is suspended; and

    (b) the landlord shall not require the tenant to pay rent.

After compliance

(5) After the landlord has complied with subsections (1) and (2), or subsection (3), as the case may be, the landlord may require the tenant to pay any rent withheld by the tenant under subsection (4).

Commencement of tenancy

9. (1) The term or period of a tenancy begins on the day the tenant is entitled to occupy the rental unit under the tenancy agreement.

Actual entry not required

(2) A tenancy agreement takes effect when the tenant is entitled to occupy the rental unit, whether or not the tenant actually occupies it.

Frustrated contracts

10. The doctrine of frustration of contract and the *Frustrated Contracts Act* apply with respect to tenancy agreements.

Covenants interdependent

11. Subject to this Part, the common law rules respecting the effect of the breach of a material covenant by one party to a contract on the obligation to perform by the other party apply with respect to tenancy agreements.

Covenants running with land

12. Covenants concerning things related to a rental unit or the residential complex in which it is located run with the land, whether or not the things are in existence at the time the covenants are made.

Minimize losses

13. When a landlord or a tenant becomes liable to pay any amount as a result of a breach of a tenancy agreement, the person entitled to claim the amount has a duty to take reasonable steps to minimize the person's losses.

Acceleration clause void

14. A provision in a tenancy agreement providing that all or part of the remaining rent for a term or period of a tenancy or a specific sum becomes due upon a default of the tenant in paying rent due or in carrying out an obligation is void.

"No pet" provisions void

15. A provision in a tenancy agreement prohibiting the presence of animals in or about the residential complex is void.

Provisions conflicting with Act void

16. Subject to section 181, a provision in a tenancy agreement that is inconsistent with this Act or the regulations is void.

ASSIGNMENT AND SUBLETTING

Assignment of tenancy

17. (1) Subject to subsections (2), (3) and (6), and with the consent of the landlord, a tenant may assign a rental unit to another person.

Landlord's options, general request

(2) If a tenant asks a landlord to consent to an assignment of a rental unit, the landlord may,

    (a) consent to the assignment of the rental unit; or

    (b) refuse consent to the assignment of the rental unit.

Landlord's options, specific request

(3) If a tenant asks a landlord to consent to the assignment of the rental unit to a potential assignee, the landlord may,

    (a) consent to the assignment of the rental unit to the potential assignee;

    (b) refuse consent to the assignment of the rental unit to the potential assignee; or

    (c) refuse consent to the assignment of the rental unit.

Refusal or non-response

(4) A tenant may give the landlord a notice of termination under section 48 within 30 days after the date a request is made if,

    (a) the tenant asks the landlord to consent to an assignment of the rental unit and the landlord refuses consent;

    (b) the tenant asks the landlord to consent to an assignment of the rental unit and the landlord does not respond within seven days after the request is made;

    (c) the tenant asks the landlord to consent to an assignment of the rental unit to a potential assignee and the landlord refuses consent to the assignment under clause (3) (c); or

    (d) the tenant asks the landlord to consent to an assignment of the rental unit to a potential assignee and the landlord does not respond within seven days after the request is made.

Same

(5) A landlord shall not arbitrarily or unreasonably refuse consent to an assignment of a

rental unit to a potential assignee under clause (3) (b).

(6) Subject to subsection (5), a landlord who has given consent to an assignment of a rental unit under clause (2) (a) may subsequently refuse consent to an assignment of the rental unit to a potential assignee under clause (3) (b).

(7) A landlord may charge a tenant only for the landlord's reasonable out of pocket expenses incurred in giving consent to an assignment to a potential assignee.

(8) If a tenant has assigned a rental unit to another person, the tenancy agreement continues to apply on the same terms and conditions and,

(a) the assignee is liable to the landlord for any breach of the tenant's obligations and may enforce against the landlord any of the landlord's obligations under the tenancy agreement or this Act, if the breach or obligation relates to the period after the assignment, whether or not the breach or obligation also related to a period before the assignment;

(b) the former tenant is liable to the landlord for any breach of the tenant's obligations and may enforce against the landlord any of the landlord's obligations under the tenancy agreement or this Act, if the breach or obligation relates to the period before the assignment;

(c) if the former tenant has started a proceeding under this Act before the assignment and the benefits or obligations of the new tenant may be affected, the new tenant may join in or continue the proceeding.

(9) This section applies with respect to all tenants, regardless of whether their tenancies are periodic, fixed, contractual or statutory, but does not apply with respect to a tenant of superintendent's premises.

18. (1) With the consent of the landlord, a tenant may sublet a rental unit to another person, thus giving the other person the right to occupy the rental unit for a term ending on a specified date before the end of the tenant's term or period and giving the tenant the right to resume occupancy on that date.

(2) A landlord shall not arbitrarily or unreasonably withhold consent to the sublet of a rental unit to a potential subtenant.

(3) A landlord may charge a tenant only for the landlord's reasonable out of pocket expenses incurred in giving consent to a subletting.

(4) If a tenant has sublet a rental unit to another person,

(a) the tenant remains entitled to the benefits, and is liable to the landlord for the breaches, of the tenant's obligations under the tenancy agreement or this Act during the subtenancy; and

(b) the subtenant is entitled to the benefits, and is liable to the tenant for the breaches, of the subtenant's obligations under the subletting agreement or this Act during the subtenancy.

(5) A subtenant has no right to occupy the rental unit after the end of the subtenancy.

(6) This section applies with respect to all tenants, regardless of whether their tenancies are periodic, fixed, contractual or statutory, but does not apply with respect to a tenant of superintendent's premises.

ENTRY INTO RENTAL UNIT OR RESIDENTIAL COMPLEX

19. A landlord may enter a rental unit only in accordance with section 20 or 21.

20. (1) A landlord may enter a rental unit at any time without written notice,

(a) in cases of emergency; or

(b) if the tenant consents to the entry at the time of entry.

(2) A landlord may enter a rental unit without written notice to clean it if the tenancy agreement requires the landlord to clean the rental unit at regular intervals and,

(a) the landlord enters the unit at the times specified in the tenancy agreement; or

(b) if no times are specified, the landlord enters the unit between the hours of 8 a.m. and 8 p.m.

(3) A landlord may enter the rental unit without written notice to show the unit to prospective tenants if,

(a) the landlord and tenant have agreed that the tenancy will be terminated or one of them has given notice of termination to the other;

(b) the landlord enters the unit between the hours of 8 a.m. and 8 p.m.; and

(c) before entering, the landlord informs or makes a reasonable effort to inform the tenant of the intention to do so.

21. (1) A landlord may enter a rental unit in accordance with written notice given to the tenant at least 24 hours before the time of entry under the following circumstances:

1. To carry out a repair or do work in the rental unit.

2. To allow a potential mortgagee or insurer of the residential complex to view the rental unit.

3. To allow a potential purchaser to view the rental unit.

4. For any other reasonable reason for entry specified in the tenancy agreement.

(2) The written notice under subsection (1) shall specify the reason for entry, the day of entry and a time of entry between the hours of 8 a.m. and 8 p.m.

22. No landlord shall restrict reasonable access to a residential complex by candidates for election to any office at the federal, provincial or municipal level, or their authorized representatives, if they are seeking access for the purpose of canvassing or distributing election material.

23. (1) A landlord shall not alter the locking system on a door giving entry to a rental unit or residential complex or cause the locking system to be altered during the tenant's occupancy of the rental unit without giving the tenant replacement keys.

(2) A tenant shall not alter the locking system on a door giving entry to a rental unit or residential complex or cause the locking system to be altered during the tenant's occu-pancy of the rental unit without the consent of the landlord.

ADDITIONAL RESPONSIBILITIES OF LANDLORD

24. (1) A landlord is responsible for providing and maintaining a residential complex, including the rental units in it, in a good state of repair and fit for habitation and for complying with health, safety, housing and maintenance standards.

(2) Subsection (1) applies even if the tenant was aware of a state of non-repair or a contravention of a standard before entering into the tenancy agreement.

25. A landlord shall not at any time during a tenant's occupancy of a rental unit and before the day on which an order evicting the tenant is executed, withhold reasonable supply of any vital service, care service or food that it is the landlord's obligation to supply under the tenancy agreement or deliberately interfere with the reasonable supply of any vital service, care service or food.

26. A landlord shall not at any time during a tenant's occupancy of a rental unit and before the day on which an order evicting the tenant is executed substantially interfere with the reasonable enjoyment of the rental unit or the residential complex in which it is located for all usual purposes by a tenant or members of his or her household.

27. A landlord shall not harass, obstruct, coerce, threaten or interfere with a tenant.

ADDITIONAL RESPONSIBILITIES OF TENANT

28. A tenant shall not harass, obstruct, coerce, threaten or interfere with a landlord.

29. The tenant is responsible for ordinary cleanliness of the rental unit, except to the extent that the tenancy agreement requires the landlord to clean it.

30. The tenant is responsible for the repair of damage to the rental unit or residential complex caused by the wilful or negligent conduct of the tenant, other occupants of the rental unit or persons who are permitted in the residential complex by the tenant.

Distress
abolished

31. No landlord shall, without legal process, seize a tenant's property for default in the payment of rent or for the breach of any other obligation of the tenant.

Tenant
applications

32. (1) A tenant or former tenant of a rental unit may apply to the Tribunal for any of the following orders:

1. An order determining that the landlord has arbitrarily or unreasonably withheld consent to the assignment or sublet of a rental unit to a potential assignee or subtenant.

2. An order determining that the landlord breached the obligations under subsection 24 (1).

3. An order determining that the landlord, superintendent or agent of the landlord has illegally entered the rental unit.

4. An order determining that the landlord, superintendent or agent of the landlord has altered the locking system on a door giving entry to the rental unit or the residential complex or caused the locking system to be altered during the tenant's occupancy of the rental unit without giving the tenant replacement keys.

5. An order determining that the landlord, superintendent or agent of the landlord has withheld the reasonable supply of any vital service, care service or food that it is the landlord's obligation to supply under the tenancy agreement or deliberately interfered with the reasonable supply of any vital service, care service or food.

6. An order determining that the landlord, superintendent or agent of the landlord has substantially interfered with the reasonable enjoyment of the rental unit or residential complex for all usual purposes by the tenant or a member of his or her household.

7. An order determining that the landlord, superintendent or agent of the landlord has harassed, obstructed, coerced, threatened or interfered with the tenant during the tenant's occupancy of the rental unit.

8. Where a notice under section 51 has been given in bad faith and the tenant vacates the rental unit as a result of the notice, an order determining that the notice has been given in bad faith and neither the landlord, the landlord's spouse nor a child or parent of one of them has occupied the rental unit within a reasonable time after that termination.

9. Where a notice under section 52 has been given in bad faith and the tenant vacates the rental unit as a result of the notice, an order determining that the notice has been given in bad faith and neither the purchaser, the purchaser's spouse nor a child or parent of one of them has occupied the rental unit within a reasonable time after that termination.

10. Where a notice under section 53 has been given in bad faith and the tenant vacates the rental unit as a result of the notice, an order determining that the notice has been given in bad faith and the landlord has not demolished, converted or repaired or renovated the rental unit within a reasonable time after that termination.

Time
limitation

(2) No application may be made under subsection (1) more than one year after the day the alleged conduct giving rise to the application occurred.

Order re
assignment,
sublet

33. (1) If the Tribunal determines that a landlord has unlawfully withheld consent to an assignment or sublet in an application under paragraph 1 of subsection 32 (1), the Tribunal may do one or more of the following:

1. Order that the assignment or sublet is authorized.

2. Where appropriate, by order authorize another assignment or sublet proposed by the tenant.

3. Order that the tenancy be terminated.

4. Order an abatement of the tenant's or former tenant's rent.

Same

(2) The Tribunal may establish terms and conditions of the assignment or sublet.

Same

(3) If an order is made under paragraph 1 or 2 of subsection (1), the assignment or sublet shall have the same legal effect as if the landlord had consented to it.

Order, repair,
comply with
standards

34. (1) If the Tribunal determines in an application under paragraph 2 of subsection

160

32 (1) that a landlord has breached the obligations under subsection 24 (1), the Tribunal may do one or more of the following:

1. Terminate the tenancy.

2. Order an abatement of the rent.

3. Authorize a repair that has been or is to be made and order its cost to be paid by the landlord to the tenant.

4. Order the landlord to do specified repairs or other work within a specified time.

5. Make any other order that it considers appropriate.

Same

(2) In determining the remedy under this section, the Tribunal shall consider whether the tenant or former tenant advised the landlord of the alleged breaches before applying to the Tribunal.

Order, subs. 32 (1), pars. 3 to 10

35. (1) If the Tribunal determines that a landlord, a superintendent or an agent of a landlord has done one or more of the activities set out in paragraphs 3 to 10 of subsection 32 (1), the Tribunal may,

(a) order that the landlord, superintendent or agent may not engage in any further activities listed in those paragraphs against any of the tenants in the residential complex;

(b) order an abatement of rent;

(c) order that the landlord pay to the Tribunal an administrative fine not exceeding the greater of $10,000 or the monetary jurisdiction of the Small Claims Court in the area where the residential complex is located;

(d) order that the tenancy be terminated;

(e) make any other order that it considers appropriate.

Same

(2) If in an application under any of paragraphs 3 to 10 of subsection 32 (1) it is determined that the tenant was induced by the conduct of the landlord, the superintendent or an agent of the landlord to vacate the rental unit, the Tribunal may, in addition to the remedies set out in subsection (1), order that the landlord pay a specified sum to the tenant as compensation for,

(a) all or any portion of any increased rent which the tenant has incurred or will

incur for a one year period after the tenant has left the rental unit; and

(b) reasonable out of pocket moving, storage and other like expenses which the tenant has incurred or will incur.

Locking systems, landlord application re: alteration

36. If a tenant alters a locking system, contrary to subsection 23 (2), the landlord may apply to the Tribunal for an order determining that the tenant has altered the locking system on a door giving entry to the rental unit or the residential complex or caused the locking system to be altered during the tenant's occupancy of the rental unit without the consent of the landlord.

Locking systems, order

37. If the Tribunal in an application under section 36 determines that a tenant has altered the locking system or caused it to be altered, the Tribunal may order that the tenant provide the landlord with keys or pay the landlord the reasonable out of pocket expenses necessary to change the locking system.

HUMAN RIGHTS CODE

Selecting prospective tenants

38. In selecting prospective tenants, landlords may use, in the manner prescribed in the regulations made under the *Human Rights Code*, income information, credit checks, credit references, rental history, guarantees, or other similar business practices as prescribed in the regulations made under the *Human Rights Code*.

PART III
SECURITY OF TENURE AND
TERMINATION OF TENANCIES

SECURITY OF TENURE

Tenancy terminated

39. (1) A tenancy may be terminated only in accordance with this Act.

Same

(2) A notice of termination need not be given if a landlord and a tenant have agreed to terminate a tenancy.

When agreement void

(3) An agreement between a landlord and tenant to terminate a tenancy is void if it is entered into,

(a) at the time the tenancy agreement is entered into; or

(b) as a condition of entering into the tenancy agreement.

When notice void

(4) A tenant's notice to terminate a tenancy is void if it is given,

(a) at the time the tenancy agreement is entered into; or

Deemed renewal where no notice

40. (1) If a tenancy agreement for a fixed term ends and has not been renewed or terminated, the landlord and tenant shall be deemed to have renewed it as a monthly tenancy agreement containing the same terms and conditions that are in the expired tenancy agreement and subject to any increases in rent charged in accordance with this Act.

Same

(2) If the period of a periodic tenancy ends and the tenancy has not been renewed or terminated, the landlord and tenant shall be deemed to have renewed it for another week, month, year or other period, as the case may be with the same terms and conditions that are in the expired tenancy agreement and subject to any increases in rent charged in accordance with this Act.

Restriction on recovery of possession

41. A landlord shall not recover possession of a rental unit subject to a tenancy unless,

(a) the tenant has vacated or abandoned the unit; or

(b) an order of the Tribunal evicting the tenant has authorized the possession.

Disposal of abandoned property, unit vacated

42. (1) A landlord may sell, retain for the landlord's own use or otherwise dispose of property in a rental unit or the residential complex if the rental unit has been vacated in accordance with,

(a) a notice of termination of the landlord or the tenant;

(b) an agreement between the landlord and the tenant to terminate the tenancy;

(c) subsection 68 (2); or

(d) an order of the Tribunal terminating the tenancy or evicting the tenant.

Where eviction order enforced

(2) Despite subsection (1), where an order is made to evict a tenant, the landlord shall not sell, retain or otherwise dispose of the tenant's property before 48 hours have elapsed after the enforcement of the eviction order.

Same

(3) A landlord shall make an evicted tenant's property available to be retrieved at a location proximate to the rental unit for 48 hours after the enforcement of an eviction order.

Liability of landlord

(4) A landlord is not liable to any person for selling, retaining or otherwise disposing of a tenant's property in accordance with this section.

Agreement

(5) A landlord and a tenant may agree to terms other than those set out in this section with regard to the disposal of the tenant's property.

NOTICE OF TERMINATION –
GENERAL PROVISIONS

Notice of termination

43. (1) Where this Act permits a landlord or tenant to terminate a tenancy by notice, the notice shall be in a form approved by the Tribunal and shall,

(a) identify the rental unit for which the notice is given;

(b) state the date on which the tenancy is to terminate; and

(c) be signed by the person giving the notice, or the person's agent.

Same

(2) If the notice is given by a landlord, it shall also set out the reasons and details respecting the termination and inform the tenant that,

(a) if the tenant does not vacate the rental unit, the landlord may apply to the Tribunal for an order terminating the tenancy and evicting the tenant; and

(b) if the landlord applies for an order, the tenant is entitled to dispute the application.

Where notice void

44. (1) A notice of termination becomes void 30 days after the termination date specified in the notice unless,

(a) the tenant vacates the rental unit before that time; or

(b) the landlord applies for an order terminating the tenancy and evicting the tenant before that time.

Exception

(2) Subsection (1) does not apply with respect to a notice based on a tenant's failure to pay rent.

Compensation when rental unit not vacated

45. (1) A landlord is entitled to compensation for the use and occupation of a rental unit by any unauthorized occupant or after the tenancy has been terminated by notice.

Effect of payment of arrears

(2) Unless a landlord and tenant agree otherwise, the landlord does not waive a notice of termination, reinstate a tenancy or create a new tenancy,

(a) by accepting arrears of rent or compensation for use or occupation of a rental unit after notice of termination of the tenancy has been given; or

(b) by giving the tenant a notice of rent increase.

NOTICE OF TERMINATION –
END OF PERIOD OR TERM OF TENANCY

Tenant's notice to terminate tenancy, end of period or term

46. A tenant may terminate a tenancy at the end of a period of the tenancy or at the end of the term of a tenancy for a fixed term by giving notice of termination to the landlord in accordance with section 47.

Period of notice, daily or weekly tenancy

47. (1) A notice under section 46, 60 or 96 to terminate a daily or weekly tenancy shall be given at least 28 days before the date the termination is specified to be effective and that date shall be on the last day of a rental period.

Period of notice, monthly tenancy

(2) A notice under section 46, 60 or 96 to terminate a monthly tenancy shall be given at least 60 days before the date the termination is specified to be effective and that date shall be on the last day of a rental period.

Period of notice, yearly tenancy

(3) A notice under section 46, 60 or 96 to terminate a yearly tenancy shall be given at least 60 days before the date the termination is specified to be effective and that date shall be on the last day of a yearly period on which the tenancy is based.

Period of notice, tenancy for fixed term

(4) A notice under section 46, 60 or 96 to terminate a tenancy for a fixed term shall be given at least 60 days before the expiration date specified in the tenancy agreement, to be effective on that expiration date.

Period of notice, February notices

(5) A tenant who gives notice under subsection (2), (3) or (4), which specifies that the termination is to be effective on the last day of February or the last day of March in any year, shall be deemed to have given at least 60 days notice of termination if the notice is given not later than January 1 of that year in respect of a termination which is to be effective on the last day of February or February 1 of that year in respect of a termination which is to be effective on the last day of March.

Notice by tenant

48. (1) A tenant may give notice of termination of a tenancy if the circumstances set out in subsection 17 (4) apply.

Same

(2) The date for termination specified in the notice shall be at least a number of days after the date of the notice that is the lesser of the notice period otherwise required under this Act and 30 days.

DEATH OF TENANT

Death of tenant

49. (1) If a tenant of a rental unit dies and there are no other tenants of the rental unit, the tenancy shall be deemed to be terminated 30 days after the death of the tenant.

Reasonable access

(2) The landlord shall, until the tenancy is terminated under subsection (1),

(a) preserve any property of a tenant who has died that is in the rental unit or the residential complex other than property that is unsafe or unhygienic; and

(b) afford the executor or administrator of the tenant's estate, or if there is no executor or administrator, a member of the tenant's family reasonable access to the rental unit and the residential complex for the purpose of removing the tenant's property.

Landlord may dispose of property

50. (1) The landlord may sell, retain for the landlord's own use or otherwise dispose of property of a tenant who has died that is in a rental unit and in the residential complex in which the rental unit is located,

(a) if the property is unsafe or unhygienic, immediately; or

(b) otherwise, after the tenancy is terminated under section 49.

Same

(2) Subject to subsections (3) and (4), a landlord is not liable to any person for selling, retaining or otherwise disposing of the property of a tenant in accordance with subsection (1).

Same

(3) If, within six months after the tenant's death, the executor or administrator of the estate of the tenant, or if there is no executor or administrator, a member of the tenant's family claims any property of the tenant that the landlord has sold, the landlord shall pay to the estate the amount by which the proceeds of sale exceed the sum of,

(a) the landlord's reasonable out of pocket expenses for moving, storing, securing or selling the property; and

(b) any arrears of rent.

Same (4) If, within the six month period after the tenant's death, the executor or administrator of the estate of the tenant, or if there is no executor or administrator, a member of the tenant's family claims any property of the tenant that the landlord has retained for the landlord's own use, the landlord shall return the property to the tenant's estate.

Agreement (5) A landlord and the executor or administrator of a deceased tenant's estate may agree to terms other than those set out in this section with regard to the termination of the tenancy and disposal of the tenant's property.

NOTICE BY LANDLORD FOR TERMINATION AT END OF PERIOD OR TERM

Notice, landlord personally, etc., requires unit **51.** (1) A landlord may, by notice, terminate a tenancy if the landlord in good faith requires possession of the rental unit for the purpose of residential occupation by the landlord, the landlord's spouse or a child or parent of one of them.

Same (2) The date for termination specified in the notice shall be at least 60 days after the notice is given and shall be the day a period of the tenancy ends or, where the tenancy is for a fixed term, the end of the term.

Earlier termination by tenant (3) A tenant who receives notice of termination under subsection (1) may, at any time before the date specified in the notice, terminate the tenancy, effective on a specified date earlier than the date set out in the landlord's notice.

Same (4) The date for termination specified in the tenant's notice shall be at least 10 days after the date the tenant's notice is given.

Where purchasing landlord personally requires unit **52.** (1) A landlord of a residential complex that contains no more than three residential units and that is subject to a tenancy agreement may give notice to the tenant on behalf of a purchaser of the residential complex to terminate the tenancy if,

(a) the landlord has entered into an agreement of purchase and sale to sell the residential complex; and

(b) the purchaser in good faith requires possession of the residential complex or a unit in it for the purpose of resi-

dential occupation by the purchaser, the purchaser's spouse or a child or parent of one of them.

Period of notice (2) The date for termination specified in the notice shall be at least 60 days after the notice is given and shall be the day a period of the tenancy ends or, where the tenancy is for a fixed term, the end of the term.

Earlier termination by tenant (3) A tenant who receives notice of termination under subsection (1) may, at any time before the date specified in the notice, terminate the tenancy, effective on a specified date earlier than the date set out in the landlord's notice.

Same (4) The date for termination specified in the tenant's notice shall be at least 10 days after the date the tenant's notice is given.

Notice, demolition, conversion or repairs **53.** (1) A landlord may give notice of termination of a tenancy if the landlord requires possession of the rental unit in order to,

(a) demolish it;

(b) convert it to use for a purpose other than residential premises; or

(c) do repairs or renovations to it that are so extensive that they require a building permit and vacant possession of the rental unit.

Same (2) The date for termination specified in the notice shall be at least 120 days after the notice is given and shall be the day a period of the tenancy ends or, where the tenancy is for a fixed term, the end of the term.

Same (3) A notice under clause (1) (c) shall inform the tenant that if he or she wishes to exercise the right of first refusal under section 56 to occupy the premises after the repairs or renovations, he or she must give the landlord notice of that fact in accordance with subsection 56 (2) before vacating the rental unit.

Earlier termination by tenant (4) A tenant who receives notice of termination under subsection (1) may, at any time before the date specified in the notice, terminate the tenancy, effective on a specified date earlier than the date set out in the landlord's notice.

Same (5) The date for termination specified in the tenant's notice shall be at least 10 days after the date the tenant's notice is given.

Conversion to condominium, security of tenure **54.** (1) Where a part or all of a residential complex becomes subject to a registered declaration and description under the *Condomin-*

ium Act on or after the day this section is proclaimed in force, a landlord may not give a notice under section 51 or 52 to a person who was a tenant of a rental unit when it became subject to a registered declaration and description under the *Condominium Act*.

Proposed units, security of tenure

(2) Where a landlord has entered into an agreement of purchase and sale of a rental unit that is a proposed unit as defined in the *Condominium Act*, a landlord may not give a notice under section 51 or 52 to the tenant of the rental unit who was the tenant on the date the agreement of purchase and sale was entered into.

Non-application of section

(3) Subsections (1) and (2) do not apply with respect to a residential complex until the day set out in subsection (4) if no rental unit in the residential complex was rented before the date prescribed for the purposes of this subsection.

Same

(4) The day on which subsections (1) and (2) begin to apply under subsection (3) is the day that is the later of,

(a) two years after the day on which the first rental unit was first rented; and

(b) two years after the date prescribed for the purposes of this subsection.

Conversion to condominium, right of first refusal

(5) If a landlord receives an acceptable offer to purchase a condominium unit converted from rented residential premises and still occupied by a tenant who was a tenant on the date of the registration referred to in subsection (1) or an acceptable offer to purchase a rental unit intended to be converted to a condominium unit, the tenant has a right of first refusal to purchase the unit at the price and subject to the terms and conditions in the offer.

Same

(6) The landlord shall give the tenant at least 72 hours notice of the offer to purchase the unit before accepting the offer.

Exception

(7) Subsection (5) does not apply when,

(a) the offer to purchase is an offer to purchase more than one unit; or

(b) the unit has been previously purchased since that registration, but not together with any other units.

Compensation, demolition or conversion

55. A landlord shall compensate a tenant in an amount equal to three months rent or

offer the tenant another rental unit acceptable to the tenant if,

(a) the tenant receives notice of termination of the tenancy for the purposes of demolition or conversion to non-residential use;

(b) the residential complex in which the rental unit is located contains at least five residential units; and

(c) in the case of a demolition, it was not ordered to be carried out under the authority of any other Act.

Tenant's right of first refusal, repair or renovation

56. (1) A tenant who receives notice of termination of a tenancy for the purpose of repairs or renovations may, in accordance with this section, have a right of first refusal to occupy the rental unit as a tenant when the repairs or renovations are completed.

Written notice

(2) A tenant who wishes to have a right of first refusal shall give the landlord notice in writing before vacating the rental unit.

Rent to be charged

(3) A tenant who exercises a right of first refusal may re-occupy the rental unit at a rent that is no more than what the landlord could have lawfully charged if there had been no interruption in the tenant's tenancy.

Change of address

(4) It is a condition of the tenant's right of first refusal that the tenant inform the landlord in writing of any change of address.

Tenant's right to compensation, repair or renovation

57. (1) A landlord shall compensate a tenant who receives notice of termination of a tenancy under section 53 for the purpose of repairs or renovations in an amount equal to three months rent or shall offer the tenant another rental unit acceptable to the tenant if,

(a) the tenant does not intend to return to the rental unit after the repairs or renovations are complete;

(b) the residential complex in which the rental unit is located contains at least five residential units; and

(c) the repair or renovation was not ordered to be carried out under the authority of this or any other Act.

Same

(2) If a tenant has given a landlord notice under subsection 56 (2) with respect to a rental unit in a residential complex containing at least five residential units, the tenant is entitled to compensation in an amount equal

to the rent for the lesser of three months and the period the unit is under repair or renovation.

58. A landlord of a residential complex that is created as a result of a severance shall compensate a tenant of a rental unit in that complex in an amount equal to three months rent or offer the tenant another rental unit acceptable to the tenant if,

(a) before the severance, the residential complex from which the new residential complex was created had at least five residential units;

(b) the new residential complex has fewer than five residential units; and

(c) the landlord gives the tenant a notice of termination under section 53 less than two years after the date of the severance.

59. Where a rental unit becomes separately conveyable property due to a consent under section 53 of the *Planning Act* or a plan of subdivision under section 51 of that Act, a landlord may not give a notice under section 51 or 52 to a person who was a tenant of the rental unit at the time of the consent or approval.

60. (1) A landlord may give a tenant notice of termination of their tenancy on any of the following grounds:

1. The tenant has persistently failed to pay rent on the date it becomes due and payable.

2. The rental unit that is the subject of the tenancy agreement is a rental unit as described in paragraph 1, 2 or 3 of subsection 5 (1) and the tenant has ceased to meet the qualifications required for occupancy of the rental unit.

3. The tenant was an employee of an employer who provided the tenant with the rental unit during the tenant's employment and the employment has terminated.

4. The tenancy arose by virtue of or collateral to an agreement of purchase and sale of a proposed unit within the meaning of the *Condominium Act* in good faith and the agreement of purchase and sale has been terminated.

(2) The date for termination specified in the notice shall be at least the number of days after the date the notice is given that is set out in section 47 and shall be the day a period of the tenancy ends or, where the tenancy is for a fixed term, the end of the term.

61. (1) If a tenant fails to pay rent lawfully owing under a tenancy agreement, the landlord may give the tenant notice of termination of the tenancy effective not earlier than,

(a) the 7th day after the notice is given, in the case of a daily or weekly tenancy; and

(b) the 14th day after the notice is given, in all other cases.

(2) The notice shall set out the amount of rent due and shall specify that the tenant may avoid the termination of the tenancy by paying that rent and any other rent that has become owing under the tenancy agreement before the notice of termination becomes effective.

(3) The notice of termination under this section is void if the tenant pays the rent that is due in accordance with the tenancy agreement before the day the landlord applies to the Tribunal to terminate the tenancy.

62. (1) A landlord may give a tenant notice of termination of the tenancy if the tenant commits an illegal act or carries on an illegal trade, business or occupation or permits a person to do so in the rental unit or the residential complex.

(2) A landlord may give a tenant notice of termination of the tenancy if the rental unit is a rental unit described in paragraph 1, 2 or 3 of subsection 5 (1) and the tenant has knowingly and materially misrepresented his or her income or that of other members of his or her family occupying the rental unit.

(3) A notice of termination under this section shall,

(a) provide a termination date not earlier than the 20th day after the notice is given; and

(b) set out the grounds for termination.

63. (1) A landlord may give a tenant notice of termination of the tenancy if the tenant or a person whom the tenant permits in the residential complex wilfully or negligently causes undue damage to the rental unit or the residential complex.

(2) A notice of termination under this section shall,

(a) provide a termination date not earlier than the 20th day after the notice is given;

(b) set out the grounds for termination; and

(c) require the tenant, within seven days, to pay to the landlord the reasonable costs of repair or to make the repairs.

(3) The notice of termination under this section is void if the tenant, within seven days after receiving the notice, makes the repair, pays the reasonable costs of repair or makes arrangements satisfactory to the landlord to pay the costs or to make the repairs.

64. (1) A landlord may give a tenant notice of termination of the tenancy if the conduct of the tenant, another occupant of the rental unit or a person permitted in the residential complex by the tenant is such that it substantially interferes with the reasonable enjoyment of the residential complex for all usual purposes by the landlord or another tenant or substantially interferes with another lawful right, privilege or interest of the landlord or another tenant.

(2) A notice of termination under subsection (1) shall,

(a) provide a termination date not earlier than the 20th day after the notice is given;

(b) set out the grounds for termination; and

(c) require the tenant, within seven days, to stop the conduct or activity or correct the omission set out in the notice.

(3) The notice of termination under subsection (1) is void if the tenant, within seven days after receiving the notice, stops the conduct or activity or corrects the omission.

65. (1) A landlord may give a tenant notice of termination of the tenancy if,

(a) an act or omission of the tenant, another occupant of the rental unit or a person permitted in the residential complex by the tenant seriously impairs or has seriously impaired the safety of any person; and

(b) the act or omission occurs in the residential complex.

(2) A notice of termination under this section shall provide a termination date not earlier than the 10th day after the notice is given and set out the grounds for termination.

66. (1) A landlord may give a tenant notice of termination of the tenancy if the number of persons occupying the rental unit on a continuing basis results in a contravention of health, safety or housing standards required by law.

(2) A notice of termination under this section shall,

(a) provide a termination date not earlier than the 20th day after the notice is given;

(b) set out the details of the grounds for termination; and

(c) require the tenant, within seven days, to reduce the number of persons occupying the rental unit to comply with health, safety or housing standards required by law.

(3) The notice of termination under this section is void if the tenant, within seven days after receiving the notice, sufficiently reduces the number of persons occupying the rental unit.

67. (1) A landlord may give a tenant notice of termination of the tenancy if,

(a) a notice of termination under section 63, 64 or 66 or under an equivalent provision of Part IV of the *Landlord and Tenant Act* has become void as a result of the tenant's compliance with the terms of the notice; and

(b) the tenant contravenes any of section 62, 63, 64 or 66 within six months after the first notice became void.

(2) The notice under this section shall set out the date it is to be effective and that date shall not be earlier than the 14th day after the notice is given.

SUPERINTENDENT'S PREMISES

68. (1) If a landlord has entered into a tenancy agreement with respect to a superintendent's premises, unless otherwise agreed, the tenancy terminates on the day on which the employment of the tenant is terminated.

167

Same
(2) A tenant shall vacate a superintendent's premises within one week after his or her tenancy is terminated.

No rent charged for week
(3) A landlord shall not charge a tenant rent or compensation or receive rent or compensation from a tenant with respect to the one week period mentioned in subsection (2).

APPLICATION TO TRIBUNAL BY LANDLORD –
LANDLORD HAS GIVEN NOTICE OF
TERMINATION

Application by landlord
69. (1) A landlord may apply to the Tribunal for an order terminating a tenancy and evicting the tenant if the landlord has given notice to terminate the tenancy under this Act or under the former Part IV of the *Landlord and Tenant Act*.

Same
(2) An application under subsection (1) may not be made later than 30 days after the termination date specified in the notice.

Exception
(3) Subsection (2) does not apply with respect to an application based on the tenant's failure to pay rent.

Landlord personally requires premises
70. (1) The Tribunal ' shall not make an order terminating a tenancy and evicting the tenant in an application under section 69 based on a notice of termination under section 51 or 52 unless the person who personally requires the rental unit files with the Tribunal a declaration certifying that the person in good faith requires the rental unit for his or her own personal use.

Same
(2) The Tribunal shall not make an order terminating a tenancy and evicting the tenant in an application under section 69 based on a notice of termination under section 51 or 52 where the landlord's claim is based on a tenancy agreement or occupancy agreement that purports to entitle the landlord to reside in the rental unit unless,

(a) the application is brought in respect of premises situate in a building containing not more than four residential units; or

(b) the landlord, the landlord's spouse or a child or parent of the landlord or his or her spouse has previously been a genuine occupant of the premises.

Demolition, conversion, repairs
71. The Tribunal shall not make an order terminating a tenancy and evicting the tenant in an application under section 69 based on a notice of termination under section 53 unless it is satisfied that,

(a) the landlord intends in good faith to carry out the activity on which the notice of termination was based; and

(b) the landlord has obtained all necessary permits or other authority that may be required to do so.

Non-payment of rent
72. (1) A landlord may not apply to the Tribunal for an order terminating a tenancy and evicting the tenant based on a notice of termination under section 61 before the notice of termination becomes effective.

Discontinuance where rent paid
(2) If an application is brought under section 69 based on a notice of termination under section 61 and if before an eviction order under the application becomes enforceable the tenant pays to the Tribunal or the landlord all the rent in arrears and compensation owing under section 45, any costs ordered by the Tribunal and the fee for making the application, that part of the application relating to arrears of rent, compensation and eviction of the tenant on the grounds of arrears of rent is discontinued and any order under it is void.

Illegal act or misrepresentation of income
73. The Tribunal may issue an order terminating a tenancy and evicting a tenant in an application referred to under section 69 based on a notice of termination under section 62 whether or not the tenant or other person has been convicted of an offence relating to an illegal act, trade, business or occupation.

Notice gives 7 days to correct
74. (1) A landlord may not apply to the Tribunal for an order terminating a tenancy and evicting the tenant based on a notice of termination under section 63, 64 or 66 before the seven day remedy period specified in the notice expires.

Application based on animals
(2) If an application based on a notice of termination under section 64 or 65 is grounded on the presence, control or behaviour of an animal in or about the residential complex, the Tribunal shall not make an order terminating the tenancy and evicting the tenant without being satisfied that the tenant is keeping an animal and that,

(a) subject to subsection (3), the past behaviour of an animal of that species has substantially interfered with the reasonable enjoyment of the residential complex for all usual purposes by the landlord or other tenants;

(b) subject to subsection (4), the presence of an animal of that species has caused the landlord or another tenant to suffer a serious allergic reaction; or

(c) the presence of an animal of that species or breed is inherently dangerous to the safety of the landlord or the other tenants.

Same (3) The Tribunal shall not make an order terminating the tenancy and evicting the tenant relying on clause (2) (a) if it is satisfied that the animal kept by the tenant did not cause or contribute to the substantial interference.

Same (4) The Tribunal shall not make an order terminating the tenancy and evicting the tenant relying on clause (2) (b) if it is satisfied that the animal kept by the tenant did not cause or contribute to the allergic reaction.

Immediate application 75. Unless specifically provided otherwise in this Act or the former Part IV of the *Landlord and Tenant Act*, a landlord who has served a notice of termination may apply immediately to the Tribunal under section 69 for an order terminating the tenancy and evicting the tenant.

Application To Tribunal By Landlord – Landlord Has Not Given Notice Of Termination

Agreement to terminate, tenant's notice 76. (1) A landlord may, without notice to the tenant, apply to the Tribunal for an order terminating a tenancy and evicting the tenant if,

(a) the landlord and tenant have entered into an agreement to terminate the tenancy; or

(b) the tenant has given the landlord notice of termination of the tenancy.

Same (2) The landlord shall include with the application an affidavit verifying the agreement or notice of termination, as the case may be.

Same (3) An application under subsection (1) shall not be made later than 30 days after the termination date specified in the agreement or notice.

Order (4) On receipt of the application, the Tribunal may make an order terminating the tenancy and evicting the tenant.

Same (5) An order under subsection (4) shall be effective not earlier than,

(a) the date specified in the agreement, in the case of an application under clause (1) (a); or

(b) the termination date set out in the notice, in the case of an application under clause (1) (b).

Set aside order (6) The respondent may make a motion to the Tribunal, on notice to the applicant, to have the order set aside within 10 days after the order is issued.

Same (7) An order under subsection (4) is stayed when a motion to have the order set aside is received by the Tribunal and shall not be enforced under this Act or as an order of the court during the stay.

Same (8) If the Tribunal sets the order aside, the Tribunal shall hear the merits of the application.

Application based on previous order, mediated settlement 77. (1) A landlord may, without notice to the tenant, apply to the Tribunal for an order terminating a tenancy or evicting the tenant if,

(a) the landlord had previously applied to the Tribunal for an order terminating the tenancy or evicting the tenant;

(b) with respect to that application, an order or a settlement mediated under section 181 provided that the landlord could apply under this section if the tenant did not meet specified conditions of the order or settlement; and

(c) the tenant has not met those conditions.

Same (2) The landlord shall include with the application a copy of the order or settlement and an affidavit setting out what conditions of the order or settlement have not been met and how they have not been met.

Same (3) An application under this section shall not be made later than 30 days after a failure of the tenant to meet a condition specified in the order or settlement.

Same (4) Subsections 76 (4), (6) and (7) apply, with necessary modifications, with respect to an application under this section.

(5) If the Tribunal sets the order aside, the Tribunal shall consider whether a failure to meet the conditions occurred.

78. If a landlord believes that a tenant has abandoned a rental unit, the landlord may apply to the Tribunal for an order terminating the tenancy.

79. (1) A landlord may dispose of property in a rental unit that a tenant has abandoned and property of persons occupying the rental unit that is in the residential complex in which the rental unit is located in accordance with subsections (2) and (3) if,

(a) the landlord obtains an order terminating the tenancy under section 78; or

(b) the landlord gives notice to the tenant of the rental unit and to the Tribunal of the landlord's intention to dispose of the property.

(2) If the tenant has abandoned the rental unit, the landlord may dispose of any unsafe or unhygienic items immediately.

(3) The landlord may sell, retain for the landlord's own use or otherwise dispose of any other items if 30 days have passed after obtaining the order referred to in clause (1) (a) or giving the notice referred to in clause (1) (b) to the tenant and the Tribunal.

(4) If, before the 30 days have passed, the tenant notifies the landlord that he or she intends to remove property referred to in subsection (3), the tenant may remove the property within that 30 day period.

(5) If the tenant notifies the landlord in accordance with subsection (4) that he or she intends to remove the property, the landlord shall make the property available to the tenant at a reasonable time and within a reasonable proximity to the rental unit.

(6) The landlord may require the tenant to pay the landlord for arrears of rent and any reasonable out of pocket expenses incurred by the landlord in moving, storing or securing the tenant's property before allowing the tenant to remove the property.

(7) If, within six months after the date the notice referred to in clause (1) (b) is given to the tenant and the Tribunal or the order terminating the tenancy is issued, the tenant claims any of his or her property that the landlord has sold, the landlord shall pay to the tenant the amount by which the proceeds of sale exceed the sum of,

(a) the landlord's reasonable out of pocket expenses for moving, storing, securing or selling the property; and

(b) any arrears of rent.

(8) Subject to subsections (5) and (7), a landlord is not liable to any person for selling, retaining or otherwise disposing of the property of a tenant in accordance with this section.

80. The landlord may apply to the Tribunal for an order terminating the tenancy of a tenant of superintendent's premises and evicting the tenant if the tenant does not vacate the rental unit within one week of the termination of his or her employment.

81. (1) If a tenant transfers the occupancy of a rental unit to a person in a manner other than by an assignment authorized under section 17 or a subletting authorized under section 18, the landlord may apply to the Tribunal for an order evicting the person to whom occupancy of the rental unit was transferred.

(2) An application under this section must be made no later than 60 days after the landlord discovers the unauthorized occupancy.

LANDLORD OR TENANT APPLICATION
OVERHOLDING SUBTENANT

82. (1) If a subtenant continues to occupy a rental unit after the end of the subtenancy, the landlord or the tenant may apply to the Tribunal for an order evicting the subtenant.

(2) An application under this section must be made within 60 days after the end of the subtenancy.

EVICTION ORDERS

83. (1) If a notice of termination of a tenancy has been given and the landlord has subsequently applied to the Tribunal for an order evicting the tenant, the order of the Tribunal evicting the tenant may not be effective earlier than the date of termination set out in the notice.

(2) Where a default order provides for the eviction of a person from a rental unit, the eviction order shall take effect 11 days after the order is issued.

84. (1) Upon an application for an order evicting a tenant or subtenant, the Tribunal may, despite any other provision of this Act or the tenancy agreement,

(a) refuse to grant the application unless satisfied, having regard to all the circumstances, that it would be unfair to refuse; or

(b) order that the enforcement of the order of eviction be postponed for a period of time.

Same (2) Without restricting the generality of subsection (1), the Tribunal shall refuse to grant the application where satisfied that,

(a) the landlord is in serious breach of the landlord's responsibilities under this Act or of any material covenant in the tenancy agreement;

(b) the reason for the application being brought is that the tenant has complained to a governmental authority of the landlord's violation of a law dealing with health, safety, housing or maintenance standards;

(c) the reason for the application being brought is that the tenant has attempted to secure or enforce his or her legal rights;

(d) the reason for the application being brought is that the tenant is a member of a tenants' association or is attempting to organize such an association; or

(e) the reason for the application being brought is that the rental unit is occupied by children and the occupation by the children does not constitute overcrowding.

No eviction before compensation, demolition or conversion (3) The Tribunal shall not issue an eviction order in a proceeding regarding termination of a tenancy for the purposes of demolition, conversion to non-residential rental use, renovations or repairs until the landlord has complied with section 55, 57 or 58, as the case may be.

No eviction before compensation, repair or renovation (4) If a tenant has given a landlord notice under subsection 56 (2), the Tribunal shall not issue an eviction order in a proceeding regarding termination of the tenancy until the landlord has compensated the tenant in an amount equal to the rent for the amount of time the landlord estimates is required to complete the repair or renovation.

Effect of eviction order 85. An order evicting a person shall have the same effect, and shall be enforced in the same manner, as a writ of possession.

OTHER LANDLORD APPLICATIONS

Arrears of rent 86. (1) A landlord may apply to the Tribunal for an order for the payment of arrears of rent if,

(a) the tenant has not paid rent lawfully required under the tenancy agreement; and

(b) the tenant is in possession of the rental unit.

Compensation, overholding tenant (2) If a tenant is in possession of a rental unit after the tenancy has been terminated, the landlord may apply to the Tribunal for an order for the payment of compensation for the use and occupation of a rental unit after a notice of termination or an agreement to terminate the tenancy has taken effect.

Same (3) In determining the amount of arrears of rent, compensation or both owing in an order for termination of a tenancy and the payment of arrears of rent, compensation or both, the Tribunal shall subtract from the amount owing the amount of any rent deposit or interest on a rent deposit that would be owing to the tenant on termination.

Compensation for damage 87. A landlord may apply to the Tribunal for an order for compensation if the tenant or a person whom the tenant permits in the residential complex wilfully or negligently causes undue damage to the rental unit or the residential complex and the tenant is in possession of the rental unit.

Compensation, misrepresentation of income 88. If a landlord has a right to give a notice of termination under subsection 62 (2), the landlord may apply to the Tribunal for an order for the payment of money the tenant would have been required to pay if the tenant had not misrepresented his or her income or that of other members of his or her family, so long as the application is made while the tenant is in possession of the rental unit.

OTHER TENANT NOTICES AND APPLICATIONS

Compensation, overholding subtenant 89. A tenant may apply to the Tribunal for an order for compensation for use and occupation by an overholding subtenant after the end of the subtenancy if the overholding subtenant is in possession of the rental unit at the time of the application.

90. Sections 61 to 67, 69, 86, 87 and 99 apply with necessary modifications with respect to a tenant who has sublet a rental unit as if the tenant were the landlord and the subtenant were the tenant.

PART IV
CARE HOMES

RIGHTS AND DUTIES OF LANDLORDS AND TENANTS

Agreement
required

91. (1) There shall be a written tenancy agreement relating to the tenancy of every tenant in a care home.

Contents of
agreement

(2) The agreement shall set out what has been agreed to with respect to care services and meals and the charges for them.

Information
to tenant

92. (1) Before entering into a tenancy agreement with a new tenant in a care home, the landlord shall give to the new tenant an information package containing the prescribed information.

Effect of
non-
compliance

(2) The landlord shall not give a notice of rent increase or a notice of increase of a charge for providing a care service or meals until after giving the required information package to the tenant.

Tenancy
agreement:
right to
consult

93. (1) Every tenancy agreement relating to the tenancy of a tenant in a care home shall contain a statement that the tenant has the right to consult a third party with respect to the agreement and to cancel the agreement within five days after the agreement has been entered into.

Cancellation

(2) The tenant may cancel the tenancy agreement by written notice to the landlord within five days after entering into it.

Entry check
condition of
tenant

94. (1) Despite section 19, a landlord may enter a rental unit in a care home at regular intervals to check the condition of a tenant in accordance with the tenancy agreement if the agreement requires the landlord to do so.

Right to
revoke
provision

(2) A tenant whose tenancy agreement contains a provision requiring the landlord to regularly check the condition of the tenant may unilaterally revoke that provision by written notice to the landlord.

Assignment,
subletting in
care homes

95. A landlord may withhold consent to an assignment or subletting of a rental unit in a care home if the effect of the assignment or subletting would be to admit a person to the care home contrary to the admission requirements or guidelines set by the landlord.

Notice of
termination

96. (1) A landlord may, by notice, terminate the tenancy of a tenant in a care home if,

(a) the rental unit was occupied solely for the purpose of receiving rehabilitative or therapeutic services agreed upon by the tenant and the landlord;

(b) no other tenant of the care home occupying a rental unit solely for the purpose of receiving rehabilitative or therapeutic services is permitted to live there for longer than two years; and

(c) the period of tenancy agreed to has expired.

Period of
notice

(2) The date for termination specified in the notice shall be at least the number of days after the date the notice is given that is set out in section 47 and shall be the day a period of the tenancy ends or, where the tenancy is for a fixed term, the end of the term.

Termination,
care homes

97. Despite section 47, a tenant of a care home may terminate a tenancy at any time by giving at least 30 days notice of termination to the landlord.

Notice of
termination,
demolition,
conversion
or repairs

98. (1) A landlord who gives a tenant of a care home a notice of termination under section 53 shall make reasonable efforts to find appropriate alternate accommodation for the tenant.

Same

(2) Sections 55 and 57 do not apply with respect to a tenant of a care home who receives a notice of termination under section 53 and chooses to take alternate accommodation found by the landlord for the tenant under subsection (1).

TRANSFERRING TENANCY

Application

99. (1) A landlord may apply to the Tribunal for an order transferring a tenant out of a care home and evicting the tenant if,

(a) the tenant no longer requires the level of care provided by the landlord; or

(b) the tenant requires a level of care that the landlord is not able to provide.

Order

(2) The Tribunal may issue an order under clause (1) (b) only if it is satisfied that,

(a) appropriate alternate accommodation is available for the tenant; and

(b) the level of care that the landlord is able to provide when combined with the community based services provided to the tenant in the care home cannot meet the tenant's care needs.

Same | (3) The Tribunal may not issue a default order in an application under this section.

Mandatory mediation | (4) If a dispute arises, the dispute shall be sent to mediation before the Tribunal makes an order.

Same | (5) If the landlord fails to participate in the mediation, the Tribunal may dismiss the landlord's application.

Rules Related To Rent

Rent in care home | **100.** If there is more than one tenancy agreement for a rental unit in a care home, the provisions of Part VI apply with respect to each tenancy agreement as if it were an agreement for a separate rental unit.

Notice of increased charges | **101.** (1) A landlord shall not increase a charge for providing a care service or meals to a tenant of a rental unit in a care home without first giving the tenant at least 90 days notice of the landlord's intention to do so.

Contents of notice | (2) The notice shall be in writing in the form approved by the Tribunal and shall set out the landlord's intention to increase the charge and the new charges for care services and meals.

Effect of non-compliance | (3) An increase in a charge for a care service or meals is void if the landlord has not given the notice required by this section, and before the landlord can take the increase the landlord must give a new notice.

Certain charges permitted | **102.** (1) Nothing in subsection 140 (1) limits the right of a landlord to charge a tenant of a rental unit in a care home for providing care services or meals to the tenant so long as the landlord has complied with the requirements of sections 92 and 101.

Same | (2) Nothing in subsection 140 (3) limits the right of a tenant or a person acting on behalf of a tenant to charge a subtenant of a rental unit in a care home for providing care services or meals to the subtenant.

PART V
MOBILE HOME PARKS AND LAND LEASE COMMUNITIES

INTERPRETATION

Part applies to land lease communities | **103.** This Part applies with necessary modifications with respect to tenancies in land lease communities, as if the tenancies were in mobile home parks.

Interpretation | **104.** A reference in this Part to a tenant's mobile home shall be interpreted to be a reference to a mobile home owned by the tenant and situated within a mobile home park of the landlord with whom the tenant has a tenancy agreement.

Rights And Duties Of Landlords And Tenants

Tenant's right to sell, etc. | **105.** (1) A tenant has the right to sell or lease his or her mobile home without the landlord's consent.

Landlord as agent | (2) A landlord may act as the agent of a tenant in negotiations to sell or lease a mobile home only in accordance with a written agency contract entered into for the purpose of beginning those negotiations.

Same | (3) A provision in a tenancy agreement requiring a tenant who owns a mobile home to use the landlord as an agent for the sale of the mobile home is void.

Landlord's right of first refusal | **106.** (1) This section applies if a tenancy agreement with respect to a mobile home contains a provision prohibiting the tenant from selling the mobile home without first offering to sell it to the landlord.

Same | (2) If a tenant receives an acceptable offer to purchase a mobile home, the landlord has a right of first refusal to purchase the mobile home at the price and subject to the terms and conditions in the offer.

Same | (3) A tenant shall give a landlord at least 72 hours notice of a person's offer to purchase a mobile home before accepting the person's offer.

Landlord's purchase at reduced price | (4) If a provision described in subsection (1) permits a landlord to purchase a mobile home at a price that is less than the one contained in a prospective purchaser's offer to purchase, the landlord may exercise the option to purchase the mobile home, but the provision is void with respect to the landlord's right to purchase the mobile home at the lesser price.

For sale signs

107. (1) A landlord shall not prevent a tenant who owns a mobile home from placing in a window of the mobile home a sign that the home is for sale, unless the landlord does so in accordance with subsection (2).

Alternative method of advertising a sale

(2) A landlord may prevent a tenant who owns a mobile home from placing a for sale sign in a window of a mobile home if all of the following conditions are met:

1. The prohibition applies to all tenants in the mobile home park.

2. The landlord provides a bulletin board for the purpose of placing for sale advertisements.

3. The bulletin board is provided to all tenants in the mobile home park free of charge.

4. The bulletin board is placed in a prominent place and is accessible to the public at all reasonable times.

Assignment

108. A landlord may not refuse consent to the assignment of a site for a mobile home on a ground set out in clause 17 (2) (b) or 17 (3) (c) if the potential assignee has purchased or has entered into an agreement to purchase the mobile home on the site.

Restraint of trade prohibited

109. (1) A landlord shall not restrict the right of a tenant to purchase goods or services from the person of his or her choice, except as provided in subsection (2).

Standards

(2) A landlord may set reasonable standards for mobile home equipment.

Responsibility of landlord

110. (1) A landlord is responsible for,

(a) removing or disposing of garbage or ensuring the availability of a means for removing or disposing of garbage in the mobile home park at reasonable intervals;

(b) maintaining mobile home park roads in a good state of repair;

(c) removing snow from mobile home park roads;

(d) maintaining the water supply, sewage disposal, fuel, drainage and electrical systems in the mobile home park in a good state of repair;

(e) maintaining the mobile home park grounds and all buildings, structures, enclosures and equipment intended for

the common use of tenants in a good state of repair; and

(f) repairing damage to a tenant's property, if the damage is caused by the wilful or negligent conduct of the landlord.

Application for relief

(2) A tenant or former tenant may apply to the Tribunal for relief as a result of a breach of the landlord's obligations under this section if the application is made within one year after the date the landlord breached the obligation.

Order

(3) In an order under this section, the Tribunal may,

(a) terminate the tenancy;

(b) order an abatement of the rent;

(c) authorize a repair that has been or is to be made and order its cost to be paid by the landlord to the tenant;

(d) order the landlord to do specified repairs or other work within a specified time;

(e) make any other order the Tribunal considers appropriate.

Same

(4) In determining the remedy under this section, the Tribunal shall consider whether the tenant or former tenant advised the landlord of the alleged breaches before applying to the Tribunal.

TERMINATION OF TENANCIES

Mobile home abandoned

111. (1) This section applies if,

(a) the tenant has vacated the mobile home in accordance with,

(i) a notice of termination of the landlord or the tenant,

(ii) an agreement between the landlord and tenant to terminate the tenancy, or

(iii) an order of the Tribunal terminating the tenancy; or

(b) the landlord has applied for an order under section 78 and the Tribunal has made an order terminating the tenancy.

Notice to tenant

(2) The landlord shall not dispose of a mobile home without first notifying the tenant of the landlord's intention to do so,

(a) by registered mail, sent to the tenant's last known mailing address; and

(b) by causing a notice to be published in a newspaper having general circulation in the locality in which the mobile home park is located.

Landlord may dispose of mobile home

(3) The landlord may sell, retain for the landlord's own use or dispose of a mobile home in the circumstances described in subsection (1) beginning 60 days after the notices referred to in subsection (2) have been given if the tenant has not made a claim with respect to the landlord's intended disposal.

Same

(4) If, within six months after the day the notices have been given under subsection (2) the tenant makes a claim for a mobile home which the landlord has already sold, the landlord shall pay to the tenant the amount by which the proceeds of sale exceed the sum of,

(a) the landlord's reasonable out of pocket expenses incurred with respect to the mobile home; and

(b) any arrears of rent of the tenant.

Same

(5) If within six months after the day the notices have been given under subsection (2) the tenant makes a claim for a mobile home which the landlord has retained for the landlord's own use the landlord shall return the mobile home to the tenant.

Same

(6) Before returning a mobile home to a tenant who claims it within the 60 days referred to in subsection (3) or the six months referred to in subsection (5), the landlord may require the tenant to pay the landlord for arrears of rent and any reasonable expenses incurred by the landlord with respect to the mobile home.

No liability

(7) Subject to subsection (4) or (5), a landlord is not liable to any person for selling, retaining or otherwise disposing of the property of a tenant in accordance with this section.

Death of mobile home owner

112. Sections 49 and 50 do not apply if the tenant owns the mobile home.

Extended notice of termination, special cases

113. If a notice of termination is given under section 53 with respect to a tenancy agreement for a mobile home owned by the tenant, the date for termination specified in the notice shall be at least one year after the date the notice is given and shall be the day a period of the tenancy ends or, where the tenancy is for a fixed term, the end of the term.

RULES RELATED TO RENT AND OTHER CHARGES

New tenant

114. (1) Despite subsection 17 (8) and section 124, if a new tenant of a site for a mobile home has purchased or has entered into an agreement to purchase the mobile home located on the site, the landlord may not charge the new tenant a rent that is greater than the last lawful rent charged plus the prescribed amount.

Same

(2) If an assignee of a tenant of a site for a mobile home has purchased or has entered into an agreement to purchase the mobile home located on the site, the assignee shall be deemed to be a new tenant for the purposes of subsection (1).

Exception

(3) Subsection 138 (11) does not apply with respect to a site for a mobile home if there is a new tenancy agreement with respect to the site and the new tenant purchased or has entered into an agreement to purchase the mobile home located on the site.

Entrance and exit fees limited

115. A landlord shall not charge for any of the following matters, except to the extent of the landlord's reasonable out of pocket expenses incurred with regard to those matters:

1. The entry of a mobile home into a mobile home park.

2. The exit of a mobile home from a mobile home park.

3. The installation of a mobile home in a mobile home park.

4. The removal of a mobile home from a mobile home park.

5. The testing of water or sewage in a mobile home park.

PROCEEDINGS BEFORE THE TRIBUNAL

Increased capital expenditures

116. (1) If the Tribunal finds that a capital expenditure is for infrastructure work required to be carried out by the Government of Canada or Ontario or a municipality or an agency of any of them, despite subsections 138 (9) and (10), the Tribunal may determine the number of years over which the rent increase justified by that capital expenditure may be taken.

Definition

(2) In this section,

"infrastructure work" means work with respect to roads, water supply, fuel, sewage disposal, drainage, electrical systems and other prescribed services and things provided to the mobile home park.

PART VI
RULES RELATING TO RENT

GENERAL RULES

Security deposits, limitation

117. (1) The only security deposit that a landlord may collect is a rent deposit collected in accordance with section 118.

Definition

(2) In this section and section 118,

"security deposit" means money, property or a right paid or given by, or on behalf of, a tenant of a rental unit to a landlord or to anyone on the landlord's behalf to be held by or for the account of the landlord as security for the performance of an obligation or the payment of a liability of the tenant or to be returned to the tenant upon the happening of a condition.

Rent deposit may be required

118. (1) A landlord may require a tenant to pay a rent deposit with respect to a tenancy if the landlord does so on or before entering into the tenancy agreement.

Amount of rent deposit

(2) The amount of a rent deposit shall not be more than the lesser of the amount of rent for one rent period and the amount of rent for one month.

Same

(3) If the lawful rent increases after a tenant has paid a rent deposit, the landlord may require the tenant to pay an additional amount to increase the rent deposit up to the amount permitted by subsection (2).

Qualification

(4) A new landlord of a rental unit or a person who is deemed to be a landlord under subsection 47 (1) of the *Mortgages Act* shall not require a tenant to pay a rent deposit if the tenant has already paid a rent deposit to the prior landlord of the rental unit.

Exception

(5) Despite subsection (4), if a person becomes a new landlord in a sale from a person deemed to be a landlord under subsection 47 (1) of the *Mortgages Act*, the new landlord may require the tenant to pay a rent deposit in an amount equal to the amount with respect to the former rent deposit that the tenant received from the proceeds of sale.

Interest

(6) A landlord of a rental unit shall pay interest to the tenant annually on the amount of the rent deposit at the rate of 6 per cent per year.

Same

(7) Where the landlord has failed to make the payment required by subsection (6) when it comes due, the tenant may deduct the amount of the payment from a subsequent rent payment.

Rent deposit applied to last rent

(8) A landlord shall apply a rent deposit that a tenant has paid to the landlord or to a former landlord in payment of the rent for the last rent period before the tenancy terminates.

Transitional

(9) A security deposit paid before the day this section is proclaimed in force shall be deemed to be a rent deposit for the purposes of this section.

Post-dated cheques

119. Neither a landlord nor a tenancy agreement shall require a tenant to provide post-dated cheques or other negotiable instruments for payment of rent.

Receipt for payment

120. A landlord shall provide free of charge to a tenant, upon the tenant's request, a receipt for the payment of any rent, rent deposit, arrears of rent or any other amount paid to the landlord.

GENERAL RULES CONCERNING AMOUNT OF RENT CHARGED

Landlord not to charge more than lawful rent

121. (1) No landlord shall charge rent for a rental unit in an amount that is greater than the lawful rent permitted under this Part.

Lawful rent where discounts offered

(2) Where a landlord offers a discount in rent at the beginning of, or during, a tenancy, the lawful rent shall be calculated in accordance with the prescribed rules.

Lawful rent where higher rent for first rental period

(3) Where the rent a landlord charges for the first rental period of a tenancy is greater than the rent the landlord charges for subsequent rental periods, the lawful rent shall be calculated in accordance with the prescribed rules.

Landlord's duty, rent increases

122. No landlord shall increase the rent charged to a tenant for a rental unit, except in accordance with this Part.

LAWFUL RENT

Lawful rent when this Act comes into force

123. Unless otherwise prescribed, the lawful rent charged to a tenant for a rental unit for which there is a tenancy agreement in effect on the day this Part comes into force shall be the rent that was charged on the day before this section came into force or, if that amount was not lawfully charged under the *Rent Control Act, 1992*, the amount that it was lawful to charge on that day.

New tenant

124. Subject to section 121, the lawful rent for the first rental period for a new tenant under a new tenancy agreement is the rent first charged to the tenant.

Assignment without consent

125. (1) If a person occupies a rental unit as a result of an assignment of the unit without the consent of the landlord, the landlord may negotiate a new tenancy agreement with the person.

Overholding subtenant

(2) If a subtenant continues to occupy a rental unit after the end of the subtenancy and the tenant has abandoned the rental unit, the landlord may negotiate a new tenancy agreement with the subtenant.

Limitation

(3) Section 124 applies to tenancy agreements entered into under subsection (1) or (2) if they are entered into no later than 60 days after the landlord discovers the unauthorized occupancy.

Deemed assignment

(4) A person's occupation of a rental unit shall be deemed to be an assignment of the rental unit with the consent of the landlord as of the date the unauthorized occupancy began if,

(a) a tenancy agreement is not entered into under subsection (1) or (2) within the period set out in subsection (3);

(b) the landlord does not apply to the Tribunal under section 81 for an order evicting the person within 60 days of the landlord discovering the unauthorized occupancy; and

(c) neither the landlord nor the tenant applies to the Tribunal under section 82 within 60 days after the end of the subtenancy for an order evicting the subtenant.

12-month rule

126. (1) A landlord who is lawfully entitled to increase the rent charged to a tenant for a rental unit may do so only if at least 12 months have elapsed,

(a) since the day of the last rent increase for that tenant in that rental unit, if there has been a previous increase; or

(b) since the day the rental unit was first rented to that tenant, otherwise.

Exception

(2) An increase in rent under section 132 shall be deemed not to be an increase in rent for the purposes of this section.

Notice of rent increase required

127. (1) A landlord shall not increase the rent charged to a tenant for a rental unit without first giving the tenant at least 90 days written notice of the landlord's intention to do so.

Same

(2) Subsection (1) applies even if the rent charged is increased in accordance with an order under section 138.

Contents of notice

(3) The notice shall be in a form approved by the Tribunal and shall set out the landlord's intention to increase the rent and the amount of the new rent.

Increase void without notice

(4) An increase in rent is void if the landlord has not given the notice required by this section, and before the landlord can take the increase the landlord must give a new notice.

Deemed acceptance where no notice of termination

128. A tenant who does not give a landlord notice of termination of a tenancy under section 46 after receiving notice of an intended rent increase under section 127 shall be deemed to have accepted whatever rent increase would be allowed under this Act after the landlord and the tenant have exercised their rights under this Act.

GUIDELINE

Guideline increase

129. (1) No landlord may increase the rent charged to a tenant or to an assignee under section 17 during the term of their tenancy by more than the guideline except in accordance with sections 130 to 139.

Guideline

(2) The Minister shall determine the guideline in effect for each calendar year as follows:

1. Determine the rent control index taking into account the weights and the three year moving averages of the operating cost categories as set out in the prescribed Table.

2. The part of the guideline allocated to operating costs is equal to 55 per cent of the percentage increase in the rent control index, rounded to the nearest 1/10th of 1 per cent.

177

3. The guideline is the sum of the part of the guideline allocated to operating costs and 2 per cent.

(3) The Minister shall have the guideline for each year published in *The Ontario Gazette* not later than the 31st day of August of the preceding year.

(4) The guideline for the calendar year 1997 and for the calendar year 1998 shall be the rent control guideline for each of those years established under the *Rent Control Act, 1992.*

AGREEMENTS TO INCREASE, DECREASE RENT

130. (1) A landlord and a tenant may agree to increase the rent charged to the tenant for a rental unit above the guideline if,

(a) the landlord has carried out or undertakes to carry out a specified capital expenditure in exchange for the rent increase; or

(b) the landlord has provided or undertakes to provide a new or additional service in exchange for the rent increase.

(2) An agreement under subsection (1) shall be in the form approved by the Tribunal and shall set out the new rent, the tenant's right under subsection (4) to cancel the agreement and the date the agreement is to take effect.

(3) A landlord shall not increase rent charged under this section by more than the guideline plus 4 per cent of the previous lawful rent charged.

(4) A tenant who enters into an agreement under this section may cancel the agreement by giving written notice to the landlord within five days after signing it.

(5) An agreement under this section may come into force no earlier than six days after it has been signed.

(6) Section 127 does not apply with respect to a rent increase under this section.

(7) Despite any deemed acceptance of a rent increase under section 128, if a landlord and tenant enter into an agreement under this section, a notice of rent increase given by the landlord to the tenant before the agreement was entered into becomes void when the agreement takes effect, if the notice of rent increase is to take effect on or after the day the agreed to increase is to take effect.

131. (1) A tenant or former tenant may apply to the Tribunal for relief if the landlord and the tenant or former tenant agreed to an increase in rent under section 130 and,

(a) the landlord has failed in whole or in part to carry out an undertaking under the agreement;

(b) the agreement was based on work that the landlord claimed to have done but did not do; or

(c) the agreement was based on services that the landlord claimed to have provided but did not do so.

(2) No application may be made under this section more than two years after the rent increase becomes effective.

(3) In an application under this section, the Tribunal may find that some or all of the rent increase above the guideline is invalid from the day on which it took effect and may order the rebate of any money consequently owing to the tenant or former tenant.

132. (1) A landlord may increase the rent charged to a tenant for a rental unit as prescribed at any time if the landlord and the tenant agree that the landlord will add any of the following with respect to the tenant's occupancy of the rental unit:

1. A parking space.

2. A prescribed service, facility, privilege, accommodation or thing.

(2) Sections 126 and 127 do not apply with respect to a rent increase under this section.

133. An agreement under section 130 or 132 is void if it has been entered into as a result of coercion or as a result of a false, incomplete or misleading representation by the landlord or an agent of the landlord.

134. A landlord shall decrease the rent charged to a tenant for a rental unit as prescribed if the landlord and the tenant agree that the landlord will cease to provide anything referred to in subsection 132 (1) with

respect to the tenant's occupancy of the rental unit.

ADDITIONAL GROUNDS FOR RENT INCREASE

Increase to maximum rent

135. (1) A landlord may increase the rent charged to a tenant of a rental unit up to the maximum rent determined under subsection (2) if the tenant of the rental unit has been a tenant of the rental unit since the day before this section is proclaimed in force.

Maximum rent

(2) For the purposes of subsection (1), the maximum rent is the amount determined by,

(a) determining the maximum rent under the *Rent Control Act, 1992* on the day before this section was proclaimed in force;

(b) adding to that amount any increases in maximum rent resulting from an order issued under section 21 of the *Rent Control Act, 1992* or a notice of carry forward issued under section 22 of that Act; and

(c) subtracting from that amount the amount of any decreases in maximum rent ordered under section 28 or 33 of the *Rent Control Act, 1992*.

REDUCTION OF RENT – MUNICIPAL TAXES REDUCED

Municipal taxes reduced

136. (1) If the municipal property tax for a residential complex is reduced by more than the prescribed percentage, the lawful rent for each of the rental units in the complex is reduced in accordance with the prescribed rules.

Effective date

(2) The rent reduction shall take effect on the prescribed date, whether or not notice has been given under subsection (3).

Notice

(3) If, for a residential complex with at least the prescribed number of rental units, the rents that the tenants are required to pay are reduced under subsection (1), the local municipality shall, within the prescribed period and by the prescribed method of service, notify the landlord and all of the tenants of the residential complex of that fact.

Same

(4) The notice shall be in writing in a form approved by the Tribunal and shall,

(a) inform the tenants that their rent is reduced;

(b) set out the percentage by which their rent is reduced and the date the reduction takes effect;

(c) inform the tenants that if the rent is not reduced in accordance with the notice they may apply to the Tribunal under section 144 for the return of money illegally collected; and

(d) advise the landlord and the tenants of their right to apply for an order under section 137.

Same

(5) The local municipality shall give a copy of a notice under this section to the Tribunal or to the Ministry, on request.

Application for variation

137. (1) A landlord or a tenant may apply to the Tribunal under the prescribed circumstances for an order varying the amount by which the rent charged is to be reduced under section 136.

Same

(2) An application under subsection (1) must be made within the prescribed time.

Determination and order

(3) The Tribunal shall determine an application under this section in accordance with the prescribed rules and shall issue an order setting out the percentage of the rent reduction.

Same

(4) An order under this section shall take effect on the effective date determined under subsection 136 (2).

LANDLORD APPLICATION FOR RENT INCREASE

Increased operating costs, capital expenditures

138. (1) (1) A landlord may apply to the Tribunal for an order allowing the rent charged to be increased by more than the guideline for any or all of the rental units in a residential complex in any or all of the following cases:

1. An extraordinary increase in the cost for municipal taxes and charges or utilities or both for the whole residential complex.

2. Capital expenditures incurred respecting the residential complex or one or more of the rental units in it.

3. Operating costs related to security services provided in respect of the residential complex by persons not employed by the landlord.

Same

(2) An increase in the cost of municipal taxes and charges or utilities is extraordinary if it is greater than the percentage increase set out for the corresponding cost category recognized in the Table referred to in subsection 129 (2).

179

(3) An application under this section shall be made at least 90 days before the effective date of the first intended rent increase referred to in the application.

(4) If an application is made under this section and the landlord has given a notice of rent increase as required, until an order authorizing the rent increase for the rental unit takes effect, the landlord shall not require the tenant to pay a rent that exceeds the lesser of,

(a) the new rent specified in the notice; and

(b) the greatest amount that the landlord could charge without applying for a rent increase.

(5) Despite subsection (4), the tenant may choose to pay the amount set out in the notice of rent increase pending the outcome of the landlord's application and, if the tenant does so, the landlord shall owe to the tenant any amount paid by the tenant exceeding the amount allowed by the order of the Tribunal.

(6) In an application under this section, the Tribunal shall make findings in accordance with the prescribed rules with respect to all of the grounds of the application and shall order the percentage rent increase that may be taken and the time period as prescribed, during which it may be taken.

(7) In making findings in an application under paragraph 2 of subsection (1), the Tribunal may disallow a capital expenditure if the Tribunal finds the capital expenditure is unreasonable.

(8) The Tribunal shall not make a finding under subsection (7) that a capital expenditure is unreasonable if the capital expenditure,

(a) is necessary to protect or restore the physical integrity of the residential complex or part of it;

(b) is necessary to maintain maintenance, health, safety or other housing related standards required by law;

(c) is necessary to maintain the provision of a plumbing, heating, mechanical, electrical, ventilation or air conditioning system;

(d) provides access for persons with disabilities;

(e) promotes energy or water conservation; or

(f) maintains or improves the security of the residential complex.

(9) The Tribunal shall not make an order with respect to a rental unit that increases the lawful rent with respect to capital expenditures or operating costs related to security services in an amount that is greater than 4 per cent of the previous lawful rent.

(10) If the Tribunal determines with respect to a rental unit that an increase in lawful rent of more than 4 per cent of the previous lawful rent is justified with respect to capital expenditures, operating costs related to security services or both, the Tribunal shall also order, in accordance with the prescribed rules, increases in rent for the following years in an amount not to exceed in any year 4 per cent of the lawful rent for the previous year, until the total increase has been taken.

Order not to
apply to new
tenant

(11) An order of the Tribunal under subsection (6) or (10) with respect to a rental unit ceases to be of any effect on and after the day a new tenant enters into a new tenancy agreement with the landlord if that agreement takes effect on or after the day that is 90 days before the first effective date of a rent increase in the order.

139. If an order is made under subsection 138 (6) with respect to a rental unit and a landlord has not yet taken all the increases in rent for the rental unit permissible under a previous order under subsection 138 (10), the landlord may increase the rent for the rental unit in accordance with the prescribed rules.

ILLEGAL ADDITIONAL CHARGES

140. (1) Unless otherwise prescribed, no landlord shall, directly or indirectly, with respect to any rental unit,

(a) collect or require or attempt to collect or require from a tenant or prospective tenant of the rental unit a fee, premium, commission, bonus, penalty, key deposit or other like amount of money whether or not the money is refundable;

(b) require or attempt to require a tenant or prospective tenant to pay any consideration for goods or services as a condition for granting the tenancy or continuing to permit occupancy of a rental unit if that consideration is in addition to the rent the tenant is lawfully required to pay to the landlord; or

(c) rent any portion of the rental unit for a rent which, together with all other rents payable for all other portions of the rental unit, is a sum that is greater than the rent the landlord lawfully may charge for the rental unit.

Same

(2) No superintendent, property manager or other person who acts on behalf of a landlord with respect to a rental unit shall, directly or indirectly, with or without the authority of the landlord, do any of the things mentioned in clause (1) (a), (b) or (c) with respect to that rental unit.

Same

(3) Unless otherwise prescribed, no tenant and no person acting on behalf of the tenant shall, directly or indirectly,

(a) sublet a rental unit for a rent that is greater than the rent that is lawfully charged by the landlord for the rental unit;

(b) sublet any portion of the rental unit for a rent which, together with all other rents payable for all other portions of the rental unit, is a sum that is greater than the rent that is lawfully charged by the landlord for the rental unit;

(c) collect or require or attempt to collect or require from any person any fee, premium, commission, bonus, penalty, key deposit or other like amount of money, for subletting a rental unit or any portion of it, for surrendering occupancy of a rental unit or for otherwise parting with possession of a rental unit; or

(d) require or attempt to require a person to pay any consideration for goods or services as a condition for the subletting, assignment or surrender of occupancy or possession in addition to the rent the person is lawfully required to pay to the tenant or landlord.

Rent deemed lawful

141. (1) Rent charged one or more years earlier shall be deemed to be lawful rent unless an application has been made within one year after the date that amount was first charged and the lawfulness of the rent charged is in issue in the application.

Increase deemed lawful

(2) An increase in rent shall be deemed to be lawful unless an application has been made within one year after the date the increase was first charged and the lawfulness of the rent increase is in issue in the application.

Delayed effect

(3) Subsections (1) and (2) shall not take effect until the day that is six months after this section is proclaimed in force.

Section 131 prevails

(4) Nothing in this section shall be interpreted to deprive a tenant after the right to apply for and get relief in an application under section 131 within the time period set out in that section.

APPLICATIONS TO TRIBUNAL BY TENANT

Reduction in rent, reduction in services

142. (1) A tenant of a rental unit may apply to the Tribunal for an order for a reduction of the rent charged for the rental unit due to a reduction or discontinuance in services or facilities provided in respect of the rental unit or the residential complex.

Same, former tenant

(2) A former tenant of a rental unit may apply under this section as a tenant of the rental unit if the person was affected by the discontinuance or reduction of the services or facilities while the person was a tenant of the rental unit.

Order re lawful rent

(3) The Tribunal shall make findings in accordance with the prescribed rules and may order,

(a) that the rent charged be reduced by a specified amount;

(b) that there be a rebate to the tenant of any rent found to have been unlawfully collected by the landlord;

(c) that the rent charged be reduced by a specified amount for a specified period if there has been a temporary reduction in a service.

Same

(4) An order under this section reducing rent takes effect on the day that the discontinuance or reduction first occurred.

181

(5) No application may be made under this
section more than one year after a reduction
or discontinuance in a service or facility.

Reduction
in rent,
reduction in
taxes
143. (1) A tenant of a rental unit may
apply to the Tribunal for an order for a reduction of the rent charged for the rental unit due
to a reduction in the municipal taxes and
charges for the residential complex.

Order (2) The Tribunal shall make findings in
accordance with the prescribed rules and may
order that the rent charged for the rental unit
be reduced.

Money
collected
illegally
144. (1) A tenant or former tenant of a
rental unit may apply to the Tribunal for an
order that the landlord, superintendent or
agent of the landlord pay to the tenant any
money the person collected or retained in
contravention of this Act, the *Rent Control
Act, 1992* or Part IV of the *Landlord and
Tenant Act*.

Prospective
tenants
(2) A prospective tenant may apply to the
Tribunal for an order under subsection (1).

Subtenants (3) A subtenant may apply to the Tribunal
for an order under subsection (1) as if the
subtenant were the tenant and the tenant were
the landlord.

Time
limitation
(4) No order shall be made under this section with respect to an application filed more
than one year after the person collected or
retained money in contravention of this Act,
the *Rent Control Act, 1992* or Part IV of the
Landlord and Tenant Act.

PART VII
VITAL SERVICES AND MAINTENANCE
STANDARDS

VITAL SERVICES

Definitions 145. In this section and sections 146 to
153.

"local municipality" has the same meaning as
in the *Municipal Act*; ("municipalité lo-
cale")

"vital services by-law" means a by-law
passed under section 146. ("règlement
municipal sur les services essentiels")

By-laws
respecting
vital services
146. (1) The council of a local municipality may pass by-laws,

(a) requiring every landlord to provide
adequate and suitable vital services to
each of the landlord's rental units;

(b) prohibiting a supplier from ceasing to
provide the vital service until a notice
has been given under subsection 147
(1);

(c) requiring a supplier to promptly restore
the vital service when directed to do so
by an official named in the by-law;

(d) prohibiting a person from hindering,
obstructing or interfering with or
attempting to hinder, obstruct or interfere with the official or person referred
to in subsection 148 (1) in the exercise
of a power or performance of a duty
under this section or sections 147 to
153;

(e) providing that a person who contravenes or fails to comply with a by-law
is guilty of an offence for each day or
part of a day on which the offence
occurs or continues;

(f) providing that every director or officer
of a corporation that is convicted of an
offence who knowingly concurs in the
commission of the offence is guilty of
an offence;

(g) authorizing an official named in the
by-law to enter into agreements on
behalf of a local municipality with
suppliers of vital services to ensure that
adequate and suitable vital services are
provided for rental units.

Exception (2) A vital services by-law does not apply
to a landlord with respect to a rental unit to
the extent that the tenant has expressly agreed
to obtain and maintain the vital services.

Contents of
vital services
by-law
(3) A vital services by-law may,

(a) classify buildings or parts of buildings
for the purposes of the by-law and designate the classes to which it applies;

(b) designate areas of the local municipality in which the by-law applies;

(c) establish standards for the provision of
adequate and suitable vital services;

Notice by
supplier

Same

Inspection

Same

Services by
municipality

Lien

(d) prohibit a landlord from ceasing to provide a vital service for a rental unit except when necessary to alter or repair the rental unit and only for the minimum period necessary to effect the alteration or repair;

(e) provide that a landlord shall be deemed to have caused the cessation of a vital service for a rental unit if the landlord is obligated to pay the supplier for the vital service and fails to do so and, as a result of the non-payment, the vital service is no longer provided for the rental unit.

147. (1) A supplier shall give notice of an intended discontinuance of a vital service for the rental unit because the landlord has breached a contract with the supplier for the supply of the vital service.

(2) The notice shall be given in writing to the clerk of the local municipality at least 30 days before the supplier ceases to provide the vital service.

148. (1) An official named in the by-law or a person acting under his or her instructions may, at all reasonable times, enter and inspect a building or part of a building with respect to which the by-law applies for the purpose of determining compliance with the by-law or a direction given under subsection 151 (1).

(2) Despite subsection (1), the official or person shall not enter a rental unit,

(a) unless he or she has obtained the consent of the occupier of the rental unit after informing him or her that he or she may refuse permission to enter the unit; or

(b) unless he or she is authorized to do so by a warrant issued under section 204.

149. (1) If a landlord does not provide a vital service for a rental unit in accordance with a vital services by-law, the local municipality may arrange for the service to be provided.

(2) The amount spent by the local municipality under subsection (1) plus an administrative fee of 10 per cent of that amount shall, on registration of a notice of lien in the appropriate land registry office, be a lien in favour of the local municipality against the property at which the vital service is provided.

Not special
lien

Certificate

Interim
certificate

Appeal

Payments
transferred

Effect of
payment

Use of
money

Accounting
and payment
of balance

Immunity

(3) Section 382 of the *Municipal Act* does not apply with respect to the amount spent and the fee, and no special lien is created under that section.

(4) The certificate of the clerk of the local municipality as to the amount spent is proof, in the absence of evidence to the contrary, of the amount.

(5) Before issuing a certificate referred to in subsection (4), the clerk shall send an interim certificate by registered mail to the registered owner of the property that is subject to the lien and to all mortgagees or other encumbrancers registered on title.

150. An affected owner, mortgagee or other encumbrancer may, within 15 days after the interim certificate is mailed, appeal the amount shown on it to the council of the local municipality.

151. (1) If the local municipality has arranged for a vital service to be provided to a rental unit, an official named in the vital services by-law may direct a tenant to pay any or all of the rent for the rental unit to the local municipality.

(2) Payment by a tenant under subsection (1) shall be deemed not to constitute a default in the payment of rent due under a tenancy agreement or a default in the tenant's obligations for the purposes of this Act.

152. (1) The local municipality shall apply the rent received from a tenant to reduce the amount that it spent to provide the vital service and the related administrative fee.

(2) The local municipality shall provide the person otherwise entitled to receive the rent with an accounting of the rents received for each individual rental unit and shall pay to that person any amount remaining after the rent is applied in accordance with subsection (1).

153. (1) No proceeding for damages or otherwise shall be commenced against an official or a person acting under his or her instructions or against an employee or agent of a local municipality for any act done in good faith in the performance or intended performance of a duty or authority under any of sections 145 to 152 or under a by-law passed under section 146 or for any alleged

183

neglect or default in the performance in good faith of the duty or authority.

(2) Subsection (1) does not relieve a local municipality of liability to which it would otherwise be subject with respect to a tort committed by an official or a person acting under his or her instructions or by an employee or agent of the local municipality.

MAINTENANCE STANDARDS

Application of prescribed standards

154. (1) The prescribed maintenance standards apply to a residential complex and the rental units located in it if,

(a) the residential complex is located in unorganized territory;

(b) there is no municipal property standards by-law that applies to the residential complex; or

(c) the prescribed circumstances apply.

Minister to receive complaints

(2) The Minister shall receive any written complaint from a current tenant of a rental unit respecting the standard of maintenance that prevails with respect to the rental unit or the residential complex in which it is located if the prescribed maintenance standards apply to the residential complex.

Complaints to be investigated

(3) Upon receiving a complaint respecting a residential complex or a rental unit in it, the Minister shall cause an inspector to make whatever inspection the Minister considers necessary to determine whether the landlord has complied with the prescribed maintenance standards.

Cost of inspection

(4) The Minister may charge a municipality and the municipality shall pay the Minister for the cost, as prescribed, associated with inspecting a residential complex in the municipality, for the purposes of investigating a complaint under this section and ensuring compliance with a work order under section 155.

Same

(5) If a municipality fails to make payment in full within 60 days after the Minister issues a notice of payment due under subsection (4), the notice of payment may be filed in the Ontario Court (General Division) and enforced as if it were a court order.

Inspector's work order

155. (1) If an inspector is satisfied that the landlord of a residential complex has not complied with a prescribed maintenance standard that applies to the residential complex, the inspector may make and give to the landlord a work order requiring the landlord to comply with the prescribed maintenance standard.

Same

(2) The inspector shall set out in the order,

(a) the municipal address or legal description of the residential complex;

(b) reasonable particulars of the work to be performed;

(c) the period within which there must be compliance with the terms of the work order; and

(d) the time limit for applying under section 156 to the Tribunal for a review of the work order.

Review of work order

156. (1) If a landlord who has received an inspector's work order is not satisfied with its terms, the landlord may, within 20 days after the day the order is issued, apply to the Tribunal for a review of the work order.

Order

(2) On an application under subsection (1), the Tribunal may, by order,

(a) confirm or vary the inspector's work order;

(b) rescind the work order, if it finds that the landlord has complied with it; or

(c) quash the work order.

PART VIII
ONTARIO RENTAL HOUSING TRIBUNAL

Tribunal established

157. (1) A tribunal to be known as the Ontario Rental Housing Tribunal in English and Tribunal du logement de l'Ontario in French is hereby established.

Tribunal's jurisdiction

(2) The Tribunal has exclusive jurisdiction to determine all applications under this Act and with respect to all matters in which jurisdiction is conferred on it by this Act.

Access to rent information

(3) The Registrar under the *Rent Control Act, 1992* shall give to the Tribunal all information contained in the Rent Registry under that Act and the Tribunal shall provide any of that information to members of the public on request.

(4) The Director of Rent Control under the *Rent Control Act, 1992* shall give to the Tribunal, for its use, all records held by the Director that may be of assistance to the Tribunal in carrying out its powers and duties under this Act.

Composition

158. (1) The members of the Tribunal shall be appointed by the Lieutenant Governor in Council.

Remuneration and expenses

(2) The members of the Tribunal who are not members of the public service of Ontario shall be paid the remuneration fixed by the Lieutenant Governor in Council and the reasonable expenses incurred in the course of their duties under this Act, as determined by the Minister.

Public servant members

(3) Members of the Tribunal may be persons who are appointed or transferred under the *Public Service Act*.

Chair and vice-chair

159. (1) The Lieutenant Governor in Council shall appoint one member of the Tribunal as chair and one or more members as vice-chairs.

Same

(2) The Chair may designate a vice-chair who shall exercise the powers and perform the duties of the chair when the chair is absent or unable to act.

Chair, chief executive officer

(3) The Chair shall be the chief executive officer of the Tribunal.

Quorum

160. One member of the Tribunal is sufficient to conduct a proceeding under this Act.

Conflict of interest

161. The members of the Tribunal shall file with the Tribunal a written declaration of any interests they have in residential rental property, and shall be required to comply with any conflict of interest guidelines or rules of conduct established by the Chair.

Power to determine law and fact

162. The Tribunal has authority to hear and determine all questions of law and fact with respect to all matters within its jurisdiction under this Act.

Members, mediators not compellable

163. No member of the Tribunal or person employed as a mediator by the Tribunal shall be compelled to give testimony or produce documents in a civil proceeding with respect to matters that come to his or her knowledge in the course of exercising his or her duties under this Act.

Rules and Guidelines Committee

164. (1) The Chair of the Tribunal shall establish a Rules and Guidelines Committee

to be composed of the Chair, as Chair of the Committee, and any other members of the Tribunal the Chair may from time to time appoint to the Committee.

Committee shall adopt rules

(2) The Committee shall adopt rules of practice and procedure governing the practice and procedure before the Tribunal under the authority of this section and section 25.1 of the *Statutory Powers Procedure Act*.

Committee may adopt guidelines

(3) The Committee may adopt non-binding guidelines to assist members in interpreting and applying the Act and the regulations made under it.

Means of adoption

(4) The Committee shall adopt the rules and guidelines by simple majority, subject to the right of the Chair to veto the adoption of any rule or guideline.

Make public

(5) The Tribunal shall make its rules, guidelines and approved forms available to the public.

Transitional

(6) The Minister of Municipal Affairs and Housing may establish temporary rules of practice and procedure and guidelines for the Tribunal and those rules and guidelines shall be in force as rules and guidelines of the Tribunal until the Rules and Guidelines Committee adopts rules and guidelines for the Tribunal.

Information on rights and obligations

165. The Tribunal shall provide information to landlords and tenants about their rights and obligations under this Act.

Employees

166. Employees may be appointed for the purposes of the Tribunal in accordance with the regulations.

Professional assistance

167. The Tribunal may engage persons other than its members or employees to provide professional, technical, administrative or other assistance to the Tribunal and may establish the duties and terms of engagement and provide for the payment of the remuneration and expenses of those persons.

Annual Report

168. (1) At the end of each year, the Tribunal shall file with the Minister an annual report on its affairs.

Further reports and information

(2) The Tribunal shall make further reports and provide information to the Minister from time to time as required by the Minister.

Tabled with Assembly

(3) The Minister shall submit any reports received from the Tribunal to the Lieutenant Governor in Council and then shall table them with the Assembly if it is in session or, if not, at the next session.

169. (1) The Tribunal, subject to the approval of the Minister, may set and charge fees,

(a) for making an application under this Act or requesting a review of an order under section 21.2 of the *Statutory Powers Procedure Act*;

(b) for furnishing copies of forms, notices or documents filed with or issued by the Tribunal or otherwise in the possession of the Tribunal; or

(c) for other services provided by the Tribunal.

(2) The Tribunal may treat different kinds of applications differently in setting fees and may base fees on the number of residential units affected by an application.

(3) The Tribunal shall ensure that its fee structure is available to the public.

170. The Tribunal may refund a fee paid for requesting a review of an order under section 21.2 of the *Statutory Powers Procedure Act* if, on considering the request, the Tribunal varies, suspends or cancels the original order.

PART IX
PROCEDURE

171. The Tribunal shall adopt the most expeditious method of determining the questions arising in a proceeding that affords to all persons directly affected by the proceeding an adequate opportunity to know the issues and be heard on the matter.

172. (1) An application shall be filed with the Tribunal in the form approved by the Tribunal, shall be accompanied by the prescribed information and shall be signed by the applicant.

(2) An applicant may give an agent written authorization to sign an application and, if the applicant does so, the Tribunal may require the agent to file a copy of the authorization.

173. (1) A tenant may combine several applications into one application.

(2) Two or more tenants of a residential complex may together file an application that may be filed by a tenant if each tenant applying in the application signs it.

(3) A landlord may combine several applications relating to a given tenant into one application, so long as the landlord does not combine an application for a rent increase with any other application.

174. (1) The parties to an application are the landlord and any tenants or other persons directly affected by the application.

(2) The Tribunal may add or remove parties as the Tribunal considers appropriate.

175. (1) An applicant to the Tribunal shall give the other parties to the application a copy of the application within the time set out in the Rules.

(2) Despite the *Statutory Powers Procedure Act*, an applicant shall give a copy of any notice of hearing issued by the Tribunal in respect of an application to the other parties to the application.

(3) A party shall file with the Tribunal a certificate of service in the form approved by the Tribunal in the circumstances set out in the Rules.

176. (1) The Tribunal may extend or shorten the time requirements related to making an application under section 138 or under section 156 in accordance with the Rules.

(2) The Tribunal may extend or shorten the time requirements with respect to any matter in its proceedings, other than the prescribed time requirements, in accordance with the Rules.

177. (1) A respondent wishing to dispute the following applications must do so by filing a dispute in writing with the Tribunal:

1. An application to terminate a tenancy or to evict a person.

2. A landlord's application for arrears of rent, compensation, damages or for the payment of money as a result of misrepresentation of income.

3. A tenant's application under section 89 (compensation, overholding subtenant).

4. A tenant's application under section 144.

5. A tenant's application claiming that a landlord unreasonably withheld consent to an assignment or subletting of a rental unit.

186

(2) The time for filing a dispute shall be,

(a) in the case of an application to terminate a tenancy or to evict a person, five days after the applicant has served the notice of hearing on the respondent; and

(b) in the case of any other application, within the time provided for in the Rules.

How notice or document given

178. (1) A notice or document is sufficiently given to a person other than the Tribunal,

(a) by handing it to the person;

(b) if the person is a landlord, by handing it to an employee of the landlord exercising authority in respect of the residential complex to which the notice or document relates;

(c) if the person is a tenant, subtenant or occupant, by handing it to an apparently adult person in the rental unit;

(d) by leaving it in the mail box where mail is ordinarily delivered to the person;

(e) if there is no mail box, by leaving it at the place where mail is ordinarily delivered to the person;

(f) by sending it by mail to the last known address where the person resides or carries on business; or

(g) by any other means allowed in the Rules.

When notice deemed valid

(2) A notice or document that is not given in accordance with this section shall be deemed to have been validly given if it is proven that its contents actually came to the attention of the person for whom it was intended within the required time period.

Mail

(3) A notice or document given by mail shall be deemed to have been given on the fifth day after mailing.

How notice or document given to Tribunal

179. (1) A notice or document is sufficiently given to the Tribunal,

(a) by hand delivering it to the Tribunal at the appropriate office as set out in the Rules;

(b) by sending it by mail to the appropriate office as set out in the Rules; or

(c) by any other means allowed in the Rules.

Same

(2) A notice or document given to the Tribunal by mail shall be deemed to have been given on the earlier of the fifth day after mailing and the day on which the notice or the document was actually received.

Time

180. Time shall be computed in accordance with the Rules.

Tribunal may mediate

181. (1) The Tribunal may attempt to mediate a settlement of any matter that is the subject of an application if the parties consent to the mediation.

Settlement may override Act

(2) Despite subsection 2 (1) and subject to subsection (3), a settlement mediated under this section may contain provisions that contravene any provision under this Act.

Exception

(3) The largest rent increase that can be mediated under this section for a rental unit that is not a mobile home or a land lease home is equal to the greater of,

(a) a rent increase up to the maximum rent permitted under section 135;

(b) the sum of the guideline and 4 per cent of the previous year's lawful rent.

Successful mediation

(4) If some or all of the issues with respect to an application are successfully mediated under this section, the Tribunal shall dispose of the application in accordance with the Rules.

Hearing

(5) If there is no mediated settlement, the Tribunal shall hold a hearing.

Money paid to Tribunal

182. (1) The Tribunal may, subject to the regulations, require a respondent to pay a specified sum into the Tribunal within a specified time where the Tribunal considers it appropriate to do so.

Rules re money paid

(2) The Tribunal may establish procedures in its rules for the payment of money into and out of the Tribunal.

Refuse to consider evidence, money not paid

(3) The Tribunal may refuse to consider the evidence and submissions of a respondent if the respondent fails to pay the specified sum within the specified time.

Where Tribunal may dismiss

183. (1) The Tribunal may dismiss an application without holding a hearing or refuse to allow an application to be filed if, in the opinion of the Tribunal, the matter is friv-

olous or vexatious, has not been initiated in good faith or discloses no reasonable cause of action.

Same (2) The Tribunal may dismiss a proceeding without holding a hearing if the Tribunal finds that the applicant filed documents that the applicant knew or ought to have known contained false or misleading information.

SPPA applies **184.** (1) The *Statutory Powers Procedure Act* applies with respect to all proceedings before the Tribunal.

Exception (2) Subsections 5.1 (2) and (3) of the *Statutory Powers Procedure Act* do not apply with respect to an application under section 137 or 143 or an application solely under paragraph 1 of subsection 138 (1).

Applications joined **185.** (1) Despite the *Statutory Powers Procedures Act*, the Tribunal may direct that two or more applications be joined or heard together if the Tribunal believes it would be fair to determine the issues raised by them together.

Applications severed (2) The Tribunal may order that applications that have been joined be severed or that applications that had been ordered to be heard together be heard separately.

Amend application **186.** (1) An applicant may amend an application at any time in a proceeding on notice, with the consent of the Tribunal.

Withdraw application (2) Subject to subsection (3), an applicant may withdraw an application at any time before the hearing begins.

Same, harassment (3) An applicant may withdraw an application under paragraph 7 of subsection 32 (1) only with the consent of the Tribunal.

Same (4) An applicant may withdraw an application after the hearing begins with the consent of the Tribunal.

Other powers of Tribunal **187.** (1) The Tribunal may, before, during or after a hearing,

(a) conduct any inquiry it considers necessary or authorize an employee of the Tribunal to do so;

(b) request an inspector or an employee of the Tribunal to conduct any inspection it considers necessary;

(c) question any person, by telephone or otherwise, concerning the dispute or authorize an employee of the Tribunal to do so;

(d) permit or direct a party to file additional evidence with the Tribunal which the Tribunal considers necessary to make its decision; or

(e) view premises that are the subject of the hearing.

Same (2) In making its determination, the Tribunal may consider any relevant information obtained by the Tribunal in addition to the evidence given at the hearing, provided that it first informs the parties of the additional information and gives them an opportunity to explain or refute it.

Same (3) If a party fails to comply with a direction under clause (1) (d), the Tribunal may,

(a) refuse to consider the party's submissions and evidence respecting the matter regarding which there was a failure to comply; or,

(b) if the party who has failed to comply is the applicant, dismiss all or part of the application.

Parties may view premises with Tribunal (4) If the Tribunal intends to view premises under clause (1) (e), the Tribunal shall give the parties an opportunity to view the premises with the Tribunal.

Findings of Tribunal **188.** In making findings on an application, the Tribunal shall ascertain the real substance of all transactions and activities relating to a residential complex or a rental unit and the good faith of the participants and in doing so,

(a) may disregard the outward form of a transaction or the separate corporate existence of participants; and

(b) may have regard to the pattern of activities relating to the residential complex or the rental unit.

Correction of deemed rent **189.** In any application made under this Act in which rent for a rental unit is in issue, the Tribunal may correct an error in deeming the amount of rent, the date it took effect or the inclusion of a service in rent and may take into account the rent, the effective date or the service that ought to have been deemed if,

(a) the amount of rent or date it took effect was deemed to be lawful or the service was deemed to be included in the rent by the operation of the *Rent Control*

Act, 1992 or the *Residential Rent Regulation Act*; and

(b) the Tribunal is satisfied that an error or omission in a document filed by a landlord or tenant led to the error in the deeming.

Conditions in order 190. (1) The Tribunal may include in an order whatever conditions it considers fair in the circumstances.

Order re costs (2) The Tribunal may order a party to an application to pay the costs of another party.

Same (3) The Tribunal may order that its costs of a proceeding be paid by a party or a paid agent or counsel to a party.

Same (4) The amount of an order for costs shall be determined in accordance with the Rules.

Order payment 191. (1) The Tribunal may include in an order the following provision:

"The landlord or the tenant shall pay to the other any sum of money that is owed as a result of this order."

Payment of order by instalments (2) If the Tribunal makes an order for a rent increase above the guideline and the order is made three months or more after the first effective date of a rent increase in the order, the Tribunal may provide in the order that if a tenant owes any sum of money to the landlord as a result of the order, the tenant may pay the landlord the amount owing in monthly instalments.

Same (3) If an order made under subsection (2) permits a tenant to pay the amount owing by instalments, the tenant may do so even if the tenancy is terminated.

Same (4) An order providing for monthly instalments shall not provide for more than 12 monthly instalments.

Default orders 192. (1) The Tribunal may make an order with respect to any of the following applications without holding a hearing if the application is not disputed:

1. An application to terminate a tenancy or to evict a person, other than an application based in whole or in part on a notice of termination under section 65.

2. A landlord's application for arrears of rent, compensation, damages or for the payment of money as a result of misrepresentation of income.

3. A tenant's application under section 89 (compensation, overholding subtenant).

4. A tenant's application under section 144 (money collected illegally).

5. A tenant's application claiming that a landlord unreasonably withheld consent to an assignment or subletting of a rental unit.

Setting order aside (2) The respondent may, within 10 days after the order is issued, make a motion to the Tribunal on notice to the applicant to have the order set aside.

Same (3) An order under subsection (1) is stayed when a motion to have the order set aside is received by the Tribunal and shall not be enforced under this Act or as an order of a court during the stay.

Same (4) The Tribunal may set aside the order if satisfied that the respondent was not reasonably able to participate in the proceeding and the Tribunal shall then proceed to hear the merits of the application.

Monetary jurisdiction of Tribunal 193. (1) The Tribunal may, where it otherwise has the jurisdiction, order the payment to any given person of an amount of money up to $10,000 or the monetary jurisdiction of the Small Claims Court in the area where the residential complex is located, whichever is greater.

Same (2) A person entitled to apply under this Act but whose claim exceeds the Tribunal's monetary jurisdiction may commence a proceeding in any court of competent jurisdiction for an order requiring the payment of that sum and, if such a proceeding is commenced, the court may exercise any powers that the Tribunal could have exercised if the proceeding had been before the Tribunal and within its monetary jurisdiction.

Same (3) If a party makes a claim in an application for payment of a sum equal to or less than the Tribunal's monetary jurisdiction, all rights of the party in excess of the Tribunal's monetary jurisdiction are extinguished once the Tribunal issues its order.

Order may provide deduction from rent (4) If a landlord is ordered to pay a sum of money to a person who is a current tenant of the landlord at the time of the order, the order may provide that if the landlord fails to pay the amount owing, the tenant may recover that amount plus interest by deducting a specified sum from the tenant's rent paid to the landlord for a specified number of rental periods.

Same

(5) Nothing in subsection (4) limits the right of the tenant to collect at any time the full amount owing or any balance outstanding under the order.

Post-judgment interest

(6) The Tribunal may set a date on which payment of money ordered by the Tribunal must be made and interest shall accrue on money owing only after that date at the post-judgment interest rate under section 127 of the *Courts of Justice Act.*

Notice of decision

194. (1) The Tribunal shall send each party who participated in the proceeding, or the party's counsel or agent, a copy of its order, including the reasons if any have been given, in accordance with section 178.

Same

(2) Section 18 of the *Statutory Powers Procedure Act* does not apply to proceedings under this Act.

Order final, binding

195. Except where this Act provides otherwise, an order of the Tribunal is final, binding and not subject to review except under section 21.2 of the *Statutory Powers Procedure Act.*

Appeal rights

196. (1) Any person affected by an order of the Tribunal may appeal the order to the Divisional Court within 30 days after being given the order, but only on a question of law.

Tribunal to receive notice

(2) A person appealing an order under this section shall give to the Tribunal any documents relating to the appeal.

Tribunal may be heard by counsel

(3) The Tribunal is entitled to be heard by counsel or otherwise upon the argument on any issue in an appeal.

Powers of Court

(4) If an appeal is brought under this section, the Divisional Court shall hear and determine the appeal and may,

(a) affirm, rescind, amend or replace the decision or order; or

(b) remit the matter to the Tribunal with the opinion of the Divisional Court.

Same

(5) The Divisional Court may also make any other order in relation to the matter that it considers proper and may make any order with respect to costs that it considers proper.

Tribunal may appeal Court decision

197. The Tribunal is entitled to appeal a decision of the Divisional Court on an appeal of a Tribunal order as if the Tribunal were a party to the appeal.

Substantial compliance sufficient

198. Substantial compliance with this Act respecting the contents of forms, notices or documents is sufficient.

Contingency fees, limitation

199. (1) No agent who represents a landlord or a tenant in a proceeding under this Act or who assists a landlord or tenant in a matter arising under this Act shall charge or take a fee based on a proportion of any amount which has been or may be recovered, gained or saved, in whole or in part, through the efforts of the agent, where the proportion exceeds the prescribed amount.

Same

(2) An agreement that provides for a fee prohibited by subsection (1) is void.

PART X
GENERAL

ADMINISTRATION AND ENFORCEMENT

Duties of Minister

200. The Minister shall,

(a) monitor compliance with this Act;

(b) investigate cases of alleged failure to comply with this Act; and

(c) where the circumstances warrant, commence or cause to be commenced proceedings with respect to alleged failures to comply with this Act.

Delegation

201. The Minister may in writing delegate to any person any power or duty vested in the Minister under this Act, subject to the conditions set out in the delegation.

Investigators and inspectors

202. The Minister may appoint investigators for the purpose of investigating alleged offences and inspectors for the purposes of sections 154 and 155.

Inspection powers of inspector, investigator

203. (1) Subject to subsection (6), an inspector or investigator may, at all reasonable times and upon producing proper identification, enter any property for the purpose of carrying out his or her duty under this Act and may,

(a) require the production for inspection of documents or things, including drawings or specifications, that may be relevant to the inspection or investigation;

(b) inspect and remove documents or things relevant to the inspection or investigation for the purpose of making copies or extracts;

(c) require information from any person concerning a matter related to the inspection or investigation;

(d) be accompanied by a person who has special or expert knowledge in relation to the subject matter of the inspection or investigation;

(e) alone or in conjunction with a person possessing special or expert knowledge, make examinations or take tests, samples or photographs necessary for the purposes of the inspection or investigation; and

(f) order the landlord to take and supply at the landlord's expense such tests and samples as are specified in the order.

Samples (2) The inspector or investigator shall divide the sample taken under clause (1) (e) into two parts and deliver one part to the person from whom the sample is taken, if the person so requests at the time the sample is taken and provides the necessary facilities.

Same (3) If an inspector or investigator takes a sample under clause (1) (e) and has not divided the sample into two parts, a copy of any report on the sample shall be given to the person from whom the sample was taken.

Receipt (4) An inspector or investigator shall provide a receipt for any documents or things removed under clause (1) (b) and shall promptly return them after the copies or extracts are made.

Evidence (5) Copies of or extracts from documents and things removed under this section and certified as being true copies of or extracts from the originals by the person who made them are admissible in evidence to the same extent as and have the same evidentiary value as the originals.

Where warrant required (6) Except under the authority of a warrant issued under section 204, an inspector or investigator shall not enter any room or place actually used as a dwelling without requesting and obtaining the consent of the occupier, first having informed the occupier that the right of entry may be refused and entry made only under the authority of a warrant.

Warrant 204. (1) A provincial judge or justice of the peace may at any time issue a warrant in the prescribed form authorizing a person named in the warrant to enter and search a building, receptacle or place if the provincial judge or justice of the peace is satisfied by information on oath that there are reasonable grounds to believe that an offence has been committed under this Act and the entry and search will afford evidence relevant to the commission of the offence.

Seizure (2) In a warrant, the provincial judge or justice of the peace may authorize the person named in the warrant to seize anything that, based on reasonable grounds, will afford evidence relevant to the commission of the offence.

Receipt and removal (3) Anyone who seizes something under a warrant shall,

(a) give a receipt for the thing seized to the person from whom it was seized; and

(b) bring the thing seized before the provincial judge or justice of the peace issuing the warrant or another provincial judge or justice to be dealt with according to law.

Expiry (4) A warrant shall name the date upon which it expires, which shall be not later than 15 days after the warrant is issued.

Time of execution (5) A warrant shall be executed between 6 a.m. and 9 p.m. unless it provides otherwise.

Other matters (6) Sections 159 and 160 of the *Provincial Offences Act* apply with necessary modifications with respect to any thing seized under this section.

Protection from personal liability 205. (1) No proceeding for damages shall be commenced against an investigator, an inspector, a member of the Tribunal, a lawyer for the Tribunal or an officer or employee of the Ministry or the Tribunal for any act done in good faith in the performance or intended performance of any duty or in the exercise or intended exercise of any power under this Act or for any neglect or default in the performance or exercise in good faith of such a duty or power.

Crown liability (2) Despite subsections 5 (2) and (4) of the *Proceedings Against the Crown Act*, subsection (1) does not relieve the Crown of any liability to which it would otherwise be subject in respect of a tort committed by an investigator, an inspector, a member of the Tribunal, a lawyer for the Tribunal or an officer or employee of the Ministry or the Tribunal.

Offences   **206.** (1) Any person who knowingly does any of the following is guilty of an offence:

1. Restrict reasonable access to the residential complex by political candidates or their authorized representatives in contravention of section 22.

2. Alter or cause to be altered the locking system on any door giving entry to a rental unit or the residential complex in a manner that contravenes section 23.

3. Withhold reasonable supply of a vital service, care service or food or deliberately interfere with the supply in contravention of section 25.

4. Harass, hinder, obstruct or interfere with a tenant in the exercise of,

    i. securing a right or seeking relief under this Act or in the court,

    ii. participating in a proceeding under this Act, or

    iii. participating in a tenants' association or attempting to organize a tenants' association.

5. Harass, coerce, threaten or interfere with a tenant in such a manner that the tenant is induced to vacate the rental unit.

6. Harass, hinder, obstruct or interfere with a landlord in the exercise of,

    i. securing a right or seeking relief under this Act or in the court, or

    ii. participating in a proceeding under this Act.

7. Seize any property of the tenant in contravention of section 31.

8. Obtain possession of a rental unit improperly by giving a notice to terminate in bad faith.

9. Fail to afford a tenant a right of first refusal in contravention of section 54 or 56.

10. Recover possession of a rental unit without complying with the requirements of sections 55, 57 and 58.

11. Coerce a tenant of a mobile home park or land lease community to enter into an agency agreement for the sale or lease of their mobile home or land lease home or to require an agency agreement as a condition of entering into a tenancy agreement.

12. Coerce a tenant to sign an agreement referred to in section 130.

Same   (2) Any person who does any of the following is guilty of an offence:

1. Furnish false or misleading information in any document filed in any proceeding under this Act or provided to an inspector, investigator, the Minister, a delegate of the Minister or any employee or official of the Tribunal.

2. Enter a rental unit where such entry is not permitted by section 20, 21 or 94 or enter without first complying with the requirements of section 20, 21 or 94.

3. Contravene an order of the Tribunal under paragraph 4 of subsection 34 (1) or clause 35 (1) (a).

4. Unlawfully recover possession of a rental unit.

5. Give a notice to terminate a tenancy under section 51 or 52 in contravention of section 54.

6. Give a notice of rent increase or a notice of increase of a charge in a care home without first giving an information package contrary to section 92.

7. Increase a charge for providing a care service or meals to a tenant in a care home in contravention of section 101.

8. Interfere with a tenant's right under section 105 to sell or lease his or her mobile home.

9. Restrict the right of a tenant of a mobile home park or land lease community to purchase goods or services from the person of his or her choice in contravention of section 109.

192

10. Require or receive a security deposit from a tenant contrary to section 117.

11. Fail to pay to the tenant annually interest on the rent deposit held in respect of their tenancy in accordance with subsection 118 (6).

12. Fail to apply the rent deposit held in respect of a tenancy to the rent for the last month of the tenancy in contravention of subsection 118 (8).

13. Fail to provide a tenant with a receipt in accordance with section 120.

14. Charge rent in an amount greater than permitted under the Act.

15. Require a tenant to pay rent proposed in an application in contravention of subsection 138 (4).

16. Charge or collect amounts from a tenant, a prospective tenant, a subtenant, a potential subtenant, an assignee or a potential assignee in contravention of section 140.

17. Fail to comply with any or all of the items contained in a work order issued under section 155.

18. Charge an illegal contingency fee in contravention of subsection 199 (1).

19. Obstruct or interfere with an inspector or investigator exercising a power of entry under section 203.

Same (3) Any landlord or superintendent, agent or employee of the landlord who knowingly harasses a tenant or interferes with a tenant's reasonable enjoyment of a rental unit or the residential complex in which it is located is guilty of an offence.

Same (4) Any person who knowingly attempts to commit any offence referred to in subsection (1), (2) or (3) is guilty of an offence.

Same (5) Every director or officer of a corporation who knowingly concurs in an offence is guilty of an offence.

Same (6) A person, other than a corporation, who is guilty of an offence under this section is liable on conviction to a fine of not more than $10,000.

Same (7) A corporation that is guilty of an offence under this section is liable on conviction to a fine of not more than $50,000.

Limitation (8) No proceeding shall be commenced respecting an offence under paragraph 1 of subsection (2) more than two years after the date on which the facts giving rise to the offence came to the attention of the Minister.

Same (9) No proceeding shall be commenced respecting any other offence under this section more than two years after the date on which the offence was, or is alleged to have been, committed.

Proof of filed documents **207.** (1) The production by a person prosecuting a person for an offence under this Act of a certificate, statement or document that appears to have been filed with or delivered to the Tribunal by or on behalf of the person charged with the offence shall be received as evidence that the certificate, statement or document was so filed or delivered.

Proof of making (2) The production by a person prosecuting a person for an offence under this Act of a certificate, statement or document that appears to have been made or signed by the person charged with the offence or on the person's behalf shall be received as evidence that the certificate, statement or document was so made or signed.

REGULATIONS

Regulations **208.** (1) The Lieutenant Governor in Council may make regulations,

1. prescribing services that are to be included or not included in the definition of care services in subsection 1 (1);

2. prescribing charges not to be included in the definition of "municipal taxes and charges" in subsection 1 (1);

3. prescribing circumstances under which one or more rental units that form part of a residential complex, rather than the entire residential complex, are care homes for the purposes of the definition of "care home" in subsection 1 (1);

4. providing that specified provisions of this Act do not apply with respect to specified classes of accommodation;

5. prescribing classes of accommodation for the purposes of clause 3 (m);

6. prescribing grounds of an application for the purposes of clause 7 (1) (b);

7. respecting the rules for making findings for the purposes of subsection 7 (2);

8. prescribing the information that shall be contained in an information package for the purposes of section 92;

9. prescribing rules for determining the amount by which rent charged to a new tenant may exceed the last lawful rent charged for the purposes of section 114;

10. prescribing services and things for the purposes of section 116;

11. prescribing rules for calculating the lawful rent which may be charged where a landlord provides a tenant with a discount in rent at the beginning of, or during, a tenancy and the rules may differ for different types of discounts;

12. prescribing rules for the calculation of lawful rent where the rent a landlord charges for the first rental period of a tenancy is greater than the rent the landlord charges for any subsequent rental period;

13. prescribing the circumstances under which lawful rent for the purposes of section 123 will be other than that provided for in section 123 and providing the lawful rent under those circumstances;

14. prescribing the Table setting out the weights and operating costs categories needed to calculate the guideline;

15. respecting rules for increasing or decreasing rent charged for the purposes of sections 132 and 134;

16. prescribing services, facilities, privileges, accommodations and things for the purposes of paragraph 2 of subsection 132 (1);

17. prescribing rules with respect to making findings in an order under section 138 and prescribing time periods during which rent increases may be taken;

18. prescribing the rules for phasing in of an increase in rent for the purposes of subsection 138 (10);

19. prescribing rules for the purposes of section 139;

20. exempting specified payments from the operation of section 140;

21. prescribing the rules for making findings for the purposes of subsection 142 (3);

22. prescribing the rules for making findings for the purposes of subsection 143 (2) and for determining the effective date for an order under section 143;

23. prescribing maintenance standards for the purposes of section 154;

24. prescribing other criteria for determining areas in which maintenance standards apply for the purposes of subsection 154 (1);

25. respecting the amount or the determination of the amount the Minister may charge a municipality for the purposes of subsection 154 (4), including payments to inspectors, overhead costs related to inspections and interest on overdue accounts;

26. prescribing information to be filed with an application to the Tribunal;

27. respecting the appointment, including the status, duties and benefits, of employees of the Tribunal for the purposes of section 166;

28. restricting the circumstances in which the Tribunal may, under section 182, require a respondent to make a payment into the Tribunal;

29. governing the management and investment of money paid into the Tribunal, providing for the payment of interest on money paid into the Tribunal and fixing the rate of interest so paid;

30. prescribing an amount for the purposes of subsection 199 (1);

31. prescribing the form of a search warrant for the purposes of section 204;

194

32. prescribing any matter required or permitted by this Act to be prescribed;

33. defining any word or expression used in this Act that has not already been expressly defined in this Act.

Same

(2) A regulation made under subsection (1) may be general or particular in its application.

PART XI
MISCELLANEOUS

AMENDMENTS, REPEALS AND TRANSITIONAL PROVISIONS RELATED TO RESIDENTIAL TENANCIES

Condominium Act

209. Subsection 51 (7) of the *Condominium Act*, as amended by the Statutes of Ontario, 1993, chapter 27, Schedule, is further amended by striking out "*Landlord and Tenant Act*" in the seventh and eighth lines and substituting "*Tenant Protection Act, 1997*".

Consumer Reporting Act

210. Subclause 8 (1) (d) (ii) of the French version of the *Consumer Reporting Act* is amended by striking out "d'un bail" in the third line and substituting "d'une convention de location".

Co-operative Corporations Act

211. (1) Subsection 171.7 (1) of the *Co-operative Corporations Act*, as enacted by the Statutes of Ontario, 1992, chapter 19, section 23, is amended by striking out "*Landlord and Tenant Act*" at the beginning and substituting "*Tenant Protection Act, 1997* the *Commercial Tenancies Act*".

(2) Subsection 171.7 (2) of the Act, as enacted by the Statutes of Ontario, 1992, chapter 19, section 23, is amended by striking out "*Landlord and Tenant Act*" in the second line and substituting "*Commercial Tenancies Act* or the *Tenant Protection Act, 1997*".

Human Rights Code

212. (1) Section 21 of the *Human Rights Code* is amended by adding the following subsection:

Prescribing business practices

(3) The right under section 2 to equal treatment with respect to the occupancy of residential accommodation without discrimination is not infringed if a landlord uses in the manner prescribed under this Act income information, credit checks, credit references, rental history, guarantees or other similar business practices which are prescribed in the regulations made under this Act in selecting prospective tenants.

(2) Section 48 of the Act, as amended by the Statutes of Ontario, 1994, chapter 27, section 65, is further amended by adding the following clause:

(a.1) prescribing the manner in which income information, credit checks, credit references, rental history, guarantees or other similar business practices may be used by a landlord in selecting prospective tenants without infringing section 2, and prescribing other similar business practices and the manner of their use, for the purposes of subsection 21 (3).

Landlord and Tenant Act

213. (1) The definition of "care services" in section 1 of the *Landlord and Tenant Act*, as enacted by the Statutes of Ontario, 1994, chapter 2, section 1, is repealed.

(2) The definition of "residential premises" in section 1 of the Act, as amended by the Statutes of Ontario, 1994, chapter 2, section 1 and 1994, chapter 4, section 1, is repealed.

(3) Section 2 of the Act, as amended by the Statutes of Ontario, 1992, chapter 19, section 25, is repealed and the following substituted:

Application

2. This Act does not apply to tenancies and tenancy agreements to which the *Tenant Protection Act, 1997* applies.

(4) Part IV of the Act is repealed.

(5) The title of the Act is repealed and the following substituted:

COMMERCIAL TENANCIES ACT

Land Titles Act

214. Paragraph 13 of subsection 44 (1) of the *Land Titles Act* is repealed.

Mortgages Act

215. (1) Section 27 of the *Mortgages Act*, as amended by the Statutes of Ontario, 1991, chapter 6, section 1, is further amended by striking out "Fifthly, in payment to the tenants of the mortgagor of the security deposits paid under section 82 of the *Landlord and Tenant Act* where the security deposit was not applied in payment for the last rent period." where it occurs and substituting "Fifthly, in payment to the tenants of the mortgagor of

the rent deposits paid under section 118 of the *Tenant Protection Act, 1997* where the rent deposit was not applied in payment for the last rent period".

(2) The definitions of "landlord", "residential premises", "tenancy agreement" and "tenant" in section 44 of the Act, as enacted by the Statutes of Ontario, 1991, chapter 6, section 2, are repealed and the following substituted:

"landlord" has the same meaning as in section 1 (1) of the *Tenant Protection Act, 1997*; ("locateur")

"rental unit" has the same meaning as in subsection 1 (1) of the *Tenant Protection Act, 1997*; ("logement locatif")

"residential complex" has the same meaning as in subsection 1 (1) of the *Tenant Protection Act, 1997*. ("ensemble d'habitation")

"tenancy agreement" has the same meaning as in section 1 (1) of the *Tenant Protection Act, 1997*; ("convention de location")

"tenant" has the same meaning as in section 1 (1) of the *Tenant Protection Act, 1997*. ("locataire")

(3) Section 45 of the Act, as enacted by the Statutes of Ontario, 1991, chapter 6, section 2, is repealed and the following substituted:

Single family home

45. (1) For purposes of this Part, a single family home is a residential complex that consists of a single dwelling unit or a primary dwelling unit and not more than two subsidiary dwelling units and that is not subject to a tenancy agreement when the mortgage is registered.

Duplexes or triplexes

(2) A residential complex that is a duplex or a triplex is not a single family home.

When number of units determined

(3) In deciding whether a residential complex qualifies as a single family home, the number of subsidiary units shall be the number that existed when the default under the mortgage occurred.

Definition

(4) For purposes of this section, "subsidiary dwelling unit" means,

(a) an apartment or a subsidiary residential unit, including premises whose occu-

pant or occupants are required to share a bathroom or kitchen facility with the owner, the owner's spouse, child or parent or the spouse's child or parent, where the owner, spouse, child or parent lives in the building in which the premises are located;

(b) a room or other subsidiary unit that is rented for residential purposes, including one that is rented to a member of the mortgagor's family or to an employee of the mortgagor.

(4) Clauses 46 (3) (a) and (b) of the Act, as enacted by the Statutes of Ontario, 1991, chapter 6, section 2, are repealed and the following substituted:

(a) tenancies of residential units and tenancy agreements whether entered into before or after the 13th day of June, 1991;

(b) mortgages, whether registered before or after the tenancy agreement was entered into, or the 13th day of June, 1991.

(5) Subsection 47 (1) of the Act, as enacted by the Statutes of Ontario, 1991, chapter 6, section 3, is repealed and the following substituted:

Person deemed to be landlord

(1) A person who becomes the mortgagee in possession of a mortgaged residential complex which is the subject of a tenancy agreement between the mortgagor and a tenant or who obtains title to the residential complex by foreclosure or power of sale shall be deemed to be the landlord under the tenancy agreement.

(6) Subsection 47 (2) of the French version of the Act, as enacted by the Statutes of Ontario, 1991, chapter 6, section 3, is amended by striking out "du bail" in the second line and substituting "de la convention de location".

(7) Subsection 47 (3) of the Act, as enacted by the Statutes of Ontario, 1991, chapter 6, section 3, is repealed and the following substituted:

Person deemed to be landlord

(3) A person who is deemed to be a landlord is subject to the tenancy agreement and to the provisions of the *Tenant Protection Act, 1997* which apply to residential complex.

(8) Subsection 47 (4) of the French version of the Act, as enacted by the Statutes of Ontario, 1991, chapter 6, section 3, is amended by

striking out "du bail" in the second line and substituting "de la convention de location".

(9) Subsection 48 (1) of the Act, as enacted by the Statutes of Ontario, 1991, chapter 6, section 3, is repealed and the following substituted:

Possession (1) No person exercising rights under a mortgage may obtain possession of a rental unit from the mortgagor's tenant except in accordance with the *Tenant Protection Act, 1997.*

(10) Subsections 50 (1), (2) and (3) of the Act, as enacted by the Statutes of Ontario, 1991, chapter 6, section 3, are repealed and the following substituted:

Mortgagee's rights after default (1) Despite section 42, a mortgagee may at any time after the default under a mortgage on a residential complex make inquiries of the mortgagor regarding the existence of any tenancy agreement and require the mortgagor to provide a list of tenants, if any.

Same (2) Despite section 42, a mortgagee at any time after default under a mortgage on a residential complex which is the subject of a tenancy agreement may,

(a) enter into the common areas of the residential complex for the purpose of inspection;

(b) demand production from the mortgagor or the mortgagor's tenant of a copy of the tenancy agreement if it is written; and

(c) demand from the mortgagor or the mortgagor's tenant any particulars of the tenancy agreement.

Mortgagee not deemed mortgagee in possession (3) The mortgagee does not become a mortgagee in possession of the residential complex by any of the acts described in subsection (1) or (2).

(11) Subsection 50 (5) of the Act, as enacted by the Statutes of Ontario, 1991, chapter 6, section 3, is amended by striking out "premises" at the end and substituting "complex".

(12) Subsection 51 (1) of the Act, as enacted by the Statutes of Ontario, 1991, chapter 6, section 3, is repealed and the following substituted:

Mortgagee not to interfere (1) No mortgagee or person acting on behalf of the mortgagee shall,

(a) deliberately interfere with a reasonable supply of any service, such as heat, fuel, electricity, gas, food or water to a rental unit or to the residential complex in which it is located, whether or not it was the mortgagor's obligation to supply the service; or

(b) substantially interfere with the reasonable enjoyment of the rental unit or of the residential complex in which it is located for all the usual purposes by the mortgagor's tenant or household with the intent of causing the mortgagor's tenant to give up possession of the rental unit or to refrain from asserting any rights under this Act, the tenancy agreement or the *Tenant Protection Act, 1997.*

(13) Subsection 52 (1) of the Act, as enacted by the Statutes of Ontario, 1991, chapter 6, section 3, is repealed and the following substituted:

Application to set aside tenancy (1) The Ontario Court (General Division) may on application by the mortgagee vary or set aside a tenancy agreement, or any of its provisions, entered into by the mortgagor in contemplation of or after default under the mortgage with the object of,

(a) discouraging the mortgagee from taking possession of the residential complex on default; or

(b) adversely affecting the value of the mortgagee's interest in the residential complex.

(14) Section 53 of the Act, as enacted by the Statutes of Ontario, 1991, chapter 6, section 4, is amended as follows:

1. Subsections (1) and (2) are repealed and the following substituted:

Termination of tenancy (1) A person described in subsection 47 (1) may obtain, under section 51 of the *Tenant Protection Act, 1997,* possession of a single family home that is the subject of a tenancy agreement in the circumstances described in this section.

Possession on behalf of purchaser (2) When a person described in subsection 47 (1) has entered into a binding agreement for the purchase and sale of a single family home, the person may obtain possession of it on behalf of a purchaser who on closing would be entitled to give notice of termination under section 51 of the *Tenant Protection Act, 1997*.

2. Subsection (5) is amended by striking out "97 of the *Landlord and Tenant Act*" in the second and third lines and substituting "43 of the *Tenant Protection Act, 1997*".

3. Subsection (6) is amended by striking out "110 of the *Landlord and Tenant Act*" in the third line and substituting "51 of the *Tenant Protection Act, 1997*".

4. Subsection (7) is repealed and the following substituted:

Order for termination of tenancy

(7) A person who has served notice may apply for an order terminating the tenancy and evicting the tenant under section 69 of the *Tenant Protection Act, 1997*.

(15) Section 55 of the French version of the Act, as enacted by the Statutes of Ontario, 1991, chapter 6, section 4, is amended by striking out "d'un bail" in the fourth line and substituting "d'une convention de location".

(16) Section 56 of the French version of the Act, as enacted by the Statutes of Ontario, 1991, chapter 6, section 5, is amended by striking out "le bail" in the last line and substituting "la convention de location".

(17) Section 57 of the Act, as enacted by the Statutes of Ontario, 1991, chapter 6, section 5, is amended by striking out "section 123 of the *Landlord and Tenant Act*" at the end and substituting "section 178 of the *Tenant Protection Act, 1997*".

Municipal Act

216. Sections 210.2 and 210.3 of the *Municipal Act*, as enacted by the Statutes of Ontario, 1994, chapter 7, section 1, are repealed.

Ontario Home Ownership Savings Plan Act

217. Subsection 5 (4) of the *Ontario Home Ownership Savings Plan Act* is amended by adding "and" at the end of clause (b) and by repealing clauses (d) and (e).

Rent Control Act, 1992

218. The *Rent Control Act, 1992* is repealed.

Rental Housing Protection Act

219. The *Rental Housing Protection Act* is repealed.

Residential Complex Sales Representation Act

220. The definition of "residential complex" in section 1 of the *Residential Complex Sales Representation Act* is amended by striking out "Part IV of the *Landlord and Tenant Act*" at the end and substituting "the *Tenant Protection Act, 1997*".

Settled Estates Act

221. (1) Paragraph 5 of subsection 2 (1) of the *Settled Estates Act* is amended by striking out "*Landlord and Tenant Act*" at the end and substituting "*Commercial Tenancies Act*".

(2) Subsection 32 (6) of the Act is amended by striking out "*Landlord and Tenant Act*" at the end and substituting "*Commercial Tenancies Act*".

Toronto Islands Residential Community Stewardship Act, 1993

222. (1) Subsection 9 (20) of the *Toronto Islands Residential Community Stewardship Act, 1993* is repealed and the following substituted:

No lease

(20) Despite this section, no lease and no tenancy agreement within the meaning of the *Tenant Protection Act, 1997* shall exist between the protected occupant and the Province of Ontario, the Trust or the owner.

(2) Subsection 28 (5) of the Act is repealed and the following substituted:

No lease

(5) Despite subsection (2), no lease and no tenancy agreement within the meaning of the *Tenant Protection Act, 1997* shall exist between the occupant of the house and the Province of Ontario, the Trust or the owner.

(3) Subsection 33 (1) of the Act, as re-enacted by the Statutes of Ontario, 1996, chapter 15, section 21, is repealed and the following substituted:

Conflicts

(1) This Act prevails in the event of a conflict between it and the *Assessment Act*, the *Building Code Act, 1992*, the *Commercial Tenancies Act*, the *Family Law Act*, the *Mortgages Act*, the *Municipal Tax Sales Act*, the *Tenant Protection Act, 1997* or the *Succession Law Reform Act*.

TRANSITIONAL

Transitional provisions

223. (1) Despite the prior repeal of the *Residential Rent Regulation Act*, that Act shall be deemed to be continued in force for the purpose only of continuing and finally disposing of the following matters:

1. An application made under that Act before August 10, 1992.

2. An appeal or review of an order made under that Act.

3. A court proceeding to which the Minister or the Rent Review Hearings Board is a party if the proceeding was commenced before August 10, 1992.

4. A court proceeding referred to in subsection 13 (5) of that Act.

(2) Despite the repeal of the *Rent Control Act, 1992*, that Act shall be deemed to be continued in force for the purpose only of continuing and finally disposing of the following matters:

1. An application made under that Act before the day this section is proclaimed in force.

2. An appeal or reconsideration of an order made under that Act.

3. A court proceeding to which the Minister, the Director, the Registrar or a rent officer is a party if the proceeding was commenced before the day this section is proclaimed in force.

4. A court proceeding in which the sum claimed exceeds the monetary jurisdiction referred to in section 30 of that Act.

5. The filing of notices of intent and the issuing of notices of carry forward under section 22 of that Act.

6. A written complaint received by the Director under section 36 of that Act.

7. The staying of orders made under section 38 of that Act and the lifting of those stays.

(3) Despite the repeal of the *Rent Control Act, 1992*, a notice of rent increase or a notice of increased charges in a care home prescribed under that Act may be used for the purposes of this Act any time within two months after this subsection comes into force.

(4) Any outstanding matter in a proceeding commenced before the day this section comes into force that would have been determined by the Minister or the Rent Review Hearings Board under the *Residential Rent Regulation Act* or by a rent officer under the *Rent Con-*

trol Act, 1992 shall be determined by the Tribunal unless the hearing has already commenced before the day this subsection comes into force.

(5) An order issued under section 38 of the *Rent Control Act, 1992* or section 15 of the *Residential Rent Regulation Act* shall remain in force with respect to a rental unit until:

(a) the work order which resulted in the order is lifted by the authority which issued the work order;

(b) the work order which resulted in the order is quashed or rescinded on appeal; or

(c) the tenant who is the tenant when this subsection comes into force or an assignee under section 17 of that tenant, is no longer the tenant of the rental unit.

(6) All orders issued under section 43 of the *Rent Control Act, 1992* or section 66 of the *Residential Rent Regulation Act* are void on the day this subsection comes into force.

(7) All work orders issued under section 37 of the *Rent Control Act, 1992* or subsection 16 (4) of the *Residential Rent Regulation Act* shall be deemed to be work orders issued under section 155 of this Act and may be lifted by an inspector where the inspector is satisfied that the work order has been complied with.

(8) Despite the repeal of Part IV of the *Landlord and Tenant Act*, that Part shall be deemed to be continued in force for the purpose only of continuing and finally disposing of any applications commenced before the day this subsection comes into force, including any appeals with respect to those applications.

(9) Despite the repeal of Part IV of the *Landlord and Tenant Act*, a notice of termination prescribed under that Act may be used for the purposes of this Act any time within two months after this subsection comes into force.

(10) Despite the repeal of the *Rental Housing Protection Act*, that Act shall be deemed to be continued in force for the purpose only of continuing and finally disposing of any proceedings commenced before the day this sub-

section comes into force, including any appeals with respect to those proceedings.

(11) Sections 54, 55, 57, 58 and 59 of this Act do not apply where a landlord has obtained approval from the municipality under the *Rental Housing Protection Act* with respect to the activities referred to in those sections.

AMENDMENTS AND REPEALS RELATED TO MUNICIPAL PROPERTY STANDARDS BY-LAWS

Building Code Act, 1992
224. (1) The definitions of "Minister" and "municipality" in subsection 1 (1) of the *Building Code Act, 1992* are repealed and the following substituted:

"Minister" means the Minister of Municipal Affairs and Housing; ("ministre")

"municipality" means a city, town, village or township. ("municipalité")

(2) Subsection 1 (1) of the Act is amended by adding the following definition:

"officer" means a property standards officer who has been assigned the responsibility of administering and enforcing by-laws passed under section 15.1. ("agent")

(3) Section 1 of the Act is amended by adding the following subsections:

Interpretation
(1.1) Except as provided in subsection (1.2), a reference to "this Act" in any provision of this Act shall be deemed to be a reference to this Act excluding sections 15.1 to 15.8.

Same
(1.2) A reference to "this Act" in subsection 1 (1) and sections 2, 16, 19, 20, 21, 27, 31, 36 and 37 includes a reference to sections 15.1 to 15.8.

(4) Subsection 2 (2) of the Act, as amended by the Statutes of Ontario, 1993, chapter 27, Schedule, is repealed and the following substituted:

Director
(2) There shall be a director of the Housing Development and Buildings Branch who shall be appointed by the Lieutenant Governor in Council.

(5) Subsection 4 (6) of the Act is amended by striking out "The Deputy Minister of Housing" at the beginning and substituting "The Deputy Minister of Municipal Affairs and Housing".

(6) Subsection 8 (7) of the Act is amended by striking out "municipal taxes" in the sixth line and in the tenth line and substituting in each case "municipal real property taxes".

(7) Subsection 15 (9) of the Act is amended by striking out "municipal taxes" in the fifth and sixth lines and in the ninth line and substituting in each case "municipal real property taxes".

(8) The Act is amended by adding the following sections:

Definitions
15.1 (1) In sections 15.1 to 15.8 inclusive,

"committee" means a property standards committee established under section 15.6; ("comité")

"occupant" means any person or persons over the age of 18 years in possession of the property; ("occupant")

"owner" includes,

(a) the person for the time being managing or receiving the rent of the land or premises in connection with which the word is used, whether on the person's own account or as agent or trustee of any other person, or who would receive the rent if the land and premises were let, and

(b) a lessee or occupant of the property who, under the terms of a lease, is required to repair and maintain the property in accordance with the standards for the maintenance and occupancy of property; ("propriétaire")

"property" means a building or structure or part of a building or structure, and includes the lands and premises appurtenant thereto and all mobile homes, mobile buildings, mobile structures, outbuildings, fences and erections thereon whether heretofore or hereafter erected, and includes vacant property; ("bien")

"repair" includes the provision of facilities, the making of additions or alterations or the taking of any other action that may be required to ensure that a property conforms with the standards established in a by-law passed under this section. ("réparation")

Adoption of policy
(2) Where there is no official plan in effect in a municipality, the council of a municipality may, by by-law approved by the Minister, adopt a policy statement containing provisions relating to property conditions.

Standards for maintenance and occupancy
(3) The council of a municipality may pass a by-law to do the following things if an official plan that includes provisions relating to property conditions is in effect in the municipality or if the council of the municipality

has adopted a policy statement as mentioned in subsection (2):

1. Prescribing standards for the maintenance and occupancy of property within the municipality or within any defined area or areas and for prohibiting the occupancy or use of such property that does not conform with the standards.

2. Requiring property that does not conform with the standards to be repaired and maintained to conform with the standards or the site to be cleared of all buildings, structures, debris or refuse and left in graded and levelled condition.

No distinction on the basis of relationship (4) The authority to pass a by-law under subsection (3) does not include the authority to pass a by-law that sets out requirements, standards or prohibitions that have the effect of distinguishing between persons who are related and persons who are unrelated in respect of the occupancy or use of a property, including the occupancy or use as a single housekeeping unit.

Provision of no effect (5) A provision in a by-law is of no effect to the extent that it contravenes the restrictions described in subsection (4).

Inspection of property without warrant 15.2 (1) Where a by-law under section 15.1 is in effect, an officer may, upon producing proper identification, enter upon any property at any reasonable time without a warrant for the purpose of inspecting the property to determine,

(a) whether the property conforms with the standards prescribed in the by-law; or

(b) whether an order made under subsection (2) has been complied with.

Contents of order (2) An officer who finds that a property does not conform with any of the standards prescribed in a by-law passed under section 15.1 may make an order,

(a) stating the municipal address or the legal description of the property;

(b) giving reasonable particulars of the repairs to be made or stating that the site is to be cleared of all buildings, structures, debris or refuse and left in a graded and levelled condition;

(c) indicating the time for complying with the terms and conditions of the order

and giving notice that, if the repair or clearance is not carried out within that time, the municipality may carry out the repair or clearance at the owner's expense; and

(d) indicating the final date for giving notice of appeal from the order.

Service and posting of order (3) The order shall be served on the owner of the property and such other persons affected by it as the officer determines and a copy of the order may be posted on the property.

Registration of order (4) The order may be registered in the proper land registry office and, upon such registration, any person acquiring any interest in the land subsequent to the registration of the order shall be deemed to have been served with the order on the day on which the order was served under subsection (3) and, when the requirements of the order have been satisfied, the clerk of the municipality shall forthwith register in the proper land registry office a certificate that such requirements have been satisfied, which shall operate as a discharge of the order.

Appeal of order 15.3 (1) An owner or occupant who has been served with an order made under subsection 15.2 (2) and who is not satisfied with the terms or conditions of the order may appeal to the committee by sending a notice of appeal by registered mail to the secretary of the committee within 14 days after being served with the order.

Confirmation of order (2) An order that is not appealed within the time referred to in subsection (1) shall be deemed to be confirmed.

Powers of committee on appeal (3) If an appeal is taken, the committee shall hear the appeal and shall have all the powers and functions of the officer who made the order and may,

(a) confirm, modify or rescind the order to demolish or repair;

(b) extend the time for complying with the order if, in the committee's opinion, the general intent and purpose of the by-law and of the official plan or policy statement are maintained.

Appeal to Ontario Court (4) The municipality in which the property is situate or any owner or occupant or person affected by a decision under subsection (3) may appeal to a judge of the Ontario Court (General Division) by notifying the clerk of the corporation in writing and by applying to the Ontario Court (General Division) for an appointment within 14 days after the sending of a copy of the decision.

Appointment (5) A judge of the Ontario Court (General Division) shall appoint, in writing, a time and place for the hearing of the appeal and may direct in the appointment the manner in which and upon whom the appointment is to be served.

Judge's powers (6) On the appeal, the judge has the same powers and functions as the committee.

Effect of decisions (7) An order that is deemed to be confirmed under subsection (2) or that is confirmed or modified by the committee under subsection (3) or a judge under subsection (6), as the case may be, shall be final and binding upon the owner and occupant who shall carry out the repair or demolition within the time and in the manner specified in the order.

Power of municipality 15.4 (1) If an order of an officer under section 15.2 (2) is not complied with in accordance with the order as deemed confirmed or as confirmed or modified by the committee or a judge, the municipality may cause the property to be repaired or demolished accordingly.

Warrantless entry (2) For the purpose of subsection (1), employees or agents of the municipality may enter the property at any reasonable time without a warrant in order to repair or demolish the property.

No liability (3) Despite subsection 31 (2), a municipal corporation or a person acting on its behalf is not liable to compensate the owner, occupant or any other person by reason of anything done by or on behalf of the municipality in the reasonable exercise of its powers under subsection (1).

Municipal lien (4) The municipality shall have a lien on the land for the amount spent on the repair or demolition under subsection (1) and the amount shall be deemed to be municipal real property taxes and may be added by the clerk of the municipality to the collector's roll and collected in the same manner and with the same priorities as municipal real property taxes.

Certificate of compliance 15.5 (1) An officer who, after inspecting a property, is of the opinion that the property is in compliance with the standards established in a by-law passed under section 15.1 may issue a certificate of compliance to the owner.

Request for certificate (2) An officer shall issue a certificate to an owner who requests one and who pays the fee set by the council of the municipality in which the property is located.

Fee for certificate (3) A council of a municipality may set a fee for the issuance of a certificate.

Property standards committee, membership and term of office 15.6 (1) A by-law passed under section 15.1 shall provide for the establishment of a committee composed of such persons, not fewer than three, as the council considers advisable to hold office for such term and on such conditions as the by-law may establish.

Filling of vacancies (2) The council of the municipality shall forthwith fill any vacancy that occurs in the membership of the committee.

Compensation (3) The members of the committee shall be paid such compensation as the council may provide.

Chair (4) The members shall elect a chair from among themselves; when the chair is absent through illness or otherwise, the committee may appoint another member as acting chair.

Quorum (5) A majority of the members constitutes a quorum for transacting the committee's business.

Secretary (6) The members shall provide for a secretary for the committee.

Duty of secretary (7) The secretary shall keep on file the records of all official business of the committee, including records of all applications and minutes of all decisions respecting those applications, and section 74 of the *Municipal Act* applies with necessary modifications to the minutes and records.

Rules of procedure and oaths (8) The committee may, subject to subsection (9), adopt its own rules of procedure and any member may administer oaths.

Where committee required to give notice (9) The committee shall give notice or direct that notice be given of the hearing of an appeal to such persons as the committee considers advisable.

Emergency order 15.7 (1) If upon inspection of a property the officer is satisfied that there is non-conformity with the standards in a by-law passed under section 15.1 to such extent as to pose an immediate danger to the health or safety of any person, the officer may make an order containing particulars of the non-conformity and requiring remedial repairs or other work to be carried out immediately to terminate the danger.

Service (2) The order shall be served on the owner of the property and such other persons affected thereby as the officer determines and a copy shall be posted on the property.

Emergency powers (3) After making an order under subsection (1), the officer may, either before or after the order is served, take any measures necessary to terminate the danger and, for this purpose, the municipality may, through its employees and agents, at any time enter upon the property in respect of which the order was made without a warrant.

No liability (4) Despite subsection 31 (2), a municipal corporation or a person acting on its behalf is not liable to compensate the owner, occupant or any other person by reason of anything done by or on behalf of the municipality in the reasonable exercise of its powers under subsection (3).

Service (5) If the order was not served before measures were taken to terminate the danger, the officer shall serve copies of the order in accordance with subsection (2) as soon as practicable after the measures have been taken, and each copy of the order shall have attached to it a statement by the officer describing the measures taken by the municipality and providing details of the amount expended in taking the measures.

Service of statement (6) If the order was served before the measures were taken, the officer shall serve a copy of the statement mentioned in subsection (5) in accordance with subsection (2) as soon as practicable after the measures have been taken.

Application to court (7) As soon as practicable after the requirements of subsection (5) or (6) have been complied with, the officer shall apply to a judge of the Ontario Court (General Division) for an order confirming the order made under subsection (1) and the judge shall hold a hearing for that purpose.

Powers of judge (8) The judge in disposing of an application under subsection (7) shall,

(a) confirm, modify or rescind the order; and

(b) determine whether the amount spent on measures to terminate the danger may be recovered in whole, in part or not at all.

Order final (9) The disposition under subsection (8) is final.

Municipal lien (10) The amount determined by the judge to be recoverable shall be a lien on the land and shall be deemed to be municipal real property taxes and may be added by the clerk of the municipality to the collector's roll and collected in the same manner and with the same priorities as municipal real property taxes.

Inspection powers of officer **15.8** (1) For the purposes of an inspection under section 15.2, an officer may,

(a) require the production for inspection of documents or things, including drawings or specifications, that may be relevant to the property or any part thereof;

(b) inspect and remove documents or things relevant to the property or part thereof for the purpose of making copies or extracts;

(c) require information from any person concerning a matter related to a property or part thereof;

(d) be accompanied by a person who has special or expert knowledge in relation to a property or part thereof;

(e) alone or in conjunction with a person possessing special or expert knowledge, make examinations or take tests, samples or photographs necessary for the purposes of the inspection; and

(f) order the owner of the property to take and supply at the owner's expense such tests and samples as are specified in the order.

Samples (2) The officer shall divide the sample taken under clause (1) (e) into two parts and deliver one part to the person from whom the sample is taken, if the person so requests at the time the sample is taken and provides the necessary facilities.

Same (3) If an officer takes a sample under clause (1) (e) and has not divided the sample into two parts, a copy of any report on the sample shall be given to the person from whom the sample was taken.

Receipt (4) An officer shall provide a receipt for any document or thing removed under clause (1) (b) and shall promptly return them after the copies or extracts are made.

Evidence (5) Copies of or extracts from documents and things removed under this section and certified as being true copies of or extracts from the originals by the person who made

203

them are admissible in evidence to the same extent as and have the same evidentiary value as the originals.

(9) Subsection 16 (1) of the Act is amended by striking out the portion before clause (a) and substituting the following:

Entry to dwellings

(1) Despite sections 8, 12, 15, 15.2 and 15.4, an inspector or officer shall not enter or remain in any room or place actually being used as a dwelling unless,

. . . . .

(10) Clauses 16 (1) (a), (c) and (d) of the Act are repealed and the following substituted:

(a) the consent of the occupier is obtained, the occupier first having been informed that the right of entry may be refused and entry made only under the authority of a warrant issued under this Act;

(a.1) a warrant issued under this Act is obtained;

. . . . .

(c) the entry is necessary to terminate a danger under subsection 15.7 (3) or 17 (3); or

(d) the requirements of subsection (2) are met and the entry is necessary to remove a building or restore a site under subsection 8 (6), to remove an unsafe condition under clause 15 (5) (b) or to repair or demolish under subsection 15.4 (1).

(11) Subsection 16 (2) of the Act is amended by inserting "or officer" after "inspector in the third line.

(12) Subsection 17 (10) of the Act is amended by striking out "municipal taxes" in the fourth line and in the eighth line and substituting in each case "municipal real property taxes".

(13) Section 19 of the Act is repealed and the following substituted:

Obstruction

19. (1) No person shall hinder or obstruct, or attempt to hinder or obstruct, a chief building official, inspector or officer in the exercise of a power or the performance of a duty under this Act.

Occupied dwellings

(2) A refusal of consent to enter or remain in a place actually used as a dwelling is not hindering or obstructing within the meaning of subsection (1) unless the inspector or officer is acting under a warrant issued under this Act or in the circumstances described in clauses 16 (1) (b), (c) or (d).

Assistance

(3) Every person shall assist any entry, inspection, examination, testing or inquiry by an inspector, chief building official or officer in the exercise of a power or performance of a duty under this Act.

Requirements

(4) No person shall neglect or refuse,

(a) to produce any documents, drawings, specifications or things required by an officer under clause 15.8 (1) (a) or (e) or an inspector under clause 18 (1) (a) or (e); or

(b) to provide any information required by an officer under clause 15.8 (1) (c) or an inspector under clause 18 (1) (c).

(14) Section 20 of the Act is repealed and the following substituted:

Prohibition

20. No person shall obstruct the visibility of an order and no person shall remove a copy of an order posted under this Act unless authorized to do so by an inspector or officer.

(15) Subsection 27 (2) of the Act is amended by striking out "third day" in the third line and substituting "fifth day".

(16) Subsection 31 (1) of the Act is amended by striking out "or an inspector" in the eighth line and substituting "an inspector or an officer".

(17) Clause 36 (1) (c) of the Act is repealed and the following substituted:

(c) contravenes this Act or the regulations or a by-law passed under section 7.

(18) Subsection 37 (2) of the Act is repealed and the following substituted:

Proof of matters of record

(2) A statement as to any matter of record in an office of the chief building official or an officer purporting to be certified by the chief building official or the officer is, without proof of the office or signature of the chief building official or officer, receivable in evidence as proof, in the absence of evidence to the contrary, of the facts stated therein in any civil proceeding or proceeding under the *Provincial Offences Act*.

204

(19) Subsections 39 (2) and (6) of the Act are repealed.

County of Oxford Act

225. (1) Subsection 59 (1) of the *County of Oxford Act* is amended by striking out "except as provided in subsections (2), (3) and (4)" in the fourth and fifth lines and substituting "except as provided in subsections (2), (3), (3.1) and (4)".

(2) Subsection 59 (3) of the Act is amended by striking out "31" in the fourth line.

(3) Section 59 of the Act is amended by adding the following subsection:

Same

(3.1) The council of an area municipality may exercise the powers provided in sections 15.1 to 15.8 inclusive of the *Building Code Act, 1992*, but in the event that there is a conflict between a by-law passed by the County Council and a by-law passed by the council of an area municipality in the exercise of such powers, the by-law passed by the County Council shall prevail.

Planning Act

226. (1) Section 31 of the *Planning Act*, as amended by the Statutes of Ontario, 1993, chapter 27, Schedule, 1994, chapter 2, section 42 and 1996, chapter 4, section 19, is repealed.

(2) Despite the repeal of section 31 of the Act, an order made under that section is continued as an order made under the corresponding provision of the *Building Code Act, 1992.*

(3) Subsection 32 (1) of the Act is amended,

(a) by striking out "section 31" in the first line and substituting "section 15.1 of the *Building Code Act, 1992*"; and

(b) by striking out "a notice has been sent under subsection 31 (6)" in the sixth and seventh lines and substituting "an order has been made under subsection 15.2 (2) of that Act".

(4) Subsection 33 (2) of the Act is amended by striking out "section 31" in the first line and substituting "section 15.1 of the *Building Code Act, 1992*".

(5) Subsection 33 (18) of the Act is amended by striking out "section 31" in the fifth line and substituting "section 15.1 of the *Building Code Act, 1992*".

(6) Subsection 33 (19) of the Act is amended by striking out "section 5 of the *Building Code*

Act" at the end and substituting "subsection 8 (1) of the *Building Code Act, 1992*".

(7) Clause 49.1 (1) (a) of the Act, as enacted by Statutes of Ontario, 1994, chapter 2, section 46, is amended by striking out "under section 31 or 67" and substituting "under section 67".

(8) Section 67.1 of the Act, as re-enacted by the Statutes of Ontario, 1996, chapter 4, section 34, is amended by striking out "31" in the second line.

Regional Municipal-ities Act

227. (1) Subsection 97 (3) of the *Regional Municipalities Act* is repealed and the following substituted:

Deemed municipality

(3) The Regional Corporation shall be deemed to be a municipality for the purposes of the *Building Code Act, 1992* and no council of an area municipality shall, except as provided under this Part, exercise any powers under that Act.

(2) Subsection 97 (4) of the Act, as re-enacted by the Statutes of Ontario, 1992, chapter 23, section 41, is repealed and the following substituted:

Costs recovered

(4) Any costs incurred by the Regional Corporation under subsection 8 (6), clause 15 (5) (b) or subsection 15.4 (1) of the *Building Code Act, 1992* or determined by a judge to be recoverable under subsection 15.7 (8) or 17 (8) of that Act may be charged to the area municipality in which the building or property is located and the area municipality shall collect the costs in the manner set out in subsections 8 (7), 15 (9), 15.4 (3), 15.7 (10) and 17 (10) of that Act and pay them to the Regional Corporation when collected.

(3) Subsection 98 (1) of the Act, as amended by the Statutes of Ontario, 1994, chapter 23, section 89, is further amended by striking out "31" in the sixth line.

(4) Section 98 of the Act, as amended by the Statutes of Ontario, 1994, chapter 23, section 89, is further amended by adding the following subsection:

Delegation of powers

(2.1) The Regional Council may delegate, for such period and on such terms and conditions as the Regional Council considers necessary, to the council of any area municipality the authority to exercise such of the powers under sections 15.1 to 15.8 inclusive of the

Building Code Act, 1992 as the Regional Council may determine.

(5) Subsection 100 (1) of the Act is amended by striking out "31" in the eighth line.

(6) Section 100 of the Act, as amended by the Statutes of Ontario, 1994, chapter 23, section 90, is further amended by adding the following subsection:

Delegation of powers

(4.1) The Regional Council may delegate, for such period and on such terms and conditions as the Regional Council considers necessary, to the council of any area municipality the authority to exercise such of the powers under sections 15.1 to 15.8 inclusive of the *Building Code Act, 1992* as the Regional Council may determine.

COMMENCEMENT AND SHORT TITLE

Commencement

228. This Act comes into force on a day to be named by proclamation of the Lieutenant Governor.

Short title

229. The short title of this Act is the *Tenant Protection Act, 1997.*

OTHER TITLES IN THE
SELF-COUNSEL SERIES

RENTAL FORM KIT FOR HOUSE AND APARTMENT IN ONTARIO
$5.95
Forms only

Includes:
- Two copies of a Residential Tenancy Agreement
- Two copies of an Application to Rent
- Two copies of a Report of Rental Premises and Contents
- An instruction sheet to enable you to comply with the laws in Ontario

RESIDENTIAL TENANCY AGREEMENT FOR ONTARIO
$5.95
Forms and Disk

Includes:
- One copy of a Residential Tenancy Agreement
- One copy of a Report of Rental Premises and Contents
- An instruction sheet to enable you to comply with the laws in Ontario
- Computer disk of the Residential Tenancy Agreement for you to use again and again. (For use with WordPerfect, MS Word, and all other PC word-processing packages.)

ORDERING INFORMATION

All prices are subject to change without notice. Books and forms are available in book, department, and stationery stores. If you cannot buy the book through a store, please use this order form. (Please print.)

Name _____

Address _____

Charge to: ❏ Visa ❏ MasterCard

Account number _____

Validation date _____

Expiry date _____

Signature_____

❏ Check here for a free catalogue

❏ YES, please send me:

_____ Rental Form Kit Ontario, $5.95

_____ Residential Tenancy Agreement for Ontario, $5.95

Please send your order to:

Self-Counsel Press
4 Bram Court
Brampton, ON L6W 3R6

Visit our Web site at:

www.self-counsel.com